THE
DOUBLE SHOTGUN

Revised, Expanded Edition

DON ZUTZ

1998 PRINTING

Winchester Press
NEW WIN PUBLISHING

1998 Printing

Library of Congress Cataloging in Publication Data

Zutz, Don.
    The double shotgun.

    Includes index.
    1. Shotguns.   I. Title.
TS536.8.Z9   1985   683.4'26   85-5111
ISBN 0-8329-0386-8

CONTENTS

Preface: 1998 Traditions v
Preface: 1995 The Changing Scene vii
Prologue: A Rich Heritage vix
1 Wingshooting Form: The Theoretical Bases 1
2 The Subtle Advantages of Double Guns 12
3 Grips and Gripping 22
4 A Flexible Field Style 33
5 Classic Locks and Actions 40
6 The Triggers 51
7 Bolting Systems on the Side-By-Sides 63
8 Bolting Complexities on the Over-Under 75
9 Gun Art 86
10 What's Left for the British? 100
11 The 12/20 Concept: When Joseph Lang Dared to Be Different . . .116
12 Those Boutique Smallbores 121
13 Datelines: The Continent 126
14 French Connections 142
15 A New World Classic; The Winchester Model 21 153
16 American Collectibles and the Parker Mystique 168
17 The Stateside Scene 180
18 Fine Boxlocks Are a Bargain! 192
19 Target-Grade Guns and Influences .197
20 Live-Pigeon Guns 213
21 The Space Age Doubles 219
Directory 222
Index 227
Epilogue: The State of the Art 233

1998 Preface:
Traditions

It has been more than twenty years since I first wrote *The Double Shotgun*. At the time, there was very little interest in the side-by-side shotgun and the fly rod. No magazines focused on the fly rod and few publications bothered to mention the double. Spinning was a far more efficient way of taking fish, and the over-under was gaining popularity in leaps and bounds.

But time changes all things. Not only is the fly rod now back in vogue, but it is the "in" thing among younger anglers. Where there were no fly fishing magazines in the past, there are at least a half dozen on the newsstands. Something about the ol' willow wand has attracted a new generation that seems to enjoy this traditional method of angling.

And the side-by-side shotgun also has developed a new following. Although experience has shown that the side-by-side isn't as effective as the O/U in competitive events, a new wave of sport hunters has adopted the horizontal double - especially in its ultra-trim English styling - for upland hunting. The side-by-side, of course, is at its best on game, be it driven or walked up.

This has been a relatively quiet market. There is not heavy discounting in fly rods or classic doubles. But the people who want this equipment are normally willing to pay for quality. This pricing is necessary, because the volume in such equipment is quite low and a manufacturer or builder must take more profit per item to exist. The point is, however, that there is again a fresh interest in those willow wands and doubles which formed the base of American sporting traditions.

As I wrote in the first edition, I am not presenting this as a definitive book on the double shotgun, nor am I listing all names and dates. My main purpose is to acquaint newcomers with the theoretical, mechanical, and historical aspects of the so-called "side-by-each." One can dig deeper into the past by consulting the many books which focus on just one brand; many such studies have come along since the publication of *Double Shotgun*. Thus, I hope this tome will serve as an enjoyable introduction to the world of doubles.

Don Zutz
Kohler, WI
April, 1998

1985 Preface:
The Changing Scene

It has been said that, the more things change, the more they remain the same.

Perhaps. But aside from the fact that doubles still have their barrels in side-by-side and over-under arrangements, many changes have indeed taken place in this field since the first edition of this book was published in 1978. The roaring inflation of the late 1970s and early 1980s impacted heavily on gunmakers, especially those who required skilled hands and substantial time to craft truly exquisite doubles. Some such makers have been able to ride out the financial storm in reasonably good shape and are continuing on in their traditional manner; others have modified their methods; and still others have foundered in the proverbial sea of red ink, their respected names now but memories.

Designs, models, manufacturing practices, prices, international dealings, distributors, quality and value—they have all changed, too, since The Double Shotgun originally appeared. Thus, because sportsmen, collectors, dealers and investors have keen interests in both classic and modern doubles, this updated second edition of The Double Shotgun has been written.

Since the form, functional and mechanical bases of doublebarreled shotguns are quite well established and proven, the first eight chapters of this book will, with minor variations and appended material, parallel those of the first edition. These lay the basis of any study of sporting doubles, and they must be kept intact for readers who are only now catching up with us old-timers.

Beginning with the ninth chapter, however, the topics will be new. Not only will they pertain to recent happenings within the world of sporting gun manufacture and craftsmanship but they will also cover some topics slanted toward the hunter, collector and investor. In other words, there is something for everyone who has the slightest interest in, or an appreciative eye for, those most cherished shotguns of all — doubles!

Putting together a book of this sort requires help from many sources and directions. The most difficult part is illustrating the new and important aspects. I cannot buy every double in the world just to photograph it; consequently, I have had to rely on other people. For their willing assistance in supplying such art, my thanks go to Herschel Chadick, Bill Jaqua, Dieter Krieghoff and Peter Powell. Thanks also to Frank Kodl, publisher of *Shotgun Sports* magazine (P.O. Box 340, Lake Havasu City, AZ 86403), for permission to use photos and excerpted material that originally appeared in his popular new publication. *Shotgun Sports* is recommended to all those interested in shotgun subjects.

Instead of putting addresses in the narrative, I have chosen to supply a directory at the end of this manuscript. There may be more names that should appear there, but letters of inquiry to such operatives went unanswered and I chose not to include them for fear that my readers might be treated similarly.

Whether there will ever be a need for a third edition of this work remains something for history to determine. Until then, keep your head down and follow through!

Don Zutz
Sheboygan, Wisconsin

Prologue:
A Rich Heritage

Our modern wingshooting techniques and shotgun designs stem from the middle of the nineteenth century, when leading British gunmakers gradually switched their emphasis from muzzle-loaded flintlocks to breechloaders based on the then-new percussion ignition system. No precise date can be given to the transition; the Age of Flint died hard. Traditionalists like Colonel Peter Hawker

Perfection of the flintlock paved the way for the modern double. This central-fire hammer gun with tang-top opening lever and beautifully engraved surfaces is just one step in the evolutionary process. The underlever served to cock both hammers. (Photo courtesy Pachmayr Gun Works)

and William Greener staunchly defended the virtues of the flintlock, which was reaching it pinnacle of perfection just as the early percussion guns were being developed, and the histories of the two ignition systems overlapped each other as Queen Victoria began her reign.

But 1851, the year of the Great Exhibition in London, is an excellent dividing line. It was then that the French gunmaker LeFaucheux exhibited what was to become the first successful breechloader, a double-barreled shotgun utilizing pinfire "cartridges" and a novel drop-down barrel feature. The gun and ignition system were simple in design, easily operated and ballistically efficient. Operated by an underlever, the LeFaucheux pivoted its barrels on a hinge pin, like the modern side-by-side, and the pinfire shotshells were simply slipped into the chambers with the pin jutting upward to receive the hammer's blow. The pin was driven into the priming mixture, detonating it to ignite the powder.

LeFaucheux's concept of a break-action breechloader was adapted by Joseph Lang, an outstanding British gunmaker who saw its practical advantages and mechanical potentials. Once this simple but apparently efficient application of the percussion system of ignition had been accepted by a foremost British gunmaker, the stage was set for spirited competition. In 1852, for example, Charles Lancaster, another British gunmaking great, developed an underlever double for centerfire shotshells and incorporated extractors that elevated the shotshells by their rims for easy removal.

But not everyone plunged into the fray. Some staunch traditionalists held firm, and a bit of snobbery showed through when some British authorities appear to have denied the French their credit as innovators. Writing in *Gunnery in 1858*, W. Greener heaped an entire chapter of abuse on the LeFaucheux invention. "The French system of breechloading firearms is a specious pretence," Greener argued, "the supposed advantages of which have been loudly boasted of; but none of these advantages have as yet been established by its most strenuous advocates. How it is that the British sportsman has become the dupe of certain men who set themselves up for respectable gun-makers, I know not. . . .There is no possibility of a breech-loader ever shooting equal to a well-constructed muzzle-loader; secondly, the gun [breechloader] is unsafe, and becomes more and more unsafe from the first time it is used; and, thirdly, it is a costly affair, both as regards the gun and the ammunition."

Greener wasn't content with that blast against the breechloader. "It is said, and said truly," he went on critically, "that a breechloader can be charged more rapidly than a muzzle-loader; but I hold this to be no advantage, for this reason — all guns can be charged more quickly than they are fired, and the tendency of all guns to absorb heat puts a limit to rapidity of firing. There are a few plans, or presumed improvements, which have some redeeming points; but in the case of breech-loading firearms, it is quite a task to find even a resemblance of one. No fear need be entertained that the use of breech-loaders will become general."

So much for the vision and prophecy of W. Greener. In less than 20 years, his son, W. W. Greener, was a ranking builder of those newfangled breechloaders.

In fact, breechloaders were already solidly established in concept and reality by the early 1860s, their merits having been proved in trials conducted and reported by England's main sporting magazine, *The Field*. Centerfire shotshells had been vastly improved by 1861, credit for the first truly modern centerfire ammunition going to Dawes of Threadneedle Street, who displayed them at the Great Exhibition of that year.

The breechloading percussion gun was further refined during the late 1860s and the 1870s, and those advances were important steppingstones to perfection. Choke boring came into use around 1866; both Pape of Newcastle and Greener of Birmingham claimed credit for the invention. The son of James Purdey the First introduced the pivoting top (tang) lever in 1870, and it gained almost universal acceptance. Perhaps the most significant innovation was a hammerless double made by Murcott of Haymarket in 1871. Called "Murcott's mouse trap," it paved the way for further experiments that eventually produced the sleek, hammerless designs of today.

Finally, the year 1875 gave us two noteworthy accomplishments. Anson and Deeley, a pair of craftsmen in the employ of Westley Richards, created a simple, inexpensive and reliable firing mechanism. Named after the craftsmen, the Anson

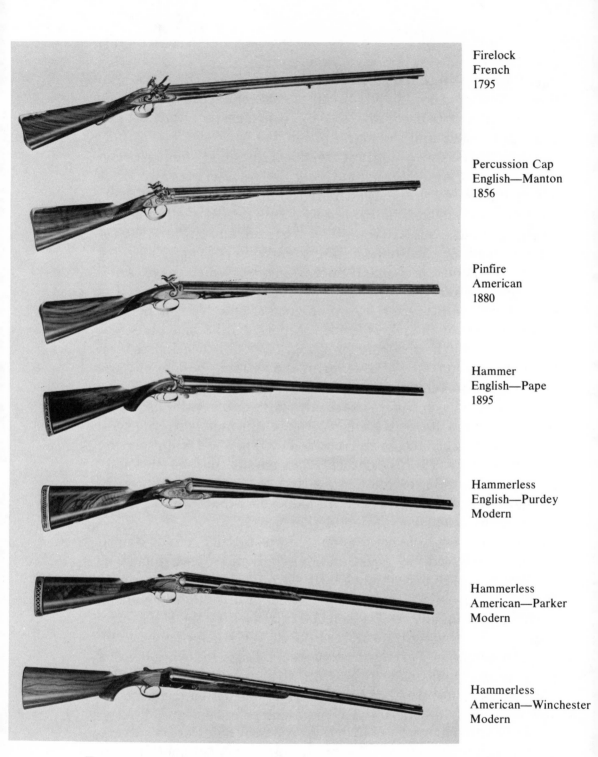

Firelock
French
1795

Percussion Cap
English—Manton
1856

Pinfire
American
1880

Hammer
English—Pape
1895

Hammerless
English—Purdey
Modern

Hammerless
American—Parker
Modern

Hammerless
American—Winchester
Modern

THE EVOLUTION OF THE DOUBLE-BARRELED SHOTGUN.

& Deeley action is still used in boxlock doubles. The second 1875 contribution was Needham's self-ejector. A Birmingham gunsmith, Needham developed the first assembly that would snap a spent case from the shotgun's chamber to facilitate reloading. However, the self-ejector was a tricky mechanism, and it wasn't perfected until the 1890s.

Thus, within 50 years gunmakers devised, developed, proved and stabilized the mechanical features of the classic side-by-side. The twentieth century's contributions were merely minor modifications of existing designs—expanded use of coil springs instead of almost total reliance on flat or V-springs, certain innovative approaches to trigger mechanisms, and, perhaps most important, the introduction of strong steel alloys for specialized applications.

This does not mean that British gunmakers fattened their fortunes by pilfering a French experimenter's idea. They had been working in the same direction but had not yet arrived at the break-action concept. In 1807, for example, the Reverend Alexander James Forsyth patented the world's first detonating lock, the beginning of the end of flint ignition. Forsyth's rather elaborate lock exploded a fulminate by utilizing hammer force on a plunger assembly tangent to the barrel's chamber. No one need be surprised that a clergyman was the first to perfect a percussion ignition system, of course. For percussion ignition is based upon the use of explosive chemicals, and men of the cloth were often the only people with training in chemistry during the late eighteenth and early nineteenth centuries.

Between 1807 and 1818, the British developed various detonating mechanisms utilizing priming pellets and paper and copper caps. Joseph Manton's 1818 patent for a percussion "tube lock" employed copper caps mounted on a nipple/tube unit that held the cap under the hammer and directed its flash straight to the powder. Manton's tube lock soon became the universal method for adapting percussion ignition to muzzleloaders, and it still is the standard for fixed-breech percussion guns. Also in 1818, Rigby made the first true Damascus barrels (earlier barrels having been fashioned from twisted horseshoe-nail stubs), while needlefire paper cartridges, which functioned on the same principle as pinfire rounds, were used by the British in the 1840s. Thus, gunmakers in England had been well on their way to sophisticated use of the percussion system prior to 1851, and given time they would undoubtedly have come to the same results as did LeFaucheux, whose drop-barrel double paired with pinfire ammunition merely speeded progress. For saving them years of experimenting and frustration, however, British gunmakers and sportsmen do owe thanks to the French.

Modern wingshooting techniques—the art and science of hitting flying targets—were refined only after percussion systems improved the speed and uniformity of ignition and ballistics. For successful wingshooting depends heavily on flawless timing between gun, gunner and ammunition, and before the advent of reliable percussion systems, such timing was impossible because of the variable ignition and ballistics of wheellock, matchlock and flintlock shotguns. Practically all game taken before the Victorian Age, including the famous grouse of the Scottish uplands, were taken "on the sit." With reliable percussion systems and the smokeless powders that came along toward the end of the nineteenth century, however, significant shot-to-shot ballistics variations were eliminated, and hunters could depend upon their equipment to take birds on the wing if their swing-and-lead technique was correct. By the beginning of the twentieth century, then, wingshooting had not only become a fashionable sport but its fundamentals had been carefully thought out and an entire code of sporting ethics had developed. Only a boor or a poacher would "ground-swat" a game bird thereafter.

As the practice of wingshooting spread, it became obvious that the dimensions and weight of flintlock guns made them unsuitable fowling pieces even if they were converted to a percussion system. The long barrels needed to burn black powder were sluggish; the rather "crooked" stock configurations, which were intended for down-the-barrel aiming at stationary targets, were less than ideal on fast-flying birds. But theorists quickly met this challenge. The role of the gripping surfaces in wingshooting was analyzed, and stock/forearm designs were changed to enhance the gun's dynamics. *Instead of the shooter having to adapt himself to the gun, the gun was refined to fit the hunter's natural movements and physical features for faster handling.*

This trend toward improved handling qualities was aided by the efficient percussion ignition system and smokeless powders, which, together, allowed the use of shorter barrels without any loss of velocity or striking power. The result was a shorter, lighter, more effective and faster-handling shotgun than the world had previously known. British and European sportsmen commonly call this responsive arm a "game gun" to differentiate it from the more ponderous waterfowl and target guns, and that term will be used throughout this book as a reference to the classic lightweight double, which, in American sporting parlance, would be an ideal upland arm.

Although flinters had debated and resisted the change to percussion ignition during the early 1800s, nothing has prompted more excitement and controversy among shotgunners than has the twentieth century's over-under. Instead of accepting each barrel arrangement as a legitimate version of the break-open double, shooters chose sides and engaged in a long, heated debate over which type was better. Traditionalists stuck with the classic simplicity and elegance of the side-by-side, arguing that the over-under was really nothing more than a "novelty" created to inspire additional sales. The more liberally minded moderns harped on the over-under's straight-line recoil, narrower sighting plane and other subtleties. Neither side has won a total victory, of course, but the debate has lost some of its fire. The over-under withstood initial attacks and is no longer considered a radical piece. By the same token, the over-under has not driven the side-by-side into obsolescence. Intelligent shooters have set emotions and traditions aside to select between the over-under and side-by-side concepts on the basis of each type's strengths and weaknesses for a specific wing-gunning application.

With that scientific approach to selection and evaluation a reality, we can now take a look in depth at the great shotguns and how to use them. It is a multifaceted study, including a concern for esthetics and artistry, mechanics and metallurgy, form and balance, line and function, theory and practice. And if beauty is indeed in the eye of the beholder, then any thorough study of shotguns must include the beholder—the human being whose tastes are expressed and whose natural actions are blended to it.

Fortunately, history and science have been kind to the shotgunners. No other segment of the sporting world, including the angler who labels himself a dry-fly purist, has a richer heritage.

Chapter 1

Wingshooting Form:
The Theoretical Bases

The human body, given a chance to react naturally, is remarkably rhythmic, precise and coordinated, and one need not be a champion athlete at the peak of his training to benefit from its abilities. They are, to varying degrees, part of everyone's makeup, an innate gift. Merely notice the swift, multiple, coordinated, evasive actions of a person whose eyes are suddenly threatened. Without a moment's hesitation, he will shut his eyes tightly, duck in a safe direction and elevate his hands to eye level. An aged person does it as automatically as a teenager. Or consider the fact that in a totally darkened room, a man can extend his forefingers and bring them directly and smoothly to the very tip of his nose. As a final observation, note the way a toddler can point precisely at the candy he wants without struggling or squinting for hand-to-eye alignment. The child's forefinger goes directly to where his master eye is looking. Neither sighting devices nor jerky contortions are needed to effect any of the above actions. Once willed by the brain, they are carried out with grace, accuracy and dispatch.

This natural (or, as some might term it, instinctive) self-centering, hand-to-eye coordination is the key to understanding classic wingshooting theory and form. You must appreciate its importance before you can properly assess the design features of a shotgun. For the gun itself, along with certain studied, refined and disciplined elements of shooting style, is merely woven into the artistic/scientific tapestry called wingshooting. The gun and special training with it are *never* the primary considerations, and anybody who insists upon stressing gun quality and flashy style

1

without initially considering basic human structure and reactions is reversing the proper order of things.

The very nature of wingshooting places heavy stress upon one's natural hand-to-eye coordination, because the shotgun is a dynamic, short-range piece that is made to be pointed quickly, swung sharply on fast-moving targets and fired without hesitation. If the shotgun shooter wishes to trigger his charge before the mark gets beyond effective range of the spreading shot pattern, he cannot dawdle by aiming carefully like a rifleman, whose firearm has much greater range. Nor is there any reason for optimum accuracy with a shotgun, since the pattern gives some leeway for human error. With properly selected choke boring and suitable ammunition, the shotgun's effective pellet distribution will cover a circular area about 25–32 inches in diameter at working ranges, thereby eliminating the need for squinty-eyed, taut-muscled, down-the-barrel aiming. The word *aim*, in fact, should be purged from any shotgunner's vocabulary and replaced by an indelible imprint of the term *point*, which implies a tolerance of slight imprecision and is far less likely to disrupt the fluidity of the shooter's natural reactions and movements.

The essence of wingshooting accuracy is utilizing hand-to-eye coordination. Humans easily point out objects by keeping their eyes focused on the mark and letting the pointing finger come up naturally.

This same natural accuracy applies if one thinks of the gun as an extension of his pointing index finger.

The most basic factor in classic wing-gunning technique, then, is a speedy, natural point made by allowing one's hands to work in natural coordination with the master eye. By eliminating doubts, hesitations and the mistaken human tendency to think one must aim every type of gun, the normal person can effect such eye-hand-gun-target alignment almost effortlessly and with more than adequate pointing accuracy. All other elements of form and style, along with all aspects of game-gun design and fit, are built on that foundation.

Because a shotgunner's hands work to his master eye, not vice versa, the use and placement of that dominant eye relative to the gun and target is of paramount importance to both shooting form and gun design. The eye's main job is focusing sharply on the flushing or passing target and remaining thus affixed during the entire sequence of gun-mounting and swinging actions. Since it cannot focus sharply on near and distant objects simultaneously, the wingshot's master eye will see the gun's upper surfaces and muzzle area only as a blur. Its focus isn't changed as the swing progresses, not even for a split-second check of the front bead's location relative to the target. When in doubt the expert puts more, not less, trust in his natural hand-to-eye coordination and continues to focus on the bird; his main adjustment is increasing swing tempo to eliminate the disruptive influence of human deliberations. Whenever a shotgunner debriefs himself after a disturbing miss or series of misses, his initial analysis of any revived "sight picture" should pivot on the rib/muzzle outline; if the recalled picture shows a sharp muzzle outline, chances are the gunner changed his focus, losing both alignment and some swing speed, by checking too precisely on the gun itself. Thus, the shotgunner uses his eyes differently than does a rifleman, who must perforce focus sharply on his arm's near sights for accurate bore alignment while seeing his target slightly blurred.

For all practical and theoretical purposes, the wingshot's master eye serves as a rear sight. Its proper place is squarely atop the comb looking directly over the center of the standing breech and straight down the bore axis of an over-under or the rib of a side-by-side. This position it must reach quickly and easily during the mounting process and hold snugly during the entire swing and follow-through. Anything less will produce the same inaccuracies that occur when a rifle's rear sight is out of adjustment.

Gun fit is a vital factor in positioning the master eye. The stock's dimensions act as a sight mount for the eye, and if the stock has such grotesque configurations that the gunner can't slip his eye in place easily and keep it there, serious bore misalignments will develop.

At this stage in a discussion of wingshooting theory there is a pressing fundamental question: What is the correct method of mounting and aligning a shotgun from a low, field-carry position if the gunner concentrates his vision sharply on the fleeting target? The classic method has been variously called the "thrust-out" or "push-out" technique, and it is predicated upon bringing the gun to the shooter's face, *not* bringing the face to the gun (as so many modern hunters mistakenly do). The great game guns are designed and, in most instances, custom-fitted to match the thrust-out system's requirements. When design and fit factors are paired with the thrust-out method, the mounting, aligning and swinging movements are blended into one smooth, graceful, accelerating action. And as the reader would expect, the thrust-out method is based entirely on the human's natural hand-to-eye coordination. Let's trace its steps by combining text with photos in sequence.

Begining with his shotgun in a field-carry position, such as in the first photo, the hunter's main job is remaining alert and having the gun under control with both hands placed for quick responses.

The assumption in the second picture is that the target has been sighted. Be it an outgoing, crossing or incoming bird, the thrust-out method now begins with two moves made in unison. The first is leaning slightly forward from the waist while also lowering the head to shooting position. This puts the shotgunner's eye (rear sight) in place, relative to both the target and the remainder of the shooter's physique, and it gives the natural hand-to-eye coordination a reference point. With his eyes now focused on the bird and with his body in a position to receive the gun, the shotgun can now be brought almost instinctively upward and in direct alignment with the moving mark. With a fine-fitted game gun, the

1. The classic thrust-out method of gun handling begins from a relaxed position with the hands placed for control and quick response. The entire technique is based on bringing the gun to the face, not the face to the gun.

2. When the target is sighted, the gunner focuses his eyes sharply on it and keeps them there during the entire mounting-swinging sequence, while taking a slight forward lean and placing his head in shooting position to receive the comb.

3. With eyes still on the rising bird, the gunner elevates the shotgun with his hands working in coordination with his master eye. When the gun's upper surfaces enter his field of vision, the hunter sees them only as a blur, depending upon natural hand-to-eye coordination for accurate alignment.

4. In the thrust-out method there is a slight extension of the gunner's arms to clear the butt of the armpit. The motion duplicates the normal pointing action one would make with arm and forefinger extended but without a gun.

5. The purpose of the thrust-out method is to attain eye-gun-target alignment first, with actual shouldering a secondary matter. Here the comb has been properly elevated to the face and brought directly under the master eye, but the buttplate is still away from the shoulder.

6. The final move is rolling the shoulder slightly forward to meet the butt. At no time does the gunner take his eyes from the target.

effort need be no greater than that used to point the leading hand and forefinger without a gun.

The lean should never be more than that shown in the second photo, and should definitely not duplicate the ludicrously exaggerated forward lean employed by many who shoot American-style skeet and trap. Skeet stances are especially horrendous. With widespread feet, many skeetmen lean so far forward the body is almost parallel with the ground! Such styles are totally inefficient afield, and skeet shooters post perfect scores using them only because skeet is a highly controlled game based upon "grooved" targets released at the shooter's command. A more upright position is mandatory for flexibility in game covers, where birds may break in any direction at any time, because an upright style lets the body pivot more freely about its vertical axis (spine).

The second part of this two-part movement is elevating the gun to bring its comb directly below the master eye, which is already centered on the target and tracking it. The elevating move is done without switching one's eyes to the gun as it comes up and enters the field of vision. If the shooter doesn't overpower his natural hand-to-eye coordination, he'll find his leading hand coming up with the gun's muzzle almost automatically on target and swinging the line of flight. In other words, the swing actually builds as the gun is brought upward to parallel the master eye's alignment, the elevating route being a slight arc instead of a straight upward jerk. The gun is not stopped or checked as its comb contacts the shooter's face or attracts his eye, but rather sweeps onward after the target with its own momentum supplying some of the energy. The third photo is an excellent example of a hunter's hands coordinating with his dominant eye. In the second photo, the lad is concentrating his gaze upon the bird, yet the gun is coming up to intercept the line of sight.

The fourth photo shows why this gun-mounting technique is called the thrust-out method. The gun is *not* brought straight up to make initial contact with the shooter's shoulder, an act that often causes butt hangup in the armpit. By a minor extension of one's arms, as the lad is doing in the fourth photo, the gun is actually thrust forward slightly toward the target as it works to the eye. This not only clears the butt from armpit hazards but it duplicates the normal action of extending one's arm and pointing without a gun. Done in a relaxed, natural manner, it enhances the potential for accurate alignment of master eye, gun muzzle and target. It also emphasizes the theory of bringing the gun to the rear sight (shooter's eye) instead of vice versa.

The trigger hand's job is to coordinate with the leading hand while elevating the stock. Nature has again endowed the human with excellent abilities in this regard: Hands work together naturally, always seeking a common plane. The best shotguns are designed to accommodate this physical virtue by a serious consideration of underlines (i.e., pistol-grip geometry and fore-end depth), a subject that will be discussed in Chapter 3.

As illustrated in the fifth photo, the comb greets the shooter's cheek while the stock's buttplate is still away from the shoulder. This is an important aspect of the thrust-out method, as the entire mounting process is predicted upon establishing a hand-to-eye alignment first, while the actual shouldering is a secondary matter.

Bringing the comb to the master eye ensures alignment, whereas rapid shouldering without concern for the eye's location means no such thing.

Once the comb has been brought directly under the master eye, the shooter's shoulder is rolled forward slightly to meet the gun butt as in the sixth photo. This is a simple physical move, but there is some confusion among shotgunners about the exact area where the butt belongs. The term *shouldering* has misled many into believing that the gun abuts the rounded shoulder muscle (deltoid), which is wrong! Some shooters with faulty notions and movements place the butt well out on their upper arm (biceps muscle), which is equally wrong. The shotgun should be slipped into the hollow spot that forms between the deltoid muscle and collarbone when the trigger arm's elbow is elevated. This provides the firmest, flattest base for the butt, and it positions the gun more directly below the master eye. Utilizing the hollow spot also negates the rolling that occurs when a shotgun's butt rests on the rounded deltoid, and it eliminates the neck-stretching needed to reach the comb when a smoothbore is placed too far out on the arm.

The thrust-out method is versatile enough to accommodate any type of swing/lead system. If a hunter uses the swing-past method, in which he starts his gun behind the bird and pulls the trigger as the blurred muzzles flash past, he can elevate the gun accordingly. And if he uses the sustained lead, meaning the gun is brought up a calculated distance ahead of the bird and swung with enough speed to hold that lead, the hunter can alter the elevating arc and intercept the bird's line of flight to suit said system. The snap shot, always of dubious effectiveness, can usually be brought off more successfully with the thrust-out method than any other mounting move; for despite the basic inaccuracies of slapdash snapping, the thrust-out method offers considerable natural pointing accuracy.

The proper leading-hand grip, as will shortly be discussed and illustrated, is vital. For the thrust-out method actually throws the gun's muzzles at and through the target, relying almost entirely on natural, coordinated movements for alignment; and the best shooting will be done by the chap who duplicates the same pointing actions he would make without a gun. This, of course, involves a pointing finger, since few normal humans point out objects with their clenched fist. Moreover, the shooter's leading hand is the boss on a straight-gripped game gun, because the trigger hand doesn't have the same controlling purchase it does on a gun equipped with the full pistol grip.

There is little doubt that trim, classic game guns are perfectly suited to the thrust-out method. The gun and the technique evolved together. However, many modern hunters with self-taught styles will initially be skeptical of push-out movements and feel awkward or uncomfortable with them. This isn't unusual. Golfers and tennis players feel the same way when they first encounter the correct gripping and swinging methods. Thus, like any other athletic move, proper shotgun handling and wingshooting must be accepted and practiced before the virtues of a dynamic game gun will be fully utilized and appreciated. Faulty gun handling handicaps the lively double, much as a duffer's antics handicap Arnold Palmer's scientifically designed golf clubs.

Chapter 2

The Subtle Advantages
of Double Guns

It would be nice if a wingshooter could point his shotgun with exactly the same ease and accuracy as when pointing his extended arm and forefinger without a gun. But just as a particle of sand can impair the keenness of one's vision when it gets in the eye, so too is even the most expensive shotgun a foreign object when it rests in a shooter's hands and must be incorporated into the pointing movement. This is not a contradiction of the concepts covered in Chapter 1, either. The natural hand-to-eye coordination stressed there is still *the* key to classic wing-gunning technique and the thrust-out mounting method. The point is that a shotgun's weight, bulk and balance place unnatural obstacles in the way of natural *perfection*. If you are alert to theoretical implications, then, you immediately realize that truly great game guns are designed, fitted and constructed to offer minimal resistance and obstruction to vital, natural and instinctive human actions. The ideal is reached when a shotgun ceases to be just a shotgun and, instead, virtually becomes a part of the shooter's anatomy. Only then can it flow with the natural fluidity of muscle movement rather than act as a hindrance to it.

Of all the shotgun designs that have evolved, it is mainly the refined double guns, be they side-by-side or over-under, that have the potential to blend mechanical features with fit, form, timing and handling requirements for near perfection. Why does the double gun excel? By virtue of its compact construction and trimness of line, the double presents optimum opportunity for pointability and balance, the refinement of which spells the difference between a truly fine game gun and just another smoothbore.

The term *pointability* can be vague and misleading, because all shotguns have it in varying degrees. Even inexpensive, klunker-type pumpguns and gas-operated autoloaders with their potbellied fore-ends can be pointed well enough to hit game and targets. In the discussion of great game guns, however, "well enough" isn't adequate. Theoretical perfection is the goal, and the nth degree of pointability isn't reached until the bore axes become an extension of the shooter's naturally pointed hand and finger; for if we accept the importance of hand-to-eye-to-target coordination in classic wingshooting theory, it then follows that any bores which sit low in the shooter's extended palm will invariably travel more accurately to the moving mark than will high-sitting barrels which, on slab-sided pumpguns and autoloaders, have their bore axis elevated so they can't possibly work along the direct line established from eye to target by the leading hand's natural position. Thus, the juxtaposition of the shooter's leading hand relative to the bore axes is vital to instinctive accuracy when the shotgun is handled rapidly afield.

The proximity of one's leading hand to the bore axes is called the "hand-to-barrel relationship." The less time there is for mounting and aligning a shotgun, the more important it becomes. The hand-to-barrel relationship for any shotgun is checked at the spot where a shooter's leading hand normally contacts the fore-end. As just stated, the best theoretical condition places the bore axes deeply in the shooter's cupped leading hand so the bores go where the hand goes.

In classic wingshooting style, in the thrust-out gun-handling method, and in the design of great game guns, the hand-to-barrel relationship takes precedence over current notions that emphasize lines without the slightest concern for function. The most prestigious over-unders derive a goodly portion of their glory from low-profile receivers and trim fore-ends, which, functioning together, bring the bores more directly in line with the exact point being made by a shooter's extended hand. The British Boss and Woodward-Purdey over-unders are classics, having remarkably shallow profiles and thin, though suitably strong, fore-ends of

A gunner's instinctive accuracy is greatly enhanced when the gun's bore axes lie immediately atop his leading hand's natural point, as shown here. Fore-end depth controls this relationship.

minimum depth. Both British-made over-unders sit deeply in the shooter's leading palm with their under barrel almost in direct contact with his natural anatomic line of point. In 12 gauge, hardly more than 3/4 inch separates the shotgunner's palm from the axis of the Boss gun's under tube. Moreover, because of the shallow receiver profile, the upper barrel of the Woodward-Purdey and Boss are kept tangent-tight to the lower member; and this, in turn, puts the upper bore's axis equally closer to the line projected by the shooter's leading hand. Even a woman can wrap her smaller fingers about the 20-gauge Woodward-Purdey, so the bores run through her cupped leading palm in the most natural fashion.

There are other excellent over-unders that have fore-ends designed for effective, natural pointing via close hand-to-barrel relationship. One is the Franz Sodia Model 24E imported by Ferlach of North America. Another is the trim, three-piece fore-end used on Merkel guns. Both the Sodia M24E and Merkel display a fore-end underline which rises gracefully from the fore-end iron to the under barrel, always bringing the shotgunner's leading hand closer to the bore axes. Italian-made Beretta over-unders, in both the inexpensive S680 series and the high-quality SO series, show minimum fore-end depth at the gripping point, and the SO series in particular has a classic, Boss-like fore-end.

It is difficult to design a side-by-side shotgun that does not have reasonably good hand-to-barrel relationship. The horizontal barrel arrangement lends itself to a trim profile, and, if the fore-end's underline sweeps ahead in harmony with the fore-end iron's underlines, there will be minimum wood between the bore axes and the shooter's leading hand at the gripping spot. Unfortunately, this potential for perfect hand-to-barrel relationship can be upset by certain American notions that demand ultra-huge beavertailed fore-ends that push the leading hand down and away from the barrels.

The ultimate hand-to-barrel relationship is when the shooter's

Merkel and Franz Sodia over-unders are made with trim fore-ends that enhance hand-to-barrel relationship. On the Merkel here, note how the leading hand surrounds the lower barrel, and how both hands are in the same plane relative to the bore axes. Thus the Merkel has fine pointing qualities despite a high standing breech.

leading hand actually cups the barrels, which happens when a side-by-side is fitted with the so-called "splinter" fore-end. The splinter fore-end is *not* intended to be a gripping surface, and using it as such is an amateurish error. Traditionally and theoretically, the gripping point on a splinter-equipped double is the barrels themselves! A shooter takes hold at whatever distance down the barrels is comfortable and effective for him. No attention is paid the splinter; its presence doesn't demand that one *must* grasp it, as so many Americans seem to believe. Indeed, any sizable human who mistakenly grips the splinter fore-end will have his arm kinked like the elbow of a southpaw beer drinker, and the acute angle will serve only to detract from natural pointing accuracy and smooth swinging action. In reality, then, the side-by-side with a splinter fore-end is the ultimate in theoretical perfection for hand-to-barrel relationship in game guns, because it allows the leading hand direct access to the bore axes; no chunky fore-end elevates the axes above the leading hand's natural pointing line.

The splinter-type fore-end is standard on all British and European game guns to take advantage of the horizontal double's subtle qualities. This gives the guns trim lines while still providing the mechanical needs of a break-action piece. To protect their hands from barrel heat, shooters of the Old World use a leather-covered hand guard that slips onto the barrels just ahead of the splinter. The hand guards are light and consequently do not spoil the beautiful balance of great game guns.

A good hand-to-barrel relationship is virtually automatic on shallow-profiled side-by-sides. Observe how the thumb parallels the bore axes to help establish alignment.

Using a bulky beavertailed fore-end generally upsets the balance of such fine guns, placing more weight ahead of the hingepin. Regaining perfect balance then becomes a testy challenge for the gunmaker's skill, because balance in a great game gun can't always be regained by the simple expedient of using greater butt density to offset the beavertail's added weight. Although a possibility, it increases overall weight and detracts from the gun's dynamics.

Handling a finely crafted double that retains excellent balance and a lively overall weight despite a beavertail is an entirely different sensation than is hefting a mass-produced beavertail-equipped double, a breed that generally suffers from weight-forward problems. Just recently, for example, I did some patterning and hunting with a low-priced side-by-side chambered for the 3-inch 12-gauge magnum shotshell. The gun's twin 30-inch barrels were heavily walled and rested atop a massive beavertail. It scaled 8½ pounds and was anything but lively. Getting it started demanded a considerable physical effort, and it was almost impossible to get on close, fast-flying birds with that muzzle-heavy item.

About the same time, however, I was able to handle a fine old Gebruder Adamy, which was also chambered for the 3-inch 12 and had 32-inch barrels, and thus should have been heavier and more cumbersome than the shorter, mass-produced side-by-side. But it wasn't! The Adamy was lighter, livelier and more responsive. It barely shaded 7½ pounds and hinted but faintly at a weight-forward condition. Made in Suhl, Germany, between 1921 and 1939, the Gebruder Adamy line of over-unders was identical to the Merkels, and it was vastly superior to my mass-produced side-by-side because craftsmen had shaped it to blend gun and gunner into theoretical perfection. The Adamy, like the Merkel, had excellent hand-to-barrel relationship, and its barrels were especially important to the weight/balance equation. Sharply tapered and relatively thin toward the muzzles, they provided a long sighting radius, high velocities and tight patterns without adding significant ounces. The result was a long-range fowling piece that had the same balance as a fast-handling upland gun, and it could be swung into action effortlessly. Such design features and craftsmanship spell the difference between a great gun and just another smoothbore.

The Browning Belgian line of over-unders was another example of how barrel tapering can affect handling qualities. The Browning catalog openly admitted that the standard and Lighting grade over-unders had a forward weight distribution, a condition that developed because of heavily walled barrels. Neither of these models had the responsiveness of a true game gun. But it's a different story with the Browning Super Light. Its barrels were apparently tapered to bring the main concentration of weight squarely between the shooter's hands, thus giving a lively characteristic as the equally weighted stock and muzzles pivot easily around the centered half-weight. The Browning Super Light, therefore, is a true game gun, whereas the heavier models fit another category by virtue of their obvious muzzle hang. Interestingly enough, a version of the Browning Super Light was on the European market long before it reached the United States, a fact that may indicate that Old World wingshots knew exactly what they wanted while Yankee and Canadian hunters were indiscriminate or sadly lacking in the knowledge of exactly what constitutes sound theoretical design in a game gun.

Since the subject of balance has now been broached, we can set aside the matter of hand-to-barrel relationship and explore this new subject relative to shotgun design and wingshooting theory. The double-barreled game gun's subtle advantage here is being built on a compact metallic nucleus that leaves its extremities open to modification as theoretical weight/balance factors decree. The same ease of modification isn't possible with pumpguns or autoloaders because of their greater length, bulk and myriad moving parts running from magazine cap into the butt. Before entering a discussion of bird-gun balance, however, a clarification of terms is necessary, for laymen frequently underestimate its complexities and importance.

There are two considerations that go into the overall evaluation of a shotgun's balance, and they must be related to avoid a simplistic approach to the subject. The first of these is "balance point"; the second, "weight distribution."

A balance point is nothing more than a spot that divides the shotgun's weight evenly fore and aft. In the well-known sport-shop test, shoppers will determine balance by resting a shotgun over an extended forefinger and shifting it until a balance point is found.

Then, with the gun teetering horizontally, the shopper proclaims it "nicely balanced" regardless of where the balance point is. This test, by itself, is of no true value in the overall evaluation of a bird gun! Every lengthy item from a crowbar to a telephone pole has a balance point, and finding said spot doesn't automatically mean overall balance is "nice." For example, barbells used by weight-lifters have a centrally located balance point—but they can also have 200 pounds of steel on either end! And despite the location of a balance point, the barbell assembly would be anything but easily handled.

The same is true for shotguns. One with thick-walled muzzles and heavy butt could still balance at a central point, but it too would be slow-starting and unwieldy. Thus, the mere act of finding a balance point means little, and overemphasizing the finger-rest test can cause one to misinterpret a shotgun's actual qualities.

Weight distribution is a more important factor in shotgun evaluation than is the basic balance point. Master craftsmen have traditionally given classic game guns what can best be described as "between-the-hands" weight distribution, meaning that at least half the gun's weight is concentrated between the shooter's trigger hand and leading hand, while the remaining weight is divided evenly throughout the butt and muzzle segments. Guns so apportioned can have their balance point directly under the knuckle pin, tangent to the knuckle's trailing edge, or a scant fraction of an inch behind the knuckle. Those with barrels of 28–30 inches may have their balance point tangent to the knuckle's leading edge or a tad farther forward. Never, however, will the balance point of a true game gun with between-the-hands balance be found any great distance ahead of the knuckle, because that would imply a distinctly muzzle-heavy situation, which is foreign to the dynamics of finely crafted game guns. The importance of between-the-hands weight concentration lies in the physical fact that a shotgun so constructed will, unless it is simply too heavy overall, pivot easily about its middle, there being relatively minor inertia in butt and muzzle sections to retard quick movement. This leaves the gun extremely responsive to work perfectly with the gunner's natural hand action and makes it a favorite for fast action in the uplands or pass shooting over normal ranges.

Upon first meeting with truly fine doubles having between-the-hands weight concentration, inexperienced shooters who have hitherto handled only long, heavy, ill-balanced repeaters find themselves excitedly announcing that quality-crafted doubles virtually "point themselves." That's an exaggeration, of course. No shotgun, however great, does much by itself except get rusty. But the neophyte's enthusiasm does reflect the vastly superior dynamics of a great game gun and proves skilled workmanship *plus* a concern for theoretical aspects can minimize the shotgun's drag upon a human's natural pointing action.

Some great shotguns have a balance point located in advance of the knuckle pin to indicate a weight-forward condition. This is legitimate when the gun has been designed with long barrels for distant shooting at waterfowl, because the heavier barrels generate a flywheel momentum that smooths the swing and carries it into a positive follow-through. But the legitimacy of a weight-forward feature does not mean the barrels can be thick-walled and massive like those of a mass-produced gun. The standard of value is based upon degrees, not extremes. And in a truly fine gun, the balance point for a weight-forward condition will be *just* ahead of the knuckle so there is no muzzle sag. Even with barrels of 30-32 inches, skilled gunmakers bring the balance point quite near the knuckle by judicious use of tapered barrels and carefully selected stock/fore-end blanks. The classic "feel" in a fine double designed to have its weight forward must not be confused with the outright muzzle-heavy hang found on ordinary guns. On the great shotguns, long barrels are draw-filed to eliminate the plummet effect of gross muzzles, and the weight is instead distributed evenly throughout the length of the tubes to give the gun a lively feel despite a forward weight adjustment.

There is a third possible weight distribution which, although seldom utilized, is legitimate for certain hunters under certain conditions. This is the rearward weight condition, a gunmaking technique that produces ultra-quick muzzle speed because the barrels are exceedingly light relative to butt/action weight. The balance point for this type of gun will be found behind the knuckle pin. These fast-starting doubles are practical in woodcock covers, grouse thickets and some bobwhite country. However, they do present definite problems for the wing-gunner: Their muzzles are so dynamic that they demand perfect coordination and timing. For

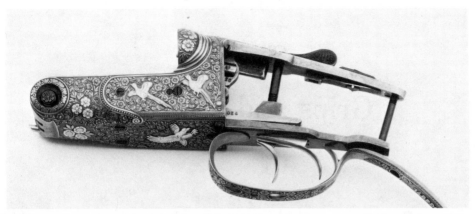

The double's subtle advantages spring from its compact, centrally located metallic nucleus. Repeaters must have working parts strung from stem to stern. This Parker frame and trigger were modified by Pachmayr Gun Works.

they are easily bossed, and aggressive hand action will slash them far ahead of the target before a poorly timed shooter can trigger the charge. Moreover, guns so weighted generate none of their own swing momentum; therefore, the shooter must display excellent form and supply his own follow-through unfailingly. The distinct and exaggerated rearward balance point is best avoided by all but the real expert who has the experience, timing and technique to handle its muzzle speed. The average shot will not only find the classic between-the-hands weight distribution adequately responsive for most wingshooting, but he will also find it smoother and more manageable.

The subtle advantages of a double gun, then, spring from its compact, centrally located action nucleus, which serves as a constant while leaving extremities that can be adjusted at will to fit weight and balance point desires along with the individual shooter's physique and the theoretical aspects of wing-gunning. Too, the double's action depth is generally shallow enough to provide a barrel arrangement that places the bore axes in very close promixity to the leading hand's natural pointing line. Repeaters cannot be modified successfully because of the greater length over which their working parts are distributed and because of the added height introduced by slab-sided receivers. But in the great doubles, skilled craftsmen have worked the subtle advantages to the nth degree of perfection.

Chapter 3

Grips and Gripping

Practically every magazine article or book chapter written about shotgun fit and design has been woefully incomplete. Writers have elaborated mainly upon those dimensions and features associated with a shotgun's upper surfaces, such as the drop at comb and drop at heel, while almost totally ignoring the importance of the lower configurations. But a proper study of shotguns requires an equal concern for both upper *and* lower lines, because the underside, supplying gripping and holding points, exerts tremendous influence on the natural ease and accuracy with which a shooter can handle and point any given gun.

The importance of a shotgun's underlines was suggested by a comment made in Chapter 2, namely, that a human's hands not only coordinate nicely with each other but that they do so with optimum efficiency when they can function on the same plane. This natural coordination can be seen in the way a housewife sweeps a floor, a farmer pitches hay, and a gardener rakes a flower bed. Be the instrument a broom, pitchfork or rake, they all have one thing in common: They keep the user's hands situated on and working along the same longitudinal plane. Any of those instruments would become unbelievably awkward if it were given a curved or S-shaped handle, because the bend would force the hands to work on different planes.

This factor is of considerable importance when the finer points of wingshooting and shotgun design are discussed. Theoretically, the fore-end and grip should be designed to keep the shooter's hands on the same plane relative to the bore axes, thus maximizing the potential for natural coordination and alignment.

When the hands are not in line they have a natural tendency

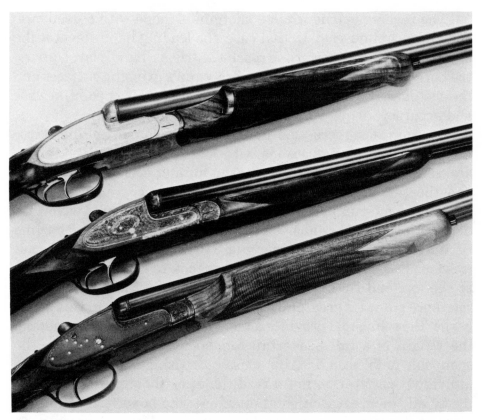

Three different fore-end designs: semi-beavertail with schnobble, splinter and full beavertail. (Photo courtesy The Orvis Company)

to seek a common level; they instinctively fight the object they hold, and, in turn, the instinctive adjustments cause varying degrees of gun tilting, which hinders alignment and pattern placement. Assume that a side-by-side with splinter fore-end has a tightly curved pistol grip. The leading hand, grasping the barrels some distance ahead of the fore-end tip, will be riding high relative to the bore axes, whereas the trigger hand will be kept lower by the full pistol grip's geometry. But when the hands fight to regain their common level, the high-riding leading hand will draw down somewhat to depress the muzzles, while the low-sitting trigger hand will work upward and elevate the butt. Depending upon the individual shotgun's dimensions, such tilting can depress the muzzles enough to obscure them below the breech and either hinder or prevent a quick, natural point.

The reverse is true when a shotgun is made with a deep fore-end and a shallow grip. In that case, the leading hand elevates the muzzles as it fights upward to reach the trigger hand's level, giving the barrels an upward tilt. Thus, a shotgun's gripping surfaces and the shotgunner's natural hand action do indeed affect pointing ease and accuracy.

Shotgun designers who understand the hands-in-line factor match a grip's configurations with fore-end's lower lines. There are basically three fore-end types: the splinter, the semi-beavertail and the full beavertail. Each can have minor variations. For instance, some gunmakers put a schnobble on the semi-beavertail. Sometimes the schnobble is used to break the long underline running from a double's trigger guard to the muzzles, in which case it is purely cosmetic. At other times, shooters who grasp a double at the fore-end tip enjoy the schnobble's swell as a palm-filling reference point for greater overall hand/gun contact. In this latter usage, the schnobble provides a more positive grip without adding the weight of a full beavertail fore-end. Normally, though, the schnobble isn't used on trim, classic British game guns. It is an individual preference, not a traditional or theoretical necessity.

Of all the great British gunmakers who honor the traditions of a splinter-type fore-end, James Purdey & Sons of London were the first to acknowledge the legitimacy of using greater-than-normal bulk and width at the tip of a splinter to fill the palm and enhance gripping qualities. It is not unusual to find a Purdey with a broader splinter-type fore-end than those applied by other famous makers. Purdey also makes a fashionable semi-beavertail that serves the same purpose. Adjustments are then effected in the handmade Purdey to retain the proper weight distribution for between-the-hands balance and weight concentration.

How are grips matched with specific fore-end types for the best hands-in-line arrangement? Classic British and European side-by-sides almost always sport the straight (English) grip in connection with a splinter or semi-beavertail fore-end. When an over-under has the low-profiled action and a slender fore-end, it is also given a straight or semi-pistol grip. Boss and Woodward-Purdey over-unders fairly shout for a straight grip, and British craftsmen insist on using it as their standard. This combination of underlines delivers the theoretically perfect blend of an excellent hand-to-barrel relationship with an efficient hands-in-line arrangement.

Certain European doubles have a semi-pistol grip accompanying the splinter or semi-beavertail fore-end, and that combination tempts laymen to argue that there is nothing truly classic about the pairing of straight grip and splinter. But anybody who has handled prestigious European doubles knows that lines alone can be deceiving. The mild sweep of a semi-pistol grip's geometry often duplicates the fit, feel and function of a straight grip. It still allows the trigger hand to ride high relative to the bores, thus keeping it in line with the leading hand's position. The semi-pistol grip, then, is hardly a radical departure from the straight grip; it serves the same theoretical purpose as the English-style grip. However, on some guns it is used to add weight and create a specific balance point, while on still others the semi-pistol

The Rolls-Royce of shotgunning: a cased Purdey with two sets of barrels. Despite favoring the splinter-type fore-end, Purdey provided slightly greater bulk at the tip to fill the shooter's palm.

The splinter-type fore-end should go with a straight English-style grip to keep the gunner's hands in line. The straight grip also allows the hand to shift when the gun has double triggers. (Photo courtesy The Orvis Company)

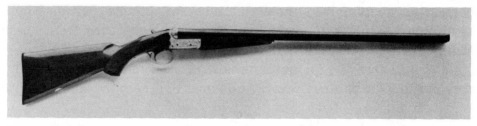

It's bad theory to pair a full pistol grip with a splinter fore-end. The trigger hand rides low, while the leading hand is placed higher as it grasps the barrel ahead of the splinter. As the hands are not on a common plane relative to the bore axes, the natural leveling action of the shooter's hands will depress the barrels.

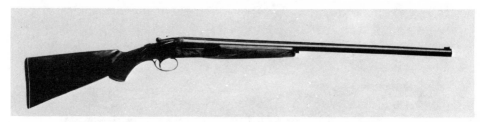

A full pistol grip works better on a side-by-side double when the fore-end is a relatively deep and full beavertail. The large fore-end lowers the leading hand so that it is closer to being in line with the trigger hand.

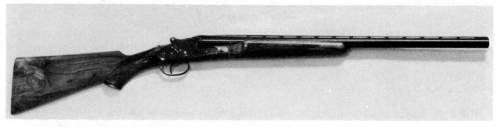

A side-by-side with a long beavertail can have a mild pistol grip and still keep both hands in the same plane. (Photo courtesy The Orvis Company)

design is used to break the monotonously long underline. Thus, like the schnobble on a fore-end, the semi-pistol grip can be mainly cosmetic.

Because the straight grip is widely misunderstood among modern shotgunners of the Western Hemisphere. I must digress here for a paragraph to discuss its past and purpose. Laymen describe the straight grip as "racy" when comparing it to the full pistol grip so common on American shotguns, and, unfortunately, they accept it solely as a matter of line without regard for function. But knowledgeable designers and critics *always* put function ahead of form and early gunmakers did just that. Without pet prejudices and preconceived notions, and unencumbered by a concern for sheer style, they developed and retained the straight grip because it met practical and theoretical needs on twin-triggered doubles having the normal (for those times) splinter fore-end. This does not especially include the supposed need for hand slippage as the shooter switches from one trigger to another, although that has traditionally been a justification for the straight grip. Trigger switching can be done as easily without sliding the entire hand, and many shooters who believe they need slippage room actually don't move their trigger hand as much as they believe they do, if at all. Instead, the straight grip has other raisons d'etre. As mentioned above, for example, the straight grip simply provides the best hands-in-line arrangement on guns having trim fore-ends. Moreover, although casual shooters will complain that a straight grip doesn't give them anything "to grab onto," that's the way it is supposed to be: The idea is to reduce the gripping power of the trigger hand so that the leading hand can dominate. For if one applies the tenets of game-gun theory—combining the thrust-out system and hand-to-eye coordination—the leading hand must perforce become the dominant member; it works to the eye, while the trigger hand merely coordinates with it. Thus, any mechanical feature that reduces the power of the trigger hand assists the physical application of theoretical elements.

Appearance, then, has nothing to do with the straight grip's development, efficiency and continued use. There were definite theoretical reasons behind it, and those reasons are still valid today when appropriate. It is wrong to use a straight grip with any or

With a full pistol grip and deep fore-end, hand-to-barrel relationship may not be ideal, but the hands will be in line—which is why this Winchester Pigeon Grade XTR Lightweight points well.

all sorts of fore-ends, especially bulky ones, simply to produce a certain profile.

The full pistol grip is best adapted to doubles having either a deep or beavertail fore-end. Fore-end depth and bulk keep the shooter's leading hand below the bore axes, and the curvature of a full pistol grip is needed to position his trigger hand at the same lower level. Hands thus depressed don't have an optimum hand-to-barrel relationship, of course, but at least a perfect hands-in-line arrangement can be salvaged if the grip's geometry is matched to the fore-end's depth.

The shooter's responsibility begins immediately after the gunmaker has given the game gun a theoretically sound combination of gripping points. He must use his hands according to design features. Grabbing the gun clumsily and thoughtlessly will frustrate the refined aspects of shotgun design and wingshooting practices.

For example, the side-by-side with a splinter fore-end is generally misused by hunters because they do not know the proper way to grip it. As already mentioned earlier, this type of shotgun is gripped at any point along the barrels that is comfortable for the shooter. The splinter is ignored; contact is purely hand-to-steel. Any mature person who grasps the barrels indifferently, however, almost surely finds himself with an immediate problem: His fingers wrap around the barrels to obstruct the sighting plane and blot out the muzzles! Thus, since a sharp picture of the target and a blurred view of the muzzles are needed as reference points for the wingshooter's master eye, a refined gripping method clearly becomes mandatory.

The proper leading-hand grip for a splinter-equipped side-by-side finds the shooter's thumb lying alongside the barrel, not

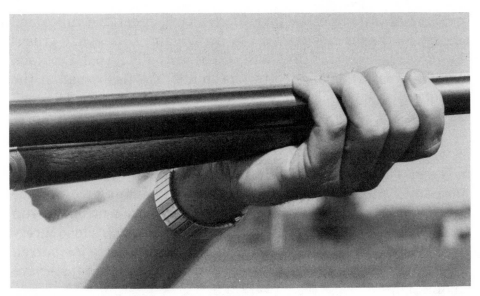

On a splinter-equipped side-by-side, the thumb lies alongside the barrel parallel to its axis while the fingers wrap around the barrels themselves, *not* the fore-end. Gripping at the fore-end tip is favored by many, because the tip fills the palm, but the grip can be anywhere along the barrels that feels comfortable.

The shooter's leading hand should grip a splinter-equipped double with the thumb lying parallel with the bore axes. The heel of the thumb blocks the left eye to ensure domination by the outside eye. However, the finger tips should *not* overlap the barrels, to obstruct the sighting plane, as shown here; they, too, must favor the barrel's side as shown above.

overlapping it, while the four fingers curl under the tubes and emerge on the far side with a rearward slant. Unless one grasps the gun at the fore-end tip, there will be virtually no palm contact. Holding pressure is applied by the thumb, the fleshy pad at the heel of the thumb, and the curled fingers. Of the four curled fingers, the index finger bears most heavily against the barrels.

It is an effective grip, although most hunters find it uncomfortable at first. The forward-pointing thumb, tangent and parallel to the bore axes, encourages a natural point via the hand-to-eye harmony. The rearward-slanting fingers, impinging on the barrel's side rather than its upper surface, help control the gun without encroaching upon the sighting plane. And an added nicety is that the fleshy thumb pad, situated boldly alongside the barrel, serves to block out the offside eye and ensure master-eye domination.

This same grip is recommended for splinter-equipped doubles with a leather handguard slipped about their barrels and side-by-sides sporting the semi-beavertail fore-end. The only slight difference might be noticeable palm contact with either of these features because of their greater bulk, but that is insignificant. The important thing is to retain the prescribed finger angles for a controlling grip while still leaving the sighting plane free of obstructions.

The leading hand's grip changes for a shotgun with a beavertail fore-end, as the added dimensions automatically keep the fingers from overlapping the sighting surface. In this gripping method, the index finger becomes the pointing digit. It is extended, and the beavertail fore-end of either a side-by-side or over-under is laid diagonally across the leading hand's cupped palm. On a side-by-side, the index finger is positioned between the tubes; on an over-under, it runs parallel to the bore axes. Viewed from the muzzles of an over-under, the index finger's tip will be roughly 6 o'clock to the lower barrel. Some shooters find the 6-o'clock location puts a strain on the hand and finger, and modify the grip by running the index finger to a more relaxed 7-o'clock point. In either case, the bore axes go wherever the pointing index finger goes, and the index finger works naturally with the master eye. The remaining three fingers curl upward, supplying just enough pressure to control recoil.

While on the subject of the leading hand's grip, I must disgress for a moment to mention the 2-inch 12-gauge. It was once a popular chambering, and practically all British gunmakers produced it. Some writers have looked upon the 2-inch 12 as a mere novelty; others have opined that it was an attempt to improve the efficiency of light charges by shortening the shot string. But I have little enthusiasm for either explanation. If any sportsman of yesteryear wanted a novelty, nothing would have been more appropriate than a sleek, racy smallbore. Moreover, the short shot string thrown by a $7/_8$-ounce charge in the 12-gauge isn't all that noticeable over the short ranges involved. The reason for the 2-inch 12's existence must be something else.

If it were possible to research the subject. I'm sure we would find that the 2-inch 12 was developed because shooters who wanted to use light-kicking game guns found the smaller gauges too narrow to grasp properly. A man-sized hand couldn't help but overlap the tubes and obstruct the sighting plane. This was especially true since the British, who developed the 2-inch 12, generally stuck with the splinter fore-end. Only the width of a 12-bore double gave these wing-gunners a substantial grip. Thus instead of going to a bonafide smallbore, they retained 12-gauge dimensions and chambered for optimum efficiency with the lighter loads. The improved pattern of the 2-incher's short shot string was therefore a bonus, not a premeditated goal.

The trigger hand's position is almost mandated by the grip's configurations. However, there is a tendency for it to creep upward on the tang of a straight or semi-pistol grip, and that tendency must be anticipated and checked. A hand that slips too high on the tang will generate a different lifting action than one properly located, and that could disrupt the natural hand-to-eye coordination or alter the hands-in-line factor. Moreover, a high-riding hand will force the trigger finger to pull upward against the trigger's geometry, which generally means greater resistance, and that heavier trigger pull could seriously affect a shooter's timing.

Regardless of the gripping surface or method, it is best if hand pressure is very light. No shotgun should ever be held tighter than necessary to control recoil, and a tender grip is especially suited to the great game guns because they are lightweight, well-balanced pieces that respond readily to hand action. Excess gripping pressure and hand action can overcontrol them, since tensed hands, which are normally accompanied by equally tight arm and shoulder muscles, impart a spastic, jerky motion to the muzzles. Thus, the prerequisite for a smooth, natural swing with a fine double is a loose, relaxed network of nerves and muscles, and that relaxed state is, at least in part, the result of a delicate touch with properly placed hands.

Chapter 4

A Flexible Field Style

Whereas modern American shotgunning style is unfortunately predicated on skeet and trap techniques, British and Continental wingshooters have come under no such disastrous influences. The dominant Old World style is still based purely on hunting usage. The result, which can be termed the "British method" because it is taught religiously in all the schools run by the foremost British gunmakers, evolved alongside the classic game gun and is a much more flexible style than the "face-the-shot" method currently in vogue in America. It allows the hunter to utilize his natural pointing attributes, to experience every thrill and advantage the trim, responsive double has to offer, and to reach that level of maximum field efficiency with only a minor concern for foot position.

Indeed, the main contrast between our Yankee face-the-shot concept and the British method lies in footwork. Ours teaches a rigidity that hinders field shooting; theirs opens the way for fast, natural movement. American skeet and trap instructors insist that the right-handed shooter's left foot must *always* be placed ahead of the right, and that the leading foot must bear somewhat more than half the body's weight. The swing then becomes a pivot-and-drive action with the leading leg acting as the pivot while the rear foot pushes the body and gun around. (The process is reversed for a left-handed shooter, of course, with the right foot always ahead.) Additionally, skeet and trap instructors insist that the feet not be positioned toward the target itself but rather along the target's line of flight where the shot will be delivered. It is from this move that the technique gets its name.

One cannot argue against facing the shot on clay targets. It works perfectly. But there is a considerable difference between clay-target games and field shooting. Tournament marksmen have the luxury of time, liberal rules that allow fully mounted and aligned guns before the target is released, and "grooved" target angles. Before the target appears, they can set their feet, adjust their weight distribution, and assume the forward tilt so common among trap and skeet shooters.

Hunters do not have the same leisure, however. They are normally out of position when game breaks cover, their feet sometimes deep in muck or clutched by bramble. Guns are generally at a low, field-carry level and must be mounted with birds already a-wing. The hunter must collect himself under pressure and make his swing with much less chance of attaining a perfect face-the-shot stance. Thus the American hunter, whatever his off-season devotion to skeet and trap, must realize that facing the shot is not a universally effective style, having definite limitations afield. It is slow, awkward and often impossible to use because it involves just one prescribed foot position.

The British method evolved long before anyone even dreamed of skeet and trap. The rigid stance requirements of those static games had no influence. In their cramped "butts" overlooking the moors, and during fast action on pheasant drives, British and Continental wingshots needed a flexible style that enabled them to slap in a quick right and left without undue concern for foot location. In many respects, those first wingshooters did what came naturally: They pivoted on their right foot on shots to the right, and they pivoted on their left foot for shots in that direction. Not only was it a natural movement, but it also left them free from mental and physical restraints. They could concentrate on the game rather than on continuous foot shuffling.

The basic ready position advocated by British experts has an even weight distribution and a relatively upright posture, and the feet are comfortably under the shooter at about shoulder width. Built on this foundation, the British method frees a shooter, both mentally and physically, to pivot in *either* direction without repositioning his feet. All he does is shift his weight slightly to

British wingshooting style allows the gunner to pivot on either leg, depending where the game flushes. If the flush is on the left, as here, the gunner plants his left foot and pivots on it, driving with the right foot.

the leg favoring the target's side while utilizing his offside foot and leg as the drive mechanism.

Let's say, for example, that a bird suddenly appears on the right side of a right-handed shotgunner. According to our American face-the-shot routine, the hunter would first have to swing his left foot and leg around, place it so his stance is opened to a spot ahead of the bird, and bring some of his weight to that leading leg as he

If the flush is on the right, the British wingshot pivots on his right foot and drives with his left. This is much faster and more natural than stepping around to get the left foot forward.

works into a forward lean. Obviously, this move would require a considerable adjustment, taking time away from the actual mounting and swinging process.

The British method, however, eliminates the excessive footwork. The hunter simply shifts his weight to the right leg and uses that member as the pivot point while mounting his gun according to the thrust-out system. Using the right leg as a pivot would be taboo under face-the-shot doctrine, of course, since it *always* demands a left-foot-forward situation for right-handed shooters.

If a bird flushes on the left side of a right-handed field gunner,

For an added thrust in making the overhead shot and for helping the body in its upward and backward rotation, the shooter's offside leg helps by driving with toe pressure and leverage. This increases the arc of the overhead swing, giving added degrees beyond what one could get from a flat-footed stance.

the British style handles it simply by moving some body weight to the left side, again without taking any step or steps toward a spot down the target's line of flight, while the right foot and leg now become the drive agents. In other words, British field technique does not dictate a rigid footwork. If the target is on the left, British experts say pivot on the left leg; if it is on the right, they are equally tolerant of pivoting on the right leg. Either move is correct among tweed-attired sportsmen.

The British shooting schools also teach a different method for overhead shots, and one would expect them to know something about this as driven game has presented them with such opportunity for more than a century. Their method is based upon getting more arc and smoothness into the swing, especially when birds are almost directly overhead. The essence of their style is predicated on foot and leg work, and it involves pushing upward with the ball and toes of the offside foot to expedite the body's upward and backward rotation. As the bird approaches, the shooter's gun-side foot remains rather firmly planted as that leg becomes the pivot point and stabilizing member. However, the offside foot begins to press upward, elevating the knee and rotating the upper body backward for freer, more fluid motion and a more positive follow-through. Once a hunter practices the technique and learns his balance and timing with it, he finds that it improves his efficiency on overhead shots beyond that of the normal flat-footed stance used and advocated in the Western Hemisphere.

The British become quite athletic about this overhead technique. They don't hesitate to get well up on the balls of their feet as they stretch upward and swing through the bird. They are tolerant of anyone who actually gets to his toes, and some famous British instructors openly advocate such aggressiveness. If the shooter is supple enough, he can arch his back and work beyond the perpendicular without engendering the wrath of a British instructor. In general, the British technique for taking overhead birds adds at least 10 degrees of comfortable and effective swing arc, while the springy footwork supplies good gun/body coordination, adequate gun speed for a smooth swing and forward allowance, and a more positive follow-through.

What shotgunners must realize, then, is that the great and

classic game guns did not evolve in a vacuum or on the artificialities of skeet and trap ranges. As the past four chapters have tried to emphasize, their lines and proportions developed as gunmakers and gunners tried to utilize every possible degree of natural human action, coordination and pointing accuracy. And as in an artistic tapestry, every element of fit, feel, function and form is a colorfully essential thread that must be properly interwoven to complete the fabric.

Chapter 5

Classic Locks and Actions

In the vernacular of shotgun authorities, a double's firing mechanisms are called "locks," while the devices used to hold its barrel and breech assemblies together are termed "bolts." The steel housing that contains the locks and bolts is either the "action body" or the "frame." These three units are inseparable, each affecting the size, style, placement and strength of the others. Therefore, any scientific evaluation of a break-open double must be based on how they complement each other under theoretical, mechanical and practical requirements.

Creating the metallic nucleus of a drop-barrel double is generally a three-step process. The gunmaker first settles on the type of locks he wishes to use, after which the frame size and style are easily determined. The bolts are selected only after the locks and frame have been established, since their job isn't merely to hold the gun together but also to compensate for whatever inherent weaknesses the first two elements may introduce. Obviously, the weaknesses aren't known until the lock and frame choices have been made.

Gunmakers encounter problems when they ignore this logical three-step process that leads from locks to frame and finally to the bolts. Some experimenters, for example, have run afoul of misfires because they built the shallowest frame possible for an over-under without giving adequate priority to the locks. Getting a powerful tumbler (hammer) blow against the over-under's lower firing pin has always been difficult because the tumbler must fall at an acute angle, and the problem is heightened as the lower tumbler's arc is further affected by reduced dimensions between the trigger plate and the lower tube's axis. The British had firing failures with some of their early versions of the over-under; the Westley Richards Ovundo was an offender because the Anson & Deeley action it employed was a poor match for the vertical barrel arrangement. The low-profiled Boss and Woodward-Purdey over-unders were flawless, thanks to powerful springs, meticulous hand fitting of hardened parts, and locks engineered specifically for the shallow frames.

Although locks can range from the simple to the sublime, they invariably fit one of three main categories: the sidelock, in which the locks are attached to separate sideplates that are fitted into the frame and stock; the boxlock, which has all the lock parts within the action frame; and the trigger-plate action, in which the lock assembly is built on the trigger plate and is introduced from the bottom of the action frame. Historically, the sidelock concept is older than the boxlock or the trigger-plate action, being mainly a sophistication of the locks used on exposed-hammer guns dating to a time before the flintlock. On the other hand, the first successful boxlock wasn't patented until 1875 when William Anson and John Deeley, who worked for Westley Richards, put the final touches on a boxlock device. By then, the American Civil War had been over for nearly a decade.

THE BOXLOCK

The Anson & Deeley lock, or variations of it, is still the universal choice in practically all boxlock side-by-sides. It is a classic in mechanical simplicity, efficiency, durability and reliability. Modern engineers in every field could do much worse than study it. As the accompanying diagram shows, the Anson & Deeley lock is composed of just five parts: the cocking rod, the mainspring, the tumbler, the sear and the sear spring. The cocking rod, tumbler and sear are pivoted to respond to the urgings of the springs.

The cocking/firing sequence of an Anson & Deeley lock is easily explained and understood. Assuming an uncocked gun, the downward (opening) rotation of the fore-end depresses the leading edge of the cocking rod, which in turn pivots the forward portion

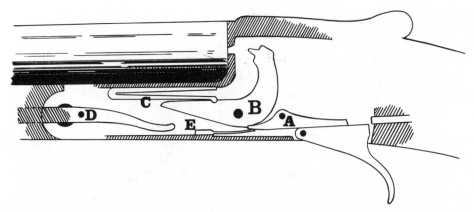

The Anson & Deeley was the first successful boxlock. When the trigger is pulled, it elevates the sear tail (A) to release the tumbler (B), which is rotated to strike the primer by the V-shaped mainspring (C). When the gun is opened, the tumbler is reset by the cocking rod (D). The sear spring (E) maintains sear/tumbler contact and supplies resistance to trigger pull. (Drawing by Dave LeGate)

American boxlocks generally have powerful coil springs rather than a V-shaped mainspring, as shown in this cutaway of the famed Parker, but the tumbler/sear arrangement is virtually identical to the original Anson & Deeley. The cutaway Parker, a one-of-a-kind item, is held by its owner, Bernard Faskell.

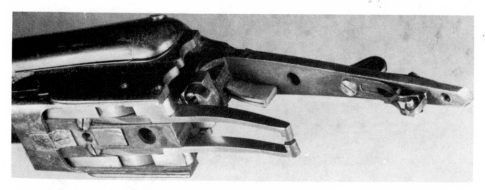

The Anson & Deeley boxlock appears very solid from outside, but does have underlying weaknesses. This 24-gauge Neumann boxlock shows the extensive machining needed to accommodate the lock works and the two transverse holes drilled for the tumbler and sear axles.

of the tumbler upward to compress the mainspring. This same act lowers the tumbler's rear segment to engage the sear, and once the sear is set, the gun is cocked.

When fired, the trigger of an Anson & Deeley lock does nothing more than elevate the sear's long tail, tipping it forward and disengaging it from the tumbler's notch. Free to pivot, the tumbler is snapped upward sharply by the V-shaped mainspring to detonate the primer. Nothing could be simpler.

THE SIDELOCK

A sidelock differs markedly from the boxlock because none of its components are supported by the frame. All lock parts are attached to a sideplate that fits inletted portions of the frame and stock. Technically speaking, the part of the stock that grips the plate is called the "jaws," while an interior metal support is known as the "bridle."

Many laymen view the sideplate mainly as an adornment, but its true beauty is that it can be removed quickly and easily for cleaning, repair and lubrication. A boxlock action is not so easily approached. Some high-quality doubles like the Holland & Holland have hand-detachable sideplates; one can remove the plate with a twist of the wrist. This is generally done by using one transverse screw and a dovetail feature. Even sidelocks that are not hand-

On a bar-action sidelock, the mainspring lies alongside the frame's action bar and has its apex pointed away from the shooter. This action is in the cocked position.

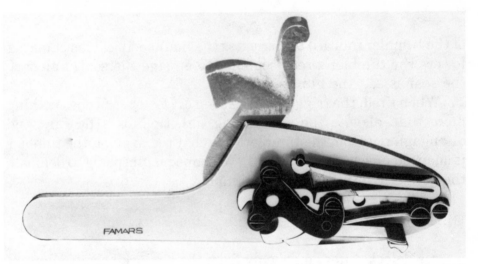

This sideplate from a Famars Castore hammer gun shows the position of a back-action sidelock. It lies behind the hammer and has its apex pointed backward toward the shooter.

detachable can be removed quicker than any boxlock can be stripped. They are normally held in place by only two screws. One is a short, forward-mounted screw that bites into the frame; the other is a long, rear-positioned screw that runs through the stock, engages the opposing plate, and draws it against the stock. On quality guns, a bushing will be fitted to accommodate this long screw for a perfectly snug fixture at a permanent location.

There are two types of sidelock arrangements, the difference between them stemming from the position of the V-shaped mainspring. These are termed the "back-action" sidelock and the "bar-action" sidelock. The back-action mechanism has its mainspring behind the trigger, apex pointed backward toward the shooter. The bar-action has its mainspring pointed forward, running alongside the extended bar of the action frame.

Many of the great shotguns have bar-action sidelocks, because they give the best sear/tumbler engagement angle. The advantage over a back-action sidelock may be slight, but properly fitted and adjusted, the crisp pulls of a bar-action give a spark of something extra.

Unfortunately, the bar-action has a weakness not encountered with back-action sidelocks: The forward location of its mainspring requires deep inletting along the action bar, reducing frame strength. Modern steels offset some of this disadvantage, but considerate gunmakers often use a top bolt, such as the Greener crossbolt, to counter the inherent weakness of a bar-action sidelock.

Safety is an important advantage held by sidelocks over boxlocks. Practically all sidelock mechanisms have an "intercepting" safety to block tumbler fall in case the sear is accidentally jarred loose. Boxlocks generally have no such secondary safety. The tangtop sliding safety of a boxlock merely controls trigger movement; it has no influence on the lock. In an Anson & Deeley lock, for instance, the long sear tails are free; and if they are given momentum by a sudden jolt, they can unseat. With nothing blocking the tumbler, an accidental discharge will occur. Holland & Holland has historically been credited with having devised the initial intercepting, or secondary, sear. But the principle is now widespread, and most British and European sidelocks employ the concept. American-made sidelocks—namely, the L. C. Smith and Baker guns—were far less sophisticated, however. Both were extremely simple mechanisms predicated on only a primary sear, and this absence of a secondary safety sear meant that either one could be fired accidentally by jarring it.

Overseas sidelocks also build a mechanical advantage into the tumbler's fall by using a "swivel" linkage between tumbler and mainspring. American-made sidelocks are without this feature, too.

High-grade over-unders have sidelocks, and the sidelock found on the Beretta SO series of guns is a classic study in strength, simplicity and safety. What is termed the bridle on most other

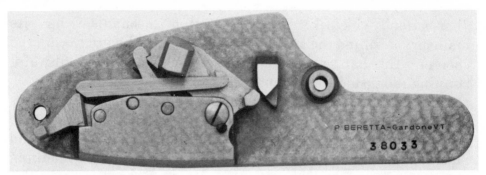

The Beretta SO sidelock is a classic example of simplicity. Its bridle and other interior projections are machined integrally, and the lock is built of very few components.

sidelocks must be built of fitted components and attached to the sideplate by screws that generally show on the outside. The Beretta's SO sideplates, however, have the bridle machined integrally, thus making the action rigid while eliminating a multitude of parts. Each SO lock requires but one screw, which holds the tumbler; three pins, on which pivot the sears; two springs, one for the sear and one for the hammer; and the major components consisting of the tumbler, main sear and safety or secondary sear. Few things in the realm of sidelocks retain the classic concept of a true sidelock while also being as elegantly simple. A polished unit is a handsome piece of the gunmaker's art.

FALSE SIDEPLATES

False sideplates are sometimes fitted to boxlock guns for the sake of ornamentation. They serve no mechanical purpose and should be detected immediately by the absence of sear and tumbler axles. Dummy sideplates merely give the engraver and inlay artist a broader canvas, and since exterior beauty is one (but *only* one) measure of the great guns, the practice is not to be criticized. Because false sideplates are generally thin, the inletting of stock and frame isn't enough to cause a genuine weakness if the basic materials and workmanship are first rate. Those who are interested in seeing a boxlock with dummy sideplates need look no further than the newest line of Browning over-unders from Belgium, the so-called Presentation series, the sideplated Citoris by Browning via Japan, and Weatherby's Japanese-made (SKB) Athena. They

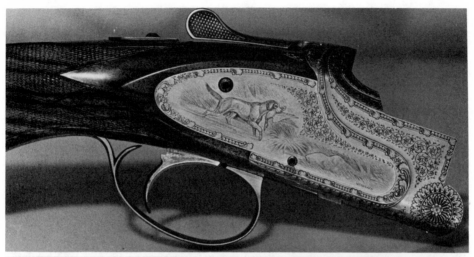

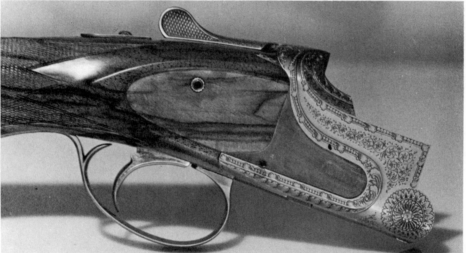

The new Presentation series of Browning Belgian-made Superposed guns can be had with false sideplates. (This one was engraved by Louis Vrancken, head of the Fabrique Nationale engraving department.) The shallow inletting does not weaken the stock significantly. Note the two bolt holes with metal bushings.

are prime examples of what false sideplates can do to enhance the looks of a double.

THE TRIGGER-PLATE ACTION

The third category of lock types, the trigger-plate action, has all lock parts connected to the trigger plate, which, of course, fits the bottom of the frame. Modern hunters will recognize it as the same principle used in repeating shotguns like the Winchester Super-X Model 1, the Model 12 pumpgun and the Remington 870 and 1100. Applied to quality doubles, however, the trigger-plate concept is more precisely fitted and adjusted than it is on production-grade repeaters.

The trigger-plate action has no weaknesses worth mentioning, but its strengths are significant. The first is that practically all trigger-plate actions are easily removed for inspection and cleaning. Perhaps more important, though, is the fact that trigger-plate assemblies sit behind the frame much like a back-action sidelock, a situation which requires no machining of the action body and consequently leaves the frame stronger.

History gives us a cloudy picture of the trigger-plate action's inception. Most writers credit James MacNaughten, who worked in Edinburgh, Scotland, during the mid-nineteenth century. But it was John Dickson, another Edinburgh gunmaker, who refined

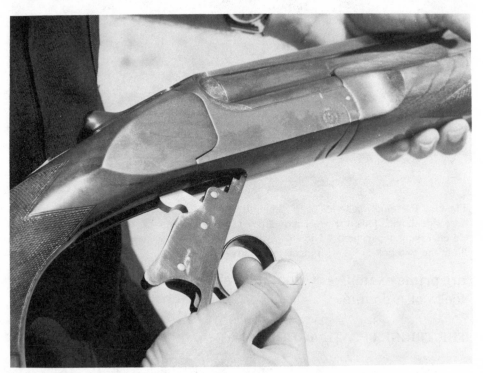

On the Perazzi guns so popular now with American trapshooters, the entire trigger and lock mechanism is neatly assembled in a compact mass atop the trigger plate, and is easily removed for cleaning or repair. It exemplifies the trigger-plate action.

Modern over-unders such as this Franchi Model 2003 have variations of the trigger-plate action. Although not readily removable like the true Dickson, they have trigger and lock components mounted directly atop the trigger plate, leaving the action body relatively free of weakening cuts and transverse holes.

the trigger-plate action and, after a legal dispute, won patent rights to it. This is not to belittle MacNaughten's efforts, of course, as I have seen some of his cased guns, and they exhibit excellent workmanship throughout. The question of who originated the trigger-plate concept may be immaterial, too, because Dickson eventually absorbed the MacNaughten enterprise.

John Dickson and Sons Ltd. is still in business at 21 Frederick Street 2, Edinburgh, Scotland. The trigger-plate action named after the firm's founder was patented in 1880 and became known as "Dickson's round action." It was a rather ingenious device, having its ejector mechanism also within the frame, whereas other types have their ejector components at least partially inside the fore-end. The lower half of the action body and the entire bar is, as the name implies, round. The bar sits well under the barrels, its geometry virtually an extension of the splinter-type fore-end's dimensions. It has nothing in common with doubles having the broad, flat floorplate.

German gunmakers jumped on the trigger-plate action with glad cries, calling it the Blitz. At least one important maker of modern doubles has also employed the trigger-plate principle. This is Perazzi of Brescia, Italy, whose target-grade over-unders have found favor among American trapshooters. The trigger-plate design gives each Perazzi extraordinary frame strength, and despite the pounding absorbed by each Perazzi tournament gun, frame failures have been nonexistent.

Some other modern over-unders of boxlock persuasion utilize the main strength of the Dickson trigger-plate action, although in classical terminology they cannot be called true round- or trigger-plate jobs. Their action bodies are not rounded; their trigger mechanisms aren't removable. However, their locks are placed behind the frame so that the body receives few, if any, weakening cuts. One glance inside over-unders like the Winchester 101, the Remington 3200, the Merkel and the Franchi 2000 series will show trigger and lock components sitting atop the trigger plate rather than inside the frame or coupled to sideplates, thus rendering the frame amply strong for magnum loads and/or continuous clay-target shooting.

Chapter 6

The Triggers

A shotgun's trigger or triggers must not be confused with its locks. They are different entities, their mechanisms entirely separate from each other. Their sole point of contact is normally on the sear's underside when the trigger's upper extension, commonly called the "blade," is elevated by the shooter's finger pressure. Thus the theory and practice of trigger design and construction is an independent topic.

It is also an important topic, since the trigger is a shooter's link with the locks. Its operation affects his timing; its design, mechanical principles, strength, assembly and fit are a measure of the gun's overall quality. A great gun deserves a great trigger so that the sportsman can get the utmost performance from refined locks.

DOUBLE TRIGGERS

The classic game gun has traditionally had double triggers. The front trigger normally fires the right barrel of a side-by-side or the lower barrel of an over-under, while the rear trigger handles the remaining left or upper tube. Generally speaking, the right barrel of a side-by-side and the lower barrel of an over-under are choked to throw more open patterns than the second barrels; hence, the hunter has an immediate choice of two patterns. Twin triggers always were, and still are, the simplest and swiftest barrel-selection method one could want.

This traditional trigger arrangement has invited some criticism from American hunters who argue that the rear trigger should control the open-bored barrel, which in stateside upland gunning is normally fired first. Recoil would then bring the front trigger backward to meet the trigger finger for an easy transition, whereas it is often difficult to go from the front trigger to the rear when recoil sends the gun backward and makes the rear trigger hard to find. In fact, the rear-to-front sequence is definitely used by the British and the Europeans on driven game: When the birds or hares appear in the distance, hunters use the tightly choked left or upper barrel first, meaning they do indeed pull the rear trigger initially, and then they switch to the front trigger for the open-bored barrel as the game nears or passes the standers or butts.

For British rough shooting, which is the equivalent of American upland gunning, the same front-to-rear sequence is employed, however, with no real complaints from British sportsmen. One reason might be that they invariably use lighter loads than do Yankee hunters, and the resulting recoil from the 1- and $1^{1}/_{16}$-ounce British game loads isn't as disruptive as the whopping belt from American high-velocity and magnum loads. I find that I can make the front-to-rear transition with no problem when hunting with the mild-recoiling 24-gauge Neumann side-by-side I love to carry, but making that same front-to-rear move has always been less swift and sure with 12- and 10-gauge magnums. Thus, on heavier recoiling guns, the rear-to-front trigger sequence may have something to recommend it.

The main reason why makers of fine, handcrafted doubles still lean to the twin-trigger setup is that it is less costly to produce and that it can be perfectly adjusted for a continuously crisp pull while still being relatively simple. The essence of gun mechanics is having the fewest number of parts to do a job. And it goes without saying that a consistently sharp trigger pull enhances one's timing and confidence. In other words, twin triggers, each one matched carefully to its individual lock, carry the gunmaker's art one step closer to perfection.

A refinement that has been worked into the double-trigger assembly is the hinged, or "articulated," front trigger, which gives in a forward direction to minimize the pounding received by the trigger finger when it pulls the rear trigger. This forward play is a standard feature on fine doubles.

Pulling the rear trigger of a double with twin triggers puts the finger in position to receive a painful rap from the front trigger when recoil sends it sharply backward.

An articulated, or hinged, front trigger, however, is spring-loaded to provide some "give" on contact and lessen the severity of the collision. This trigger unit is found on the French Vouzelaud side-by-side.

Twin triggers are simple, nothing more than the exposed trigger and an interior, high-sitting "blade" that rises to contact the lock sears. This one is from an Ansley H. Fox; the leading trigger has been pulled.

SINGLE TRIGGERS

Although the single trigger does appear to offer a shooter operational speed and ease, it is not universally accepted. Old-line gunmakers genuinely believe the twin-trigger arrangement is far superior because of its simplicity, dependability and perfect pull. Conversely, they view the single trigger as too complex, prone to breakdowns and malfunctions, and lacking the desirable crispness. These gunmakers are often joined in their opposition to single triggers by live-pigeon competitors who, shooting for substantial prizes, demand the utmost dependability.

But the single trigger does have some advantages even if it does sacrifice the final degrees of mechanical perfection attainable with twin triggers. Obviously, it eliminates the need to shift one's trigger hand for the second shot, which can be a distracting move for the unpracticed or maladroit hunter. Too, the single trigger is better adapted to climates where the hunter must wear gloves. (This latter point is not so important to British and European sportsmen, many of whom hunt in mild climates.) Based on these factors, the single trigger's popularity has spread.

A casual shooter might believe that making a single trigger is easy—that one only needs a mechanical device that trips each sear in turn. But it isn't that simple!

Designing and building a single trigger for the double-barreled shotgun or rifle is complicated by a little-known phenomenon called either the "intermediate" or "involuntary" pull. When a shoulder arm recoils, it carries the trigger hand backward with it. At some point, however, the recoiling arm meets resistance and rebounds. The rebounding action thereupon drives the trigger forward against the shooter's still-flexed finger, and the shooter *involuntarily* unseats the second lock. (Indeed, involuntary pull explains why hunters who naively put two fingers into the guard of a twin-triggered double frequently clean both barrels even though they command only one shot; the remaining, unfired trigger is loosened unwittingly when the gun rebounds.) This all happens so quickly that a gunner cannot avoid it by his own actions. Only mechanical means can negate firing because of involuntary pull by delaying the second trigger/sear engagement on a single-triggered double until the effects of rebound movement have quieted.

Some theorists also believe that involuntary firing occurs because, under recoil disturbances, a shooter grabs instinctively at his gun to regain his original grip. This instinctive grabbing, coming immediately after the first recoil sensations register on the nervous system, supposedly includes a tightening of the trigger finger, which in turn produces an involuntary second pull *not* commanded by the shooter. Instinctive grabbing may cause involuntary firing, but rebound factors constitute a better explanation and a more universal cause.

In reality, then, a shooter actually pulls a single trigger three times while getting off both barrels of a double under controlled firing. The initial pull, a consciously willed effort, unseats the first barrel's sear; the second, or involuntary pull, occurs during that intermediate period when rebound and/or instinctive forces apply; and the third is again a consciously willed pull that trips the remaining sear to fire the second barrel.

The single-trigger mechanism of a double-barreled shotgun,

then, must be designed and timed to negate the involuntary pull by providing an intermediate pause between sear engagements. For if no mechanical consideration were involved, the shooter's involuntary action would trigger the second barrel immediately after the first while the piece was still misaligned by recoil energy. It would give almost the same sensation as a fully automatic weapon or a faulty firearm that "doubles."

Gunmakers circumvent the involuntary-pull phenomenon by working delays into the single trigger, thus prolonging the time between trigger disengagement with the first sear and engagement of the second. There are two distinctly different methods of engineering a delay factor in single triggers. One is called the "three-pull" system; the other is simply known as a "delay-type" or "timing-type" mechanism.

As its name implies, the three-pull system requires three definite pulls to fire just two barrels. The first pull fires the initial tube, after which the trigger shifts to a second, or intermediate, stop position that prevents immediate engagement of the opposite sear. The involuntary trigger pull then releases the trigger from this intermediate notch, whereupon it swings to the remaining sear. When dry-fired, a double with a three-pull single trigger requires three positive trigger pulls to complete the sequence. With live ammunition, however, the involuntary pull is hidden by recoil disturbances, and the shooter must consciously will only the first and third pulls.

Very few gunmakers use the three-pull system, but Woodward, Holland & Holland and Boss have experimented with it. The Woodward over-under and Boss guns still utilize it. In collaboration with Thomas Woodward, Henry W. Holland patented a three-pull trigger in 1897. The trigger was based on a slide that fitted over the trigger blade and was free to move forward with each pull of the trigger. The slide had a stubby arm protruding from each side to engage its respective sear. When the gun was cocked, the slide occupied its most rearward position and contacted the right sear. At trigger pull, the right sear was released and the slide urged forward by a front-mounted coil spring. The slide then stopped at an intermediate position, contacting no sear, until the involuntary pull unseated it. Then it snapped forward to contact the left sear.

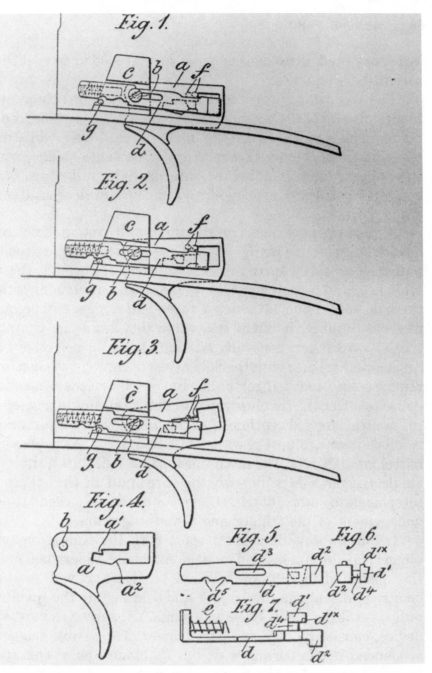

The 3-pull single trigger, designed with a definite intermediate stop to negate the mischievous involuntary pull, was patented in 1897 by Henry W. Holland and Thomas Woodward. The mechanism was based on a slide (5) that rode the trigger blade (4). When cocked (as in 1) the slide's right arm engaged the right sear. After firing the first barrel, the slide was released to move forward at the impulse of a front-mounted coil spring and to stop at a second, or intermediate, notch (2) which was a "neutral" position that contacted neither sear. Involuntary pull then freed the slide from its intermediate notch so that it could move forward again to engage the left sear (3). Thus, three distinct trigger pulls were needed to complete the firing cycle. (Photo courtesy Holland & Holland)

57

When dry-fired, three distinct pulls were needed to carry it through a right-left sequence.

The Woodward over-under's single trigger has three upright blades instead of the normal one. Arranged side by side, the right blade reaches up to engage the under barrel's sear, while the left blade contacts the over barrel's sear. The center blade, which is the trigger itself, handles the intermediate pull. Each blade is activated in turn by a spring-drawn slide that releases after every trigger pull.

A single trigger based on the three-pull system is not readily adapted to selective firing. Regardless of its mechanics, the three-pull trigger needs spring energy to carry it through the firing sequence, and a spring exerts its power in only one direction on these devices. Thus, although a three-pull trigger can be made to perform reliably, it offers less versatility than the timing-type trigger, which can generally be engineered for selective firing.

A single trigger with the delay-type or timing-type mechanism requires only two trigger pulls. But it also needs a mechanical pause to offset the involuntary pull, for if the single trigger is not in "neutral" for a short time after the initial voluntary trigger pull, recoil-caused involuntary action will discharge the double's second barrel prematurely. The mechanical pause built into a timing-type single trigger contrasts with the three-pull in that there is no intermediate stop notch. Other means are used to delay engagement of the trigger and remaining sear.

Inventors have had great sport with the timing-type single trigger, fashioning myriad models. An easily understood unit was that patented in 1898 by William W. Greener, who used recoil energy to disengage the trigger and sears while the involuntary pull was taking place. Greener's single trigger was a most simple device, consisting of a two-part trigger. The visible trigger was suspended in the normal way, but its blade was a separate part that was pivoted to the trigger's web and held in place by light spring pressure. In its upright posture, the pivoted blade could contact the sear tails of both right and left locks. Under recoil forces, however, the pivoted blade took on its own momentum, overcame the spring pressure, and rotated to a backward location away from the sear tails. The blade did not pivot forward again until recoil-induced momentum wore off. But by that time the involuntary pull had come and gone, too.

An important consideration in Greener's single trigger was the spring's strength. If it was too powerful, the pivoted blade couldn't generate enough momentum to break free and swing away from the sears. The involuntary pull would then find the trigger blade and sears still in contact, and an unwilled discharge would follow. Thus, though Greener's concept was excellent, it needed refining.

Modern designers of single triggers have done just that: They have refined Greener's approach to utilizing recoil energy rather than sheer spring pressure to effect an intermediate delay. Indeed, Greener's single trigger is not unlike the barrel-selection device on Winchester's Model 21. The mechanically exceptional Model 21

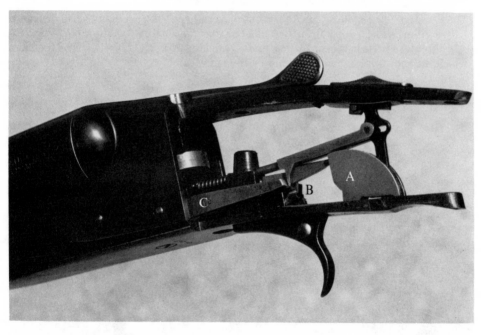

The single trigger mechanism of the Winchester Model 21 uses recoil energy to disengage the trigger blade and sear tails during the so-called "intermediate" period. Recoil forces send the timing weight (A) forward as the gun moves backward, and as the timing weight rotates forward it pushes the barrel selector mechanism and trigger blade (B) from beneath the sear tails (C). When recoil subsides and the gun rebounds completely, the timing weight returns to normal, as shown here. This mechanism is from a production-grade pre-1960 Model 21.

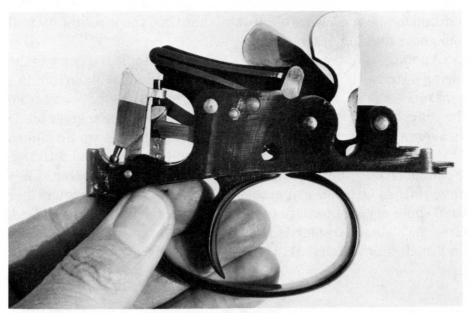

The Perazzi trigger plate action for the MX-8 over-under has a timing-type single trigger with a pillarlike sear lifter directly under the sear. The timing weight is coupled to the sear lifter by a little loop over the top, and it stands as an upright block behind the lifter, which, as shown here, has just released the right tumbler.

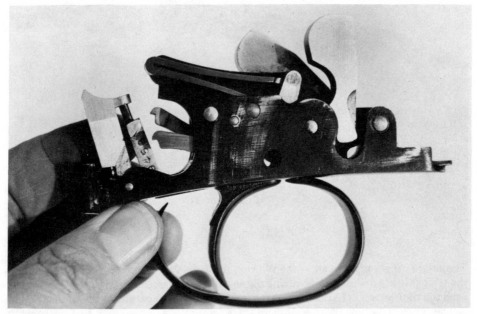

When the gun recoils, the rear-mounted timing weight takes on its own momentum and, on rebound, remains in a rearward position away from the sears so that intermediate firing will not occur when rebound drives the trigger into the shooter's finger. When a spring overcomes the timing weight's inertia, it moves back into position to contact the remaining sear.

The Lard Patent is shown here on an L. C. Smith gun prior to trigger pull (above) and after (below). The patent was based on a hooking principle that utilized considerable linkage and numerous parts. To thwart involuntary pull, a hook on the tail of the trigger linkage engaged a reversed hook on a rear-mounted pillar (as indicated by the pointer). An inertia weight, mounted directly alongside the hooks, helped hold them together during recoil/ rebound disturbances.

has a movable trigger blade, but it has been sophisticated for dependable performance by the inclusion of a massive timing block connected to it by a lengthy linkage. A heavy timing weight takes on and retains recoil-generated momentum more reliably than does just a small, pivoted trigger blade of slight weight.

Finally, Lard's Patent of 1899 is an interesting single trigger of the delay type. Originally used by Westley Richards, it came to the New World where, in 1905, it was introduced as the Hunter One Trigger on L. C. Smith guns.

The Lard trigger is based on a hooking principle. When the trigger is pulled, a hook on the tail of the trigger linkage rises to engage another hook jutting down from a rear-mounted pillar. Involuntary pull cannot occur while these hooks are joined, because the hooks must drop free before the second sear is activated. And there are two forces working to keep the hooks engaged during recoil and rebound. First, the hooks remain coupled whenever the shooter's finger retains any pressure on the trigger. But even if the shooter releases the trigger, the hooks will remain joined because of an inertia weight's action. Set alongside the hooks, this spring-urged weight swings forward under recoil motion to hold the trigger tail's hook in an elevated, engaged position. This forward action of the timing weight differs markedly from that of other devices, most of which are designed to hang in a rearward location at rebound.

Westley Richards no longer uses the Lard device, and in America it died with the L. C. Smith line. The mechanism had too many parts, the original Westley Richards unit running to 24 pieces for selective firing and 19 pieces for nonselective work. Among modern doubles, only the Remington 3200 still has such long and extensive trigger linkage. Most other makers have long since switched to the more compact triggers with the fewest possible moving parts.

Chapter 7

Bolting Systems
on the Side-by-Sides

Whenever a double-barreled shotgun is fired, there are three simultaneous forces that must be controlled to keep the gun from opening and to minimize the strain placed on the frame. Early gunmakers ran afoul of these destructive forces immediately after converting to the drop-barrel concept. Indifferently devised and poorly fitted bolts failed to control the brute forces, and, with firing pressures and vibrations bearing heavily on the action body, the inferior steels of that era yielded quickly. Frames cracked; barrels loosened. But it wasn't long until the early makers of breechloading shotguns developed sound mechanical means for bolting the gun closed while also alleviating the strain placed on the frame. The best of these bolting systems have come down to us and are still used, individually and in combinations, by modern gunmakers. This chapter and the next will review the outstanding bolting systems, their theoretical bases and their specific applications.

Before entering a discussion of the forces and the successful bolting systems, however, it must be noted that there are subtle differences between the ways they apply to side-by-side and over-under shotguns. This chapter will focus on the basic forces and the bolting systems as they relate to the conventional side-by-side, while the next chapter will cover the over-under's peculiarities.

The trio of potentially destructive forces that work on drop-barrel doubles are commonly listed as the axial force, the radial force and the bending force. The stress line of each is illustrated in the accompanying diagram.

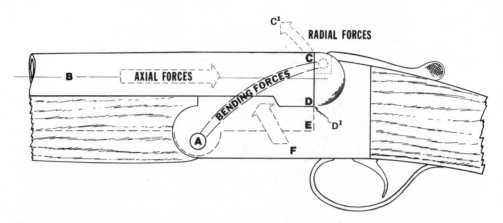

When a shotgun is fired, the frame feels three distinct and potentially destructive forces. The axial force (B) tends to separate the barrel face from the standing breech (C-D). The radial force, caused by the barrel's downward muzzle thrust, causes a lifting action at the breech end (arc C-C[1]). The bending force works like a first-class lever against the frame, exerting pressure at the angle of the frame (D) to threaten cracking (D-D[1]) at that point. The arrow at point F indicates a general fulcrum location. (Drawing by Dave LeGate)

Axial forces (designated B) are those that occur in an action/reaction manner parallel to the bore axis and perpendicular to the standing breech. If this force went unchecked, it would blow the standing breech away from the barrels at every shot.

The radial force (designated C-C[1]) pertains to the rotational movement of the barrel assembly around the hinge or knuckle pin of a drop-barrel shotgun.

These first two forces are easily controlled by any number of bolting methods to prevent gun opening. But the third factor, the bending force (A-C), complicates things considerably and argues against indiscriminate bolt selection, haphazard placement and sloppy fit. For the single most important job of a double's bolting system is minimizing the bending force's impact on the action frame. All other factors and features are secondary.

To understand the bending force and the methods used to dampen it, we must remember two things. The first is that a drop-barrel's action frame is L-shaped. Its upright portion is the standing breech; the horizontal extension is the "action bar" or, more simply stated, the "bar." The upper surface of the bar is called either the "action flat" or the "water table." The point where the standing breech and bar meet is termed the "angle of the frame." The importance of this physical form will soon become obvious.

Secondly, it must be remembered that all firearm barrels vibrate under firing pressures, beginning with a powerful downward plunge of the muzzle. This muzzle action duplicates the downward flip taken by a flyrod's tip at the start of each backcast.

Now, if we combine the frame's L-shaped outline with the knowledge that barrels vibrate, we can visualize the bending force's effect and begin to appreciate the finer theoretical and mechanical approaches to controlling it. Essentially, the bending force works against the frame like a first-class lever: With the barrel assembly's rear segment somehow bolted to the water table and/or standing breech, the pressure from the muzzle's initial downward thrust uses the knuckle pin as a fulcrum to exert pressure on the bar. The force of this prying action is felt at the angle of the frame, and if the bolting system and/or steels are of dubious quality, the frame can crack along the jagged line D-D[1] on the diagram.

Besides using high-quality steel, gunmakers try to prevent cracking by putting a slight radius at the juncture of water table and standing breech, by matching frame size to ammunition potency, and by selecting and installing perfectly fitted and positioned bolts. The radius is easily explained. If the juncture of the water table and standing breech were left at a sharp 90-degree angle, the apex of that angle becomes a wedge-shaped weak point. It minimizes molecular strength at that vital point and invites cracking. A radius, however, strengthens that critical spot by acting like a brace and by distributing the pressure over a broader area. It does not, in other words, allow a concentration of pressure at one critical point. Time has proved that a radius here need not be so huge as to deface the elegance of a fine double, and a buyer must be critical of any double made without it.

Action size is an obvious deterrent to cracking. Assuming quality steel with certain elasticity, the added molecules offer greater rigidity. The same is true in riflery; a heavy target or varmint barrel vibrates less violently than does a lightweight sporter barrel. Carried to an extreme, though, this approach of countering bending pressure with beefed-up frames will create excessively heavy guns and thereby obliterate the lively handling characteristics of the classic game gun.

Many of the great gunmakers have overcome this dilemma by

offering frames scaled to match the ammunition. Current literature from the respected firm of Westley Richards, for example, warns that magnum loads should not be used in the firm's standard-weight doubles because "the high off-centre forces involved will strain and distort action and bolting mechanisms." Westley Richards recommends its sturdier frames for magnum ammunition, listing such guns at 8 pounds or slightly more. This contrasts markedly with the normal "Best" Westley Richards 12-gauge game gun, which, built for the normal 1- to $1^1/_{16}$-ounce British hunting loads, scales but a delicate 6 pounds 4 ounces. When loads of 1¼ ounces are indicated, the Westley Richards action body is increased somewhat for an overall gun weight of 6 pounds 10 ounces.

The immortal American Parkers were also available in several frame styles. The standard 12-gauge Parker often had a No. 2 frame to withstand the most powerful loads of that day, but on special order the 12-gauge Parker could be had with a smaller No. 1½ frame. Some 12s were further refined by pairing them with a No. 1 frame, which was the standard 16-gauge Parker action body. This produced a delightful upland gun for use with mild loads.

Parker Brothers adapted the 20-gauge No. 0 frame to 16-gauge barrels for anyone wanting a light, slender version of this intermediate bore. Some 20-gauge Parkers have been found with the elegant 28-gauge No. 00 frame escorting 20-gauge tubes. Thus, the great gunmakers have manipulated frame size to meet weight, line and strength requirements.

UNDERBOLTS

Scientifically selected bolts, properly placed and fitted, are bulwarks against firing pressures. The most common method of holding a break-open gun's barrel assembly against the water table is some form of underbolting, the idea being as old as breechloaders themselves. LeFaucheux's break-action pinfire had a single underbolt that was operated by a long underlever.

The famous American Parker doubles, developed in 1865, bore a version of the underlever; a sliding lifter bar located in front of the trigger guard operated the bolt. The lifter bar was retained until 1882, when it was replaced by the now conventional top lever.

The Purdey double-underbite bolting method consists of two lumps reaching down from the barrel flat. The lumps have notches—"bites"—to receive a lug that works back and forth in the action bar. This method holds the barrels securely to the water table, but doesn't eliminate gaping at the top of the barrel/breech junction. (Photo courtesy Pachmayr Gun Works)

After 1870, however, the British and European makers gravitated to a double underbolting practice first introduced by Purdey. The Purdey double underbolt has two "lumps" extending from the barrel flat. Both lumps have notches, formally called "bites," to receive a lug that works back and forth in the bar. When the barrels are rotated into position, the rear lump depresses an action release that sends the lug popping forward to engage the bites, thus supplying a two-point hold-down pressure along the gun's longitudinal plane. Pivoting the top lever retracts the lug.

Americans have not been inclined to accept Purdey precepts. Our foremost doubles use other underbolting concepts, which will be discussed when the particular guns are encountered.

CROSSBOLTS

Underbolting alone does not counter the destructive trio of firing forces. Tests have shown that, with just underbolts in operation, the barrels can still separate from the standing breech, and this gaping action works against the bolts and the angle of the frame. British gunmakers responded to the inadequacies of

The early American Parkers had a bolting system known as a "lifter bar." In its locked position, the lifter bar hardly added to the gun's classic lines. Pushing up the bar released the bolt and allowed the barrels to drop open.

underbolting by introducing "top fasteners," which held the barrel face to the standing breech. The most famous of these top bolts is William W. Greener's crossbolt, which is a round steel rod working horizontally through the shoulders of the standing breech, alias the "fences," to fit a corresponding hole in the rib extension. (Matchlock, flintlock and caplock hammer guns were normally fitted with a vertical shield behind the point of ignition to protect the shooter's eyes from sparks, gases and cap fragments. These vertical shields became known as "fences." Technically, hammerless doubles do not have the same feature. However, traditionalists, especially the British, have insisted on applying the term to the rounded shoulders of the standing breech, and I will do so herein.) Operating in unison with the tang lever, the crossbolt's bite frustrates axial and radial forces while also dampening the harmful impulses of bending pressures. It is therefore one of the most versatile, if not the most versatile, of all top fasteners, because its placement and power oppose all three adverse forces. Not all other top bolts can do that.

Since the Greener crossbolt is insurance against cracking and premature looseness, it finds favor with overseas gunmakers who fashion lightweight game guns on boxlocks and bar-action sidelocks, both of which have their frames weakened internally by transverse holes, inletting and machined areas. The Central Europeans, along with some of the Belgian and Spanish shotgun makers, have used it extensively.

The Greener crossbolt has been widely copied, and in many instances disastrously so. The proper fit and form are essential for utmost efficiency, but producers of garden-grade doubles have taken undue liberties with Mr. Greener's invention while still capitalizing on his famous name. Claiming their product has a "Greener-*type*" crossbolt, they have inserted square or flat crossbolts instead of the original round bolt; and, in some cases, they have given the rib extension nothing more than a notch or pair of stubby arms. In quest of high profits, these makers have also done horrible jobs of fitting. The resulting bolt is but a Christmas-tree ornament. Extensions open at the rear or offering only stubby arms cannot retard axial forces or hold securely against bending pressures.

The true Greener crossbolt always uses a round bolt. Properly

The Greener crossbolt, properly fitted, is still the most effective method of pinning the barrel faces tightly against the standing breech to prevent gaping and to alleviate the strain placed on the angle of the frame.

fitted, the dowel's rear half holds securely against the barrels' thrusts; and, even on a relatively small-diameter bolt, the rear half of its circumference provides a considerable bearing surface. In turn, the rib extension need be drilled with only a small hole, thereby leaving it stronger than if it were cut for a square bolt with equal bearing surface.

THE DOLL'S HEAD

The "doll's head" is a second bolting method used to hold the barrels tightly against the standing breech. Originated by Westley Richards, the doll's head is a metallic lump or swelling, which, located at the breech end of a rib extension, fits a corresponding cavity between the rounded shoulders of a side-by-side.

Although Westley Richards used a circular doll's head, that pattern isn't mandatory. American gunmakers became especially

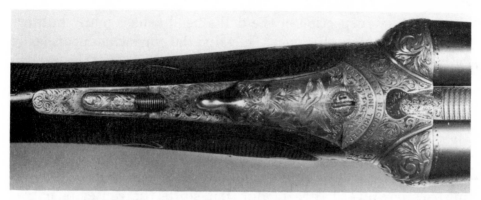

A Westley Richards game gun, showing the doll's head first devised by Westley Richards. Note the sideclips to minimize lateral gaping.

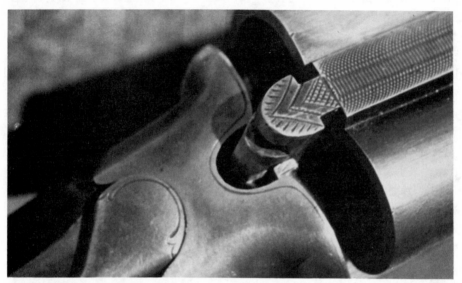

A stride forward was made in the efficiency and longevity of the doll's head bolting device when Dan LeFever devised the square-shouldered doll's head shown here to mitigate against splaying the barrel extension groove.

skeptical of the round-shaped doll's head. In the late 1800s, Dan LeFever observed that it tended to act as a wedge that splayed the slough cut into the standing breech for the barrel extension, and this spreading of the slough produced an obvious looseness between the barrel faces and the standing breech. LeFever thereupon patented a square-shouldered doll's head, thus eliminating the wedge effect. The hammerless Parkers followed suit, expanding the LeFever square-shouldered concept into a husky rectangular doll's head that gave the barrel extension a T-shaped outline.

A cursory inspection of the doll's head causes many hunters to be skeptical of its efficiency. They find the gun swings open easily for loading and unloading and, consequently, doubt that the swollen extension can actually retard firing forces. On a theoretical basis, their fear is unwarranted. The gun does indeed open smoothly when operated manually by the shooter, because the barrel assembly's pivot point is then the knuckle pin. But the pivot point changes when the barrels are bolted down firmly at discharge. Then the barrel's entire length becomes an action radius as it follows the muzzle's downward thrust, and that shifts the center of barrel movement back from the knuckle to a new point directly below the angle of the frame. This gives a radically different arc to the barrel's motion, one that is sharply down immediately ahead of the standing breech rather than lazily upward as in the case of normal loading/unloading rotation, and the leading surface of the doll's head comes fully into play as it restrains forces on the barrel assembly. The moral behind this dissertation, then, is that the budding expert must evaluate a bolting system by visualizing force lines and assessing performance under actual firing pressures. Casually opening and closing the piece proves little or nothing about a bolt's effectiveness.

To be truly effective, however, the doll's head must fit perfectly. Anything less will allow the barrels to slam forward under firing pressures and turn loose the trio of destructive forces.

Gunmakers have used sundry other top fasteners, but the Greener and the doll's head are the most effective. Those of significance will be discussed as individual guns are surveyed in following chapters.

DYNAMIC AND STATIC ACTION

Whatever its form or type, the bolt is no good unless all parts bear precisely. Sloppily fitted bolts encourage gun damage through "dynamic action." For when the bolts are loosely fitted, the main segments of a break-action gun take on their own momentum before bolting surfaces make contact, and the contact takes the form of a collision. The frame and stock stab backward as recoil sets in,

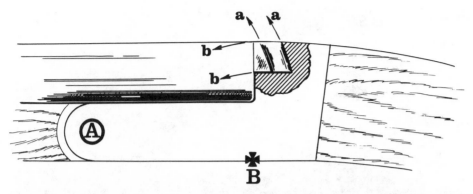

Although the doll's head allows easy opening about the knuckle pin (point A, arc a-a) for loading and unloading, its leading surfaces nevertheless dampen the impact of firing forces on the angle of the frame and bar. On firing, the barrel's entire length becomes an action radius operating about point B in arc b-b, which draws the doll's head's leading surfaces downward and against its recess. (Drawing by Dave LeGate)

while the barrels plunge downward and hump (rotate) under radial and bending forces. Obviously, since these paths taken by the major components are in opposite directions, each part takes on its own momentum. And although part movement is extremely short prior to the collision of bolting surfaces, the momentum factor cannot be ignored. Repeated with each shot, it becomes a hammerlike blow that eventually batters the metal and sets the bolting surfaces farther apart, thus allowing each part to generate even more momentum with successive shots for heightened hammering.

The opposite of dynamic action is "static action." If two or more parts of a bolting system are joined so tightly they remain solidly intact and move as a single unit under firing forces, they are said to be "static." This is the ideal bolt fit, as tightly wedded parts can't develop their own momentum to hammer each other. However, since bolt wear and the ensuing dynamic action are inevitable, the prerequisite for a great gun is action body strength to counter bolt wear.

What might confuse some readers is the fact that not all components of a side-by-side are drawn totally tight. A gun that can't flex will destroy itself in short order; thus, some relief is provided at crucial points. The barrel flat and water table should not touch except for a short distance immediately ahead of the standing breech. This minute clearance, hardly wide enough to accommodate a thin sheet of paper, keeps the barrels' downward

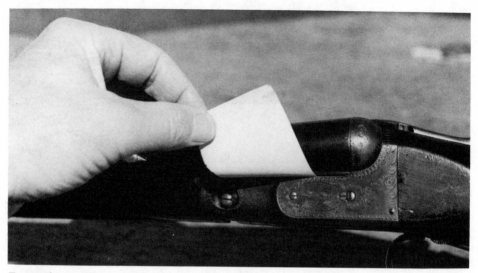

Except for a short segment immediately ahead of the standing breech, the barrel flats do not rest heavily on the action flats of a side-by-side. The slight gap prevents the barrels' downward thrust from exerting all its destructive bending force on the knuckle and the full length of the flats.

pressure from working directly against the action bar. Similarly, the rear lump is generally given slight clearance. In other words, the great gunmaker is like an understanding parent who is both flexible and rigid at the appropriate times and places.

Sideclips are a final feature intended to control the side-by-side's ruinous, exaggerated flexings. When a horizontal double is fired, its barrels tend to kick in their respective directions and open, or "gape," at the breech. This sideways wrenching can exert damaging stresses and speed overall loosening. The sideclips, which are earlike appendages angling forward from either side of the standing breech, were devised to minimize the amount of lateral gaping. Additionally, sideclips enhance the beauty of doubles by lending a curvy geometry to the standing breech.

Sideclips were always adjusted by craftsmen who smoked the surfaces, mated them to find the high spots, and then filed tenderly until the barrel face was perfectly tapered to match the sideclip's angle. It was a job that demanded patience plus artistry with a file. And it was also a job that made the great guns greater.

Chapter 8

Bolting Complexities
on the Over-Unders

Because of its greater depth, the over-under presents different design problems than does the shallow-framed side-by-side. The bending force is again the crux of the problem, because the upper barrel's elevated position gives it added leverage against the frame whenever its muzzle slams downward under initial firing dynamics. Luckily, the over-under has inherent strength in its high, U-shaped walls, and modern steels have further bolstered the frame's resistance to cracking. The vertical barrel arrangement also lends some rigidity. But continued shooting can extract its toll as vibrations either find a weak spot or create one; hence, bolt selection and strategic placement are still a vital part of the design of any stacked-barrel double.

Theoretically, the best over-under has a profile no higher than necessary to accommodate the barrel faces and a floorplate. This minimum depth, along with properly matched gripping points, provides the nucleus for the ideal hand-to-barrel and hands-in-line relationship so vital to natural pointing/swinging accuracy. It also keeps the bore axes low relative to the comb line and supporting hands so that recoil is more nearly on a straight line with the shoulder and is, therefore, less apparent than it would be from higher-sitting barrels that buck above the comb line squarely into one's face. And from a mechanical point of view, the low profile reduces the amount of leverage a vibrating upper barrel can apply against the frame.

Despite these inherent niceties of the low-profiled over-under, gunmakers have not flocked to the concept. The British did much to develop it, but their current prices are so stiff that few shooters can appreciate the fine points worked into the guns! The Italians are now employing the shallow frame beautifully, however, and they are outpacing the rest of the world in this respect. But the other European makers remain loyal to the high-profiled over-under, as do most American manufacturers. The only American shallow-profiled over-under is Ruger's Red Label.

Where does one draw the line between a shallow-profiled over-under and a high-framed one? It is an arbitrary matter, of course. On the 12-gauge gun, however, the outstanding shallow-framed models measure less than 2.50 inches through the standing breech, and some flirt openly with 2.40 inches. The classic Woodward-Purdey, which has long set standards for low-profiled over-unders, averages just 2.437 inches at that point. I have checked some Berettas at 2.43 to 2.44 inches, while over-unders made by the Zolis, including the stylish Weatherby Regency, reach just 2.49 inches. The Japanese, while not yet given much respect as makers of sporting guns, have nevertheless held the 12-gauge SKB at only 2.47 inches.

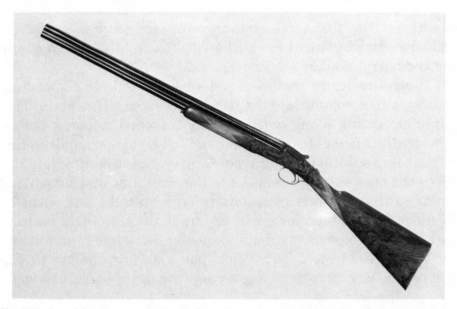

The Woodward-Purdey over-under is the epitome in a low-profiled vertical double; it has barely more height through the standing breech than is necessary to accommodate the barrel faces.

On the other hand, Browning's Superposed and its many imitators are significantly higher. I have taken the vernier caliper to Brownings of various vintages and have found them between 2.585 and 2.60 inches. The over-under made in Japan under Charles Daly (Sloan's) supervision ran a lofty 2.65 inches. Thus, there can be a full $\frac{1}{5}$-inch difference between low- and high-framed over-unders. And although that fraction may not sound impressive to readers and casual shooters, it is indeed a fine point that is noticeable to the sophisticated wingshot and discriminating shotgun fancier.

Bolting complexities are the main reason why many double-gun makers have stuck with the high-framed over-under. When the modern over-under was in its infancy, knuckle pins and underbolting had become entrenched; and gunmakers of Central Europe, taking their lead from Gebruder Merkel of Suhl, used the same methods of pivoting and joining their over-unders. The resulting guns had considerable frame depth, generally being 2½ inches or more through the standing breech, and the barrels' high location gave them potentially damaging leverage against the angle of the frame.

To offset the impact of bending forces against the steels of that era, Merkel guns were given a pair of steel "arms" that flowed down from a square-shouldered breech to bolster the angle. The arms, which many people now mistakenly consider stylish rather than functional, have been retained throughout the Merkel guns' history and have been widely copied.

Merkel bolting was very elaborate, combining the knuckle pin hook, Purdey-type double underbites, and a version of the Greener crossbolt. The knuckle pin and double underbites took up room, thus forcing the barrels skyward and causing the high profile. The barrel faces were held to the standing breech by Gustav Kersten's adaptation of the Greener crossbolt. Obviously, the true Greener's centered barrel extension couldn't be fitted on an over-under, but Kersten placed extensions on both sides of the upper barrel and fitted them to slots cut in the broad breech top. This method of top bolting has been named after its originator, but it is not universally acclaimed; for although it does reinforce the angle of the frame against bending pressures, it is also an obstacle to easy loading and unloading.

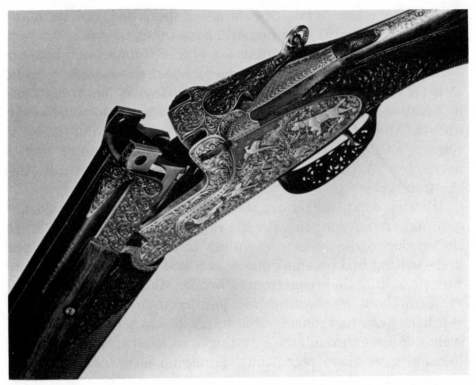

The Merkel over-under was given a version of the Greener crossbolt called the Kersten, after its inventor, Gustav Kersten.

Some critics view the Merkel's complex bolting system as an expensive anachronism, negated by the improved steels that have virtually eliminated frame cracking. Those who now make decisions at Gebruder Merkel have lent a trusting ear to the critics and modified the former quadruple bolting method. Only the most expensive Merkel, the Model 303E, still retains the underbites and Kerstens. All other lesser models have given up the Purdey-type double underbites for simple lumps that fit machined cavities in the floor. The Kerstens are still very much in evidence, however, and contribute much to each gun's basic tightness.

Merkel craftsmen have met the challenge of precise bolt fit, but the same cannot be said for copies of their product. Some excellent gunsmiths have shown me Merkel-shaped imitations, which, coming from the Iberian Peninsula and the Carinthian Alps, carried poorly adjusted bolts. The guns were in for repairs caused by dynamic action, and each had fired but a few thousand shotshells.

Because of the Kersten's effectiveness, the Merkel has always been given a relatively short, light frame without any fear of damage from bending forces. Belgian Brownings, on the other hand, compensated for the lack of a top fastener with a markedly heavier frame. A 12-gauge Merkel on my rack weighs just 6¾ pounds despite 28-inch barrels, a solid rib and dense European walnut. Conversely, my first Browning Superposed with 26-inch barrels, ventilated rib and less-dense walnut scaled a whopping 8¼ pounds. Browning has since introduced a "Super Light" over-under that shaves more than a full pound from the standard gun, but the Super Light is recommended for use only with light loads. Despite some criticism of the Merkel's quadruple bolting, then, the Kersten feature does impart an obvious strength to a light-framed, high-profiled gun.

Browning over-unders also fit the high-frame category. Besides a generous knuckle pin, they have two bolting features beneath the lower barrel. One is an underbite that runs completely across the barrel face; the other is a pair of lumps that reach down to fit cavities in the floor. This arrangement keeps all bolts on basically the same horizontal plane, but the absence of a top fastener leaves the upper barrel free to separate from the standing breech on firing and, in turn, exert a bending pressure on the frame and assembly. Browning over-unders have not failed at the angle of the frame, their salvation undoubtedly resting with quality steels and ample mass at critical points. However, experience tends to indicate that Browning over-unders and copies thereof will loosen much sooner than will a top-bolted Merkel, especially when the upper barrel is used extensively.

British gunmakers reacted more creatively to the over-under concept than did Central Europeans. Instead of taking the easy route and adopting the conventional knuckle pin/underbolt setup, they emphasized low-profile types for their many subtle advantages. The resulting Woodward, Boss and Holland & Holland over-unders thus became the ultimate harmonies of theory, strength, trimness and workmanship. It would be virtually impossible to make an over-under with less depth or more elegance.

The bolting systems used on shallow-framed guns, along with their mechanical principles, are most interesting. To begin, low-profiled over-unders cannot be pivoted on the standard knuckle pin because that takes too much space beneath the barrels. This problem was solved by the introduction of bifurcated lumps (also called "trunions"), which are round, buttonlike appurtenances found on opposing sides of the lower barrel. Machined to fit matching recesses in the frame, bifurcated lumps serve as elevated pivot points that allow the under barrel to snuggle cozily into the depths of a shallower U-shaped bar.

Aside from their influence on frame depth, bifurcated lumps also play a desirable role in controlling bending forces. By elevating the pivot point relative to the bore axes, they reduce the leverage factor. This seems especially important in relation to the upper barrel, and the Italian over-unders make almost universal use of the trunion system to prevent damage to their low, light frames.

Unless I am badly mistaken, it appears that low-profiled over-unders have longer action bars than do the high-breeched types. If so, the extra bar length is predicated on sound theory. Beginning with Westley Richards, it has been held that increasing the distance between the pivot and the rearmost bolt lends strength to any action by reducing the angle at which bending forces can work against the frame. By combining the high-sitting bifurcated lumps with a longer bar, then, clever designers have taken some strain off low, light-framed over-unders. This same idea was used on Winchester's Model 21, which has an action bar longer than that found on most other horizontal doubles. Thus, what unsophisticated shooters see only as line and style is often the application of certain mechanical principles.

Lacking underbolts, the low-profiled over-under is held together by bolts placed tangent to or above the lower barrel's axis. The Woodward-Purdey and Boss over-unders have bites cut into each side of the barrel face, and lugs working through the face of the standing breech fit them. This uniquely simple approach means that the barrel faces of the Woodward-Purdey and Boss guns are actually lumps, and it eliminates the need for appendages. On the Holland & Holland over-under, a pair of short extensions curve upward on each side of the lower barrel and match recesses in the breech face. When the gun is closed, a bolt impinges on the flat-topped surface of the extensions. Americans see very few of those great old British guns nowadays, but the crossbolt system being

used on Ruger's new over-under is a reasonable facsimile of the
Holland & Holland idea.

Woodward-Purdey and Holland & Holland over-unders have
side lugs, which, when perfectly fitted, relieve the stresses of all
firing forces. As with the doll's head, however, most casual
observers do not understand how side lugs can dampen destructive
forces when guns so equipped will swing open with relative ease.
Again, we must remember that a double's opening radius is
different from its vibrational radius, and explaining the side lugs'
effectiveness parallels that of the doll's head: When the gun is
opened for loading or unloading, the bifurcated lumps act as the
pivot, and the barrels rotate about them. At discharge, however,
the entire barrel length becomes an action radius, applying
downward leverage from breech to muzzle; and the forward
rotational movement of the barrels causes the side lugs to engage
heavily and retard potentially damaging dynamic action. The
considerable surface presented by side lugs, as compared to the

In the shallow-framed Boss over-under the need for space-consuming underlumps was
eliminated by machining the bites into the barrel face. Bolts working through the standing
breech enter the bites. This elegant Boss is from the collection of William W. Jaqua. (Photo
by Dave Phillips)

minor surface of a doll's head, renders it a most effective means of controlling barrel motion.

The exciting Italian over-unders generally employ side lugs with a version of the Holland & Holland horizontal crossbolt. They invariably engage perfectly on finely crafted Fabbri, Famars and Perazzi guns, and this bolting combination makes them, along with the Woodward-Purdey, the most solidly constructed of all modern shallow-framed over-unders.

Beretta over-unders have always been trim, and the current S 680 line follows suit. It also has a most interesting bolting system, which, like that of the former BL line, gives both strength and trimness in one compact package. Twin bolts, shaped like stubby truncated cones, project from each side of the standing breech to engage matching holes in the barrel assembly's side-mounted recoil lugs. The cones retract when the tang lever is pivoted for opening; they are sprung forward again when, upon being closed, the upper barrel contacts a release button in the curvature of the standing breech. This means there are no barrel extensions or crossbolts cluttering the breech area. Moreover, it keeps the two principal bolting features—the barrel recoil lugs and the twin bolts—merged so that the protruding cones help pin down the lugs. The conelike bolts, spring-urged, automatically adjust for wear.

The handsome handmade Berettas known to Americans as the SO series have a different bolting system from that of the less costly S 680 series of Beretta over-unders. Given a broad-shouldered standing breech reminiscent of the Merkel, the SO guns retain side-mounted recoil lugs but lack the cone-shaped bolts. Instead, bending pressures are controlled by short extensions, which, located on each side of the upper barrel, fit slots in the breech face to contact a flat crossbolt. This same version of the crossbolt is found on the Italian-made Regency over-under imported by Roy Weatherby.

Aside from the new Ruger, America's only try at a low-profiled over-under was Remington's Model 32. Both the Ruger and Remington are production-grade guns, of course, and they cannot be confused with the truly great ones. But the Model 32's bolting system is worth mentioning, because it is used variously throughout the world by other manufacturers.

The original Model 32 used a very simple arrangement. Axial

The Beretta SO over-unders (above) have side lugs that nest into matching cuts in the receiver wall, and they have minor extensions that protrude from the side of the upper barrel into the face of the standing breech where a flat crossbolt impinges upon them to control radial forces. The lower-priced Berettas, such as the former BL (below) and now the S 680 series, have no crossbolt but are secured against radial action by a pair of truncated cones that work out from the breech face and engage recesses in the lugs on either side of the upper barrel.

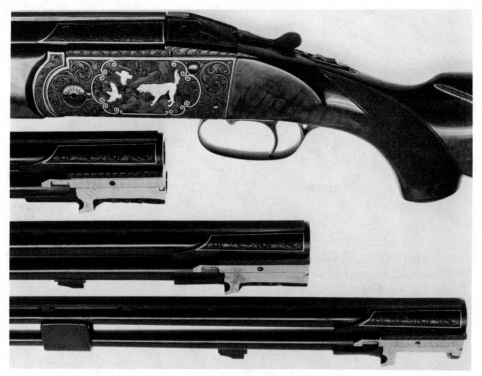

The Model 32 Krieghoff shown here, like the Valmet, Savage 330, and Remington 32 and 3200, has a sliding top bolt that moves back and forth, impinging upon the top barrel's upper surface.

forces were controlled by the bifurcated lumps; radial and bending actions were restricted by a novel sliding "top lock" that moved back and forth atop the standing breech. When the gun was closed, the top lock slid forward to cover the rearmost segment of the upper barrel and apply a hold-down pressure; when the gun was opened, the hoodlike top lock retracted and allowed the barrels to rotate about the trunions. This technique put bolting pressure rather high on the upper barrel, but the system was apparently adequate because the shallow nature of the overall design reduced the leverage angle between the bifurcated lumps and the lofty top lock. The heavy, boxy frame on the M32 was undoubtedly a factor, too.

When Remington brought out its successor to the original Model 32, the current Model 3200, it made some changes. The top lock was retained, but the lower barrel was depressed to emphasize straight-line recoil. This shift put greater distance between the bifurcated lumps and the top lock, meaning the upper barrel again had good leverage against the frame. Remington thus added massive side lugs to the barrel assembly, matching them to machined cuts in the frame's walls, for better control of firing forces.

In conclusion, then, it must be repeated that the upper barrel's leverage against the frame is a paramount consideration in evaluating or designing any over-under's bolting system. Proper fit is equally important, of course. The dynamic action permitted by sloppily fitted bolts will batter an over-under, loosening it quickly, especially when the high-sitting upper barrel brings its added leverage into play.

Chapter 9

Gun Art

Double shotguns can be viewed as tools, as works of art or as a combination of both. A typical hunter or farmer may think purely in terms of the former quality, meaning he will evaluate only the gun's utility; if it puts game on the table and keeps pests out of the barnyard, the gun has done its job. At the opposite extreme, an investor or collector may view a gun only for its esthetics and monetary value.

Carrying one's criteria to such extremes is unfortunate, of course. Great doubles are more than just tools or investments. They have the best qualities of each. They are made for efficient handling and field performances as well as being skillfully assembled and finished. The fact is that the truly outstanding gunmakers still build a double for certain hunting use and add the decor thereafter. Thus, we must never lose sight of the fact that a double's mechanics and dynamics are just as important to overall gun evaluation as are the artistic embellishments known as checkering, carving, engraving, inlaying and finishing.

But once we've considered design features and handling qualities, we must take note of the finish and other decor, something that hereafter will be combined into the term *gun art*. We must do so because artists need critics. The point is that not every double is a treasure. Old guns aren't automatically "fine"; all engraving isn't automatically valuable. Many old guns are simply klunkers; much engraving is amateurish. Before one can jump to any conclusions about the quality and the value of a gun's art, then, he must apply some critical standards.

A truly fine gun is one in which all-around excellence has been achieved by attention to details. That, of course, means hand work must be involved. Our modern machines may in fact be adjusted to cut repetitiously to almost negligible tolerances, but in the final step it is the human eye, along with the human hands, that must judge the results. Machines themselves have no concept of beauty. This explains why truly fine guns—i.e., those blessed with

On a well-made shotgun, careful attention must be given to the barrels' shape, smoothness, concentricity and regulation for point of impact. This is the barrel filer at William Powell & Son (Gunmakers) Ltd., of Birmingham, England, builders of Best Quality handmade sidelocks and boxlocks.

delightful handling qualities and attractive decor—are so expensive: The time and the talent that go into them must be rewarded. In Europe and on the British Isles, for example, guns are considered true works of art, and the people in general expect to pay for them since handmade doubles are indeed one-of-a-kind pieces.

By what standards are doubles assessed? There are several checkpoints that even an inexperienced hunter or beginning gun buff can pinpoint. After that, only time, experience and research will improve one's judgments and sense of value.

The first checkpoint is metal-to-metal fit. If this isn't properly done, the gun should never have been carried through to the final stages. On a truly fine gun, the working parts should be polished and carefully hand-fitted to one another. One reason why the older classics were so beautifully fitted is that gunsmithing assemblers were artists with files. If a part didn't fit correctly, they made it fit. Their personal pride didn't permit sloppy workmanship. As a result of such careful handwork, guns worked crisply: Triggers were snappy, ejectors were positive, bolts closed with a snap, and locks were finely adjusted. On the outside, metallic surfaces should be perfectly mated, and sharp edges are taboo. There must be no machine marks anywhere. The barrels, both inside and out, must be polished so smoothly that there is no "wave" effect whatsoever, and bores should be perfectly straight. And all of this is just a beginning!

A gun does not need to be bathed in engravings to be considered artistically finished. There is such a thing as too much art work, and there are distasteful patterns. Thus, the true measure of engraving isn't how much but rather how well it is done and how attractive it is on a given specimen. Early in man's history, he adorned his caves with pictures of the animals he hunted, and that practice has been carried through to modern firearms. Such scenes aren't needed to enhance the esthetics of a double, however, as artistically applied border scroll can go a long way toward satisfying one's appetite for art. When bird or game scenes are used, they should jibe with the quarry for which the gun is being built; a deer scene on a grouse gun, for instance, is more than somewhat incongruous.

Gun artistry can extend to the double's very butt, as is illustrated by this beautifully and extensively engraved skeleton buttplate on a Parker A-1 Special.

Not all of the "engraving" found on modern guns is done by hand with cutting instruments. Don't be fooled! Hand engraving cannot be applied to guns selling for a few thousand dollars or less. Many of these guns are engraved with the roll-on method or by chemical etching. Sometimes the chemically or mechanically applied engravings are finished by an engraver who cuts a few fast lines with a hammer and chisel so that the manufacturer can advertise hand engraving; however, those guns do not carry the same value as those with engraving done totally by hand. The roll-on method is generally easily detected: The displaced metal must go somewhere, and it normally shows up as a slight roll or bulge alongside the cut. Both the Japanese and the Italians have developed very fine roll-on equipment. This is not to belittle the guns with etched or rolled-on engravings, because many of them have pleasing scenes and do put a more handsome gun into the hands of an average sportsman who doesn't have tens of thousands of dollars to spend. But a buyer must be aware of the cheaper, less valuable engraving methods so that he isn't duped.

For all practical purposes, there are three types of hand-engraving methods. They are known by various names throughout the world, but my main audience will probably understand them best as 1) fine-line engraving, 2) deep-relief engraving and 3) bank-note engraving.

Fine-line engraving is the basic approach to engraving. It is sometimes referred to as hammer-and-chisel engraving, and the Italians call it scriber engraving or *punta e martello* (scriber and hammer) in Italian. The scriber is a hand-held cutter that provides a good grip and then tapers sharply to a rhomboid point for precise cutting. The tool has a flat head so that it can be tapped by the hammer. It is worked at an angle of 25-30 degrees, and the depth of the groove depends upon the force of the hammer blow. Sometimes the engraver works along laid out lines; sometimes he merely visualizes the pattern and works on a blank surface. Practically all scroll is cut with a scriber, and many outdoor scenes are also outlined by the method.

Scenes cut only by the fine-line approach tend to be flat and totally unlifelike. They lack detail and depth. A lot of the early American doubles, such as the lower grades of Parkers, Foxes,

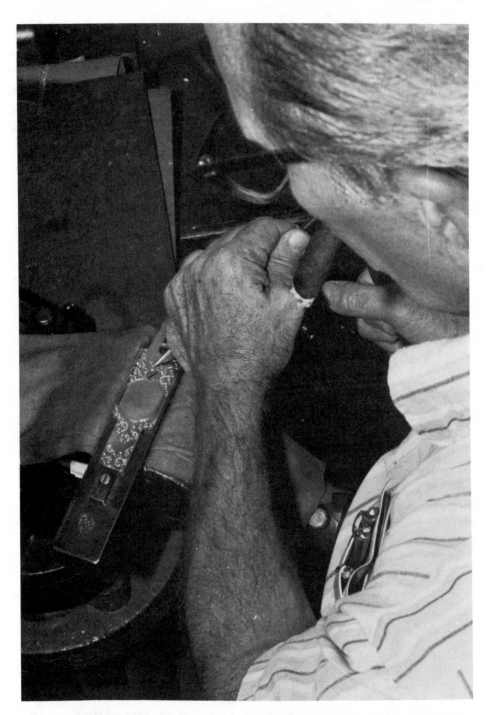

Scroll being applied to the floorplate of a Winchester Model 21 by now-retired Winchester engraver Nick Kusmeth. Yes, skilled engravers can smoke cigars on the job!

Smiths and LeFevers, had little more than flat, scriber-cut bird or hunting scenes of little artistic merit. The birds had round bodies topped by equally round heads, and they stood upon sticklike legs that could have been drawn by any third grader. The 2E and 3E L. C. Smiths have such sketchy art, as does the Grade B Parker Damascus shown here. One would have to leave his sense of reality in bed before he could appraise these as valued works of art; nevertheless, they command an undue sum of money, perhaps because of their scarcity—or perhaps because the buyers lack taste. However that statement may be received, my readers must admit that much of the game and hunting decor found on early American doubles leaves something to be desired.

There is a second step to enhancing the quality of fine-line engraving. This is done with a follow-up tool known as a "shader," which is similar to the scriber except that it lacks a sharp point for cutting but instead has a wider front end with multiple grooves. The distance between grooves will vary according to the individual tool. A shader's purpose is to cut parallel grooves to produce a

One way to assess a piece of engraving is to take a close-up photo and enlarge the negative. In this case, the engraving from a Grade B Parker Damascus double isn't very impressive; it lacks detail and lifelike qualities, although the scroll is reasonably good.

shaded area beside the lines originally cut by the sharp scriber. The shader, therefore, does what its name implies: It creates a dark, contrasting surface to set off the pattern. Any fine-line job that shows up without some shader work obviously has been done cheaply.

The second type of engraving is deep relief, also known as chasing. It could be defined as a further sophisticiation of the hammer-and-chisel method for the purpose of creating a third dimensional effect. Before chasing even begins, the engraver cuts the pattern's outline with a scriber and hammer. Once that outlining is completed, he cuts away metal with the scriber to provide a deeper background; and it is only after the metal has been removed, leaving the roughly raised outline and the deeper background, that chasing begins.

Essentially, chasing does *not* involve further metal removal. Chaser tools are used to shape the remaining metal in a sculpturelike method. The top part of a chaser tool, which is generally shorter than a scriber or a shader, is flat to receive the inevitable hammer blows. The working end, however, has various shapes such as semicircles, points, oblongs, hemispheres, diamonds or checkered surfaces. The engraver selects the tool that best matches the form he wishes to produce and then works via hammer taps. What this means, of course, is that deep-relief engraving is the gun artist's answer to sculpture, and it involves the compression of metal rather than the removal of it. Obviously, chasing tools are very finely made to permit the precise formation of feathers and eyes.

When deep-relief engraving is used, the great examples will have lifelike qualities. There will be perfectly detailed heads, bodies and facial expressions; the foregrounds and backgrounds will be in perspective. And there will be some strategic shading to emphasize depth according to the scene. Some scroll patterns are also done with the chaser method, and gunmakers from Italy, Ferlach and Suhl do so regularly.

The third form of engraving is entirely different in nature than either scriber or chaser engraving. Known commonly as bank-note engraving, it is also termed "graver" or *bulino* by the Italians. Whatever its name, this method doesn't involve the cutting of steel.

Instead, *bulino* engraving utilizes sharply pointed shafts to cut furrows or to place dots into the metal. No hammer is employed; the entire force comes from the engraver's hand. To facilitate handling, each graver tool has a sizable, palm-filling knob. Moreover, each tool can have a different type of point for various applications.

Among the experts, *bulino* engraving is considered to permit the ultimate in game and animal scenes. The Italians have also used it magnificently for creating scenes derived from mythology and history. Its beauty stems from both the possibility of achieving minute detail with the finest gravers plus the manipulation of the dots and lines to create the right shades. The closer the lines and dots, the darker the area becomes. Likewise, *bulino* engravers angle the dots and lines according to the way they want the light to affect their final product. Very few engravers have truly mastered the heights of *bulino* engraving, and most of them are Italians. The combination of scriber-and-hammer scroll and *bulino* scenes are extensively applied to the great Italian doubles like the Famars and Fabbri guns.

When evaluating engraving jobs, the buyer should check for sharpness. There should be no sharp edges. A sensitive finger run over the pattern will detect such a fault. Sharp edges reduce the value of an engraving job.

The very best engravings have amazing detail, much of which

Considerable detail and shading give this bulino-engraved scene depth and lifelike qualities. The gun is a Famars Castore hammer double made in Brescia, Italy. The scroll was done via the chasing technique, also to provide depth.

can't be seen by the naked eye. A magnifying glass is needed to pick up such perfection. Another way of assessing the details is by taking a close-up photo of some portion of the engraved scene and then enlarging it. Enlargements will quickly detect excellence as well as faults.

Before leaving the subject of engraving, it must be noted that this art can be cleverly used as camouflage to cover up an otherwise poorly made gun. Moreover, gun buyers are often duped into believing that an engraver needs tremendous amounts of time, and that any hand engraving is therefore bound to be expensive. Nothing is further from the truth. Many engraving jobs are quickly done; a talented engraver can do a considerable amount of work in one day. If anything is overpriced in today's double gun market, it is the work of an engraver. I will conclude with the words of W. W. Greener, who, in *The Gun and Its Development,* wrote: ". . . engraving being a comparatively cheap process, badly made and inexpensively produced guns had a few additional shillings spent upon the engraving, and were sold as, and represented to be, guns of good quality, if not the highest grade." Greener thereupon suggested that monies so spent would be better off used to improve the overall mechanical qualities of the same gun. Amen!

ACTION BODY COLORING

The quality doubles have action bodies that are either blued, case-hardened for a beautifully deep mottled effect, or case-hardened for a gray exterior.

Each finish has its own attractions, although blued receivers are terribly common nowadays. The classic gunmakers were said to have burnished all metal components after polishing, the work being done with a hand-held, hard-stick burnisher. The purpose was to close the steel's grain even further than the routine polishing closed it; the end result was a deeper gloss and color. The extent to which hand burnishing is still employed is unknown. Perhaps new polishing techniques have outmoded it.

Mottled case coloring can be a joy to behold. Guns finished in this manner often do not need engraving; they are exceedingly attractive as they come from the quench, and engraving can actually obliterate more beauty than it adds. Of course, case-hardening was done to strengthen the action body, but when it also lends beauty, it serves a 2-in-1 function.

Classic case hardening was done by placing the steels in a cast-iron pot with animal charcoal (parched bone dust). The pot was placed over a bright coal fire, and the gun parts were entirely covered by the charcoal for 1-1½ hours. The old-time finishers used no gauges to determine the length of heating but rather let experience be their guide. They could tell at a glance when it was ready. Upon removal from the pot, each metal component was quenched in cold water. The carbon absorbed by the steel produced a hard surface and produced a bluish mottling over the entire piece. This is a time-consuming step in gunmaking, and many modern companies have dropped it in favor of the simpler, less expensive blue job. Perazzi once put a gorgeous case color on the Mirage and the MX-8, but they now wear only a flat blue.

There is a second approach to case-hardening, one that puts a gray hue on the action body. Merkel guns are one of the most common examples of this method. To achieve the overall gray color, the red-hot action body is plunged into a solution of prussiate of potash instead of being quenched in cold water.

Thus, there can be some artistry in the coloring and hardening of a gun's action body. Unfortunately, however, they seem to be dying skills, perhaps priced out of the market by inflation factors. Cheaper body finishes are being used. The Spanish, for example, employ an oil-dip method to case-color some action bodies and sideplates, but it doesn't seem to have the same depth and beauty as the original charcoal method. Guns selling for less than $3,000 can have everything from plated bodies to sparkly silver ones made of brushed steel. Some are nitrited for hardness, which makes engraving difficult if not impossible.

THE WOODEN ACCOUTREMENTS

There is also artistry in the making of stocks and fore-ends and the finishing of same. For optimum strength, the grain of a fine

Very little wood carving is done on shotguns these days, but if it is it should have the lifelike artistry and detail of this pistol grip and cheek carving by G. Granger of St. Etienne, France.

gun's stock should run parallel to the bottom line of that stock so that the grain runs directly through the grip toward the receiver. Untrained eyes often look for the grain to run with the top of the stock, which is wrong. If a stock has some fancy swirls and contrasts, it may require careful eyeballing to detect the flow of the grain. The outstanding gunmakers, especially those of England and Europe, tend not to use blanks that extend fancy figures into the grip or wrist segment of a stock, but instead they prefer a straight grain in that region. Some Americans get upset when they see expensive guns without fancy grain throughout the stock and fore-end, but the gunmaker's concern for strength, especially in the trim straight-gripped guns, is paramount.

Added strength through the stock's wrist segment is the reason why long tangs are given straight-gripped guns. These long tangs run well back from the trigger guard, and many people mistakenly view them as pure decor. The long tang isn't necessary on most production-grade doubles because they have a sturdy draw bolt connecting them to the action body. When a long undertang is put on a modern mass-produced double, it is mainly cosmetic. On a double that does not have a draw bolt, it is a necessity.

The classic doubles have trim lines that are sharp and straight. Lines that curve, bulge, sway or hump are hardly first class. On a truly fine gun, the straight lines will cause a viewer's eyes to race from one end to the other. Target-grade doubles may well have more girth, but field guns should be stocked and finished for fast action.

Inletting cuts of a truly fine gun will appear to have been made with a razor. They are exceedingly sharp and devoid of the radius that crude cutting produces along edges.

Checkering, to be judged excellent, must find every diamond sharply cut and filed, and there should be no overruns. This is a master checkerer at work in the Krieghoff plant of Ulm, West Germany.

The checkering on a fine gun will have at least 24 lines per inch, and it could run to 32 lines per inch. The finer it gets, the more a craftsman's skill is challenged. To a certain degree, however, unduly tight checkering is senseless and purely cosmetic, for a point is reached where it no longer offers a grip but rather becomes smooth to the touch. An absolutely perfect job of 24-26 lines per inch seems preferable to anything finer if the gun is going to be used afield. This amount tests the craftsman's skill while still providing a semblance of a grip.

To be judged excellent, hand checkering must show no overruns at the border, the individual diamonds must be geometrically perfect throughout, and each one must be sharply pointed by a curved finishing file. A classic diamond is three times as long as it is wide, but variations occur among the nations and their styles. Skip-a-line checkering has never been accepted on truly fine guns, and expert checkerers seldom apply a border. In the trade, a border is considered nothing more than a convenient way for fumble-fingered amateurs to cover up mistakes and overruns. In checking the quality of any job, always inspect the workmanship to the edge rather than merely jumping to a conclusion by looking at the center of a pattern; for oftentimes center diamonds are made perfectly while those along the edges are left flat-topped and geometrically imperfect.

Before making any rapid assumptions about a double's value, then, inspect the artistry very closely. Has as much attention been given to the details of fitting and the interior as to the exterior gloss and floss? Be critical of the finesse points. If it is priced like a work of original art, make certain that the artists gave it their honest best.

Chapter 10

What's Left for the British?

They're gone now—Churchill, Atkin, Grant, Lang, Evans, Watson, Greener, Cogswell & Harrison, Lancaster, Jeffery, Rigby and others with less famous names like Claybough and Webley & Scott. British gunmakers all, they succumbed to the harsh realities of wars, inflations, depressions and the lack of talented, dedicated craftsmen who were willing to apprentice themselves at low starting wages. And with the market for ultra-expensive British guns continually threatened by other nations that have developed their own fine-gun industries and talented people, there is always the question of what's left for the British? Can those who remain— Purdey, Holland & Holland, Powell, W. & C. Scott, Westley Richards, and Boss — survive in the face of rising costs and dwindling markets? Can they satisfy customers with their quality? Will they frustrate former buyers or turn away potential trade with their ever-lengthening lag times, which often run two to three years while down payments and intermediate payments are requested?

These are more than moot questions, as is attested to by the history of collapses and/or mergers of once prestigious London and Birmingham houses. The world's economy will play a role, but no one can predict it with any certainty. And, as always, there will be the customers' moods and the impact of aggressive competition from nations that have advanced their technology to build equally fine guns faster and at lower prices.

Some of the keenest observers of the gun world have opined that the ranking British gunmakers are, in fact, their own worst enemy. This does not mean the way they treat one another or compete among themselves. It means within their own houses. For some British sporting gunmakers have stubbornly clung to antique

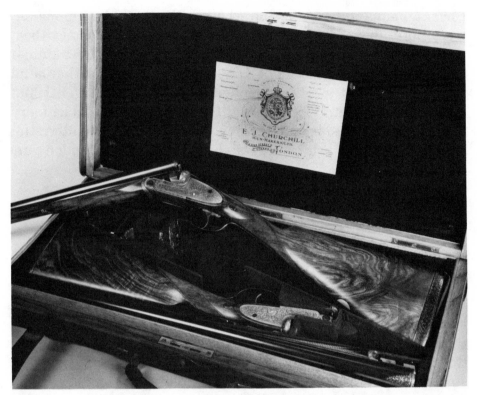

A pair of matched game guns, such as this pair from E. J. Churchill, are considered the epitome of fine shotguns. However, inflation, the lack of skilled workers, wage escalations, and perhaps even poor business practices have greatly reduced the number of such grand old British gunmakers and, in varying degrees, have cut into overall quality while sending prices soaring. Like so many others, the name of Churchill has fallen from active British gunmakers.

methods of gunmaking, relying heavily on extensive, if not total, hand cutting; and such hand labor, costly as it is, can be deemed a waste of time and money when spent on the mere roughing process that advanced machines can do in minutes. But, with a stiff upper lip, they plunge on according to their traditions—directly into bankruptcy. The only alternative to financial failure, of course, is trimming the work force, increasing prices drastically, stretching production times—and praying that the firm's prestigious name will still attract clientele.

Where do those changes leave the British now? There have always been two gunmaking centers in England, and their business attitudes and approaches have differed. Those centers are

Birmingham and London. And whereas the Birmingham makers have built many fine, handcrafted guns, they have also been interested in utilizing improved production techniques and in expanding their markets. The London makers, on the other hand, have been content to sit back and wait for well-heeled gentlemen to pay enormous sums for guns built without the aid of machinery. These divergent business philosophies have produced an interesting situation that will bear some watching to see if the London guns will survive.

THE LONDON GUNS TODAY

The name of Purdey is one of the most respected in gunmaking circles, due to the leadership in early gunmaking provided by the Purdey family and the firm's penchant for only high-quality guns and equipment. To a certain degree, however, the pinnacle to which the Purdey name has risen is also due to a generous sporting press that has continuously praised the firm to give it virtually legendary status. If the press had been as doting to another maker, Purdey might not have fared as well; for it is certain that many other gunmakers have turned out examples equal to any Purdey, and tests published in *American Rifleman* indicated that the American-made Winchester Model 21 could withstand more shooting than a Purdey and still remain tight.

Purdey's was founded in 1814 when James Purdey (the Elder) started his own business in Leicester Square. Prior to that he had worked for both Joseph Manton and the Forsyth Gun Company in London. In 1826, Purdey took over the Manton works on Oxford Street, and in 1843, his son, James (the Younger), became an apprentice. When James Purdey the Elder died in 1863, James the Younger assumed control; and it was he who expanded the business and built the now-famous Audley House (1881) where the company's showrooms are still located. James the Younger died in 1909, and since then a series of chairmen and managing directors have held sway.

In all those years, however, nothing much has changed. Purdey guns remain mainly handmade, the prices are high, and the

A Purdey game gun with a ruffed grouse scene engraved on the sideplates along with gentle leaf scroll. Although the grouse are relatively lifelike, a critic of gun art might say he has seen better.

delivery time is extensive. There is only one grade of gun, the so-called Best Gun. The prices supplied this author late in 1984 placed the hammerless ejector side-by-side at £12,500 in 12, 16 and 20 gauges, while the 28 gauge and 410 bore listed at £13,500. The hammerless over-under ejector gun had a base price of £17,500. A beavertail fore-end cost £600; an articulated front trigger was priced at £150; and a single trigger could be had for an extra £575.

Purdey's sole concession to the world market thus far has been a model called the American and Continental side-by-side gun, which is a bit heavier than the standard British game gun and, apparently, has somewhat thicker barrels for the robust ammunition used outside of the United Kingdom. The price of this heftier Purdey side-by-side is the same as that of their standard gun, namely, £12,500 in 12, 16 and 20 gauges. As in the Purdey game gun, 28-gauge and .410-bore models will have a rounded action body. At something better than $12,000 dollars, however, the American style Purdey will hardly cut into the business enjoyed by Remington, Winchester and Browning. Thus, Purdey remains an elitist affair.

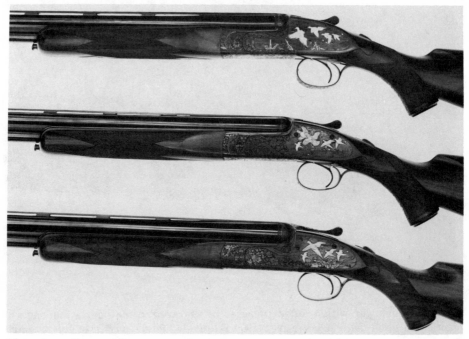

About the only prestigious over-under still being built in England is the Purdey, shown here in three different gauges with inlaid bird scenes. The top member is the only .410-bore over-under ever built by Purdey. All have Ken Hunt inlays and engraving. (Photo courtesy of Jaqua's Fine Guns, Findlay, Ohio)

The current situation at Holland & Holland appears identical to that of Purdey's. The emphasis is still on ultra-expensive guns, handmade and priced beyond the typical sportsman's ability to pay. When I asked Holland & Holland for current prices and a catalog, I was given no prices and was told that a catalog wasn't available because they were too expensive, although one was being contemplated. An American who is used to advertising must wonder if this is the correct austerity measure. However, it does represent the passive nature of the London gunmakers.

The most notable demonstrative move by Holland & Holland has been the assembly of various sets of special guns fitted to elaborate gun cabinets. These were made in 1968, 1970 and the final in 1977 to commemorate the Queen's Silver Jubilee.

Another commemorative set was commissioned in 1983 to commemorate the 1908 founding of the Wildfowler's Association of Great Britain and Ireland, which has recently changed its name to the British Association for Shooting and Conservation. To celebrate this organization's 75th anniversary, a set of six magnificent side-by-sides was made up and provided an upright cabinet made of blind curl mahogany and inlaid on all four sides with blond boxwood strips in a geometrical design featuring squares, rectangles and intersecting lines. The entire collection is known as the Wildfowler and Wader set and is comprised of two standard 12 bores, two standard 20 bores, a 3-inch-chambered wildfowling gun and a neat 28 gauge. Each panel of each gun is engraved with a different species of waterfowl. The No. 1 gun, for example, has a pair of barnacle geese on the right lock, two red-breasted geese on the left lock, and white-fronted geese on the underside of the action. The gun's knuckle joints bear the heads of whooper and mute swans, while the opening lever carries the head of a common crane. The remaining furniture uses specific aquatic vegetation in place of scroll, the left fence showing common sea lavender while the right fence shows sea aster. The accompanying photos show the right lockplate of the No. 5 gun, which is engraved with a pair of Mandarin ducks with a seashell, and the underside of the No. 3 gun's action body, which illustrates Canada geese.

No price was given for the Wildfowler and Wader collection. Exceptional though the project is, it nevertheless reflects the

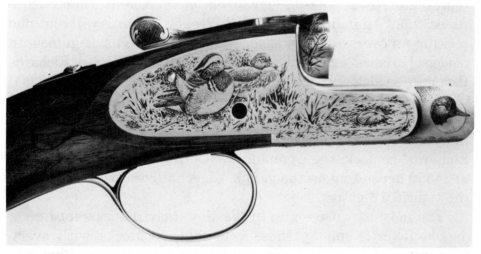

The right lockplate of gun No. 5 in Holland & Holland's Wildfowl and Wader collection showing a pair of Mandarin ducks and a seashell.

London gunmaker's obsession with the ultimate rather than giving some consideration to the remaining 99.9 percent of the market.

BIRMINGHAM BRIGHT SPOTS

Whereas the London gunmakers have always been somewhat passive, doting on prestige, the Birmingham makers have always exhibited a more aggressive tendency while still building sporting guns that rival and, in some instances, equal those of the London greats. Moreover, it has always seemed that the Birmingham gunmakers are more open-minded to innovations, both in their gunmaking and their business efforts to attract trade. Some of this may trace to the Greeners, whose publications served as advertising; and some may trace to the inception of the Birmingham Small Arms (BSA) operation, in which numerous small craftsmen of the guild joined forces for more effective marketing and production. Whatever the motivation, however, the Birmingham gunmakers are outpacing the London chaps when it comes to generating a market.

Westley Richards is one example of this spirited thrust. Representatives of Westley Richards attend some important stateside trade shows, and the company had a display booth and representative at the 1984 convention of the National Rifle Association. All indications are that Westley Richards will continue seeking an overseas market for its line of three basic game-gun models. Foremost among this trio of designs is the Westley Richards Best gun, a sidelock of traditional trimness to sell for about $13,000 in its basic form, which includes double triggers and fine scroll engraving. Engraving patterns with game or hunting scenes and inlays are available at extra cost. Opposite the sidelock is Westley Richards' boxlock, the Connaught, at prices ranging from $4250 to $4500 depending on the gauge; the smallbores cost more than the typical 12 gauge.

The most expensive gun in Westley Richards' current line is an old favorite among those who fancy boxlocks with every refinement. This is simply called the Detachable Lock Shotgun, and it is made with removable Anson & Deeley-type locks that are readily accessible via a hinged floorplate. The action body and locks require extensive fitting and finishing, and the 1984 price was $14,000, making it the highest-priced boxlock sans options. At one point not too long ago, it seemed that the Detachable Lock Shotgun would fade away, but Westley Richards has kept it alive by pricing it at the equivalent of a sidelock, which, on a business basis, justifies its existence.

W. & C. SCOTT

Another British gunmaker that has begun taking a more aggressive approach to the American and world market is W. & C. Scott, a gun line that has had a long up-and-down history and a dizzying number of name changes. The interesting thing about W. & C. Scott is that, contrary to the current trend of British gunmakers going out of business, it is a revitalized company that was organized in 1980 on the ruins of the former Webley & Scott concern. Thus, despite having the name of Scott, which reaches back through 150 years of British gunmaking, the present firm of W. & C. Scott is spanking new as enterprises go.

The name of Scott entered British gunmaking annals in the early 1820s when William Scott (1806-1883), the son of a Suffolk farmer, began working in the gun trade. He started his own shop in 1834 at 79 Weaman Street, Birmingham, and in 1840 he was joined by his brother, whereupon the company took the style William & Charles Scott. This was at first a rather general gunmaking venture, but by the late 1840s, the Scotts were putting greater emphasis on high-grade doubles. Eventually, two of William's sons joined the company, and it became known as W. & C. Scott & Son in 1858. The elder Scott was held in such high regard by the British gunmaking community that, in 1861, he was made a Guardian of the Birmingham Proof House.

The wars of the 1800s, including the American Civil War, made this a prosperous period for gunmakers; and after moving about, the company built a new factory, the Premier Works, at 123 Lancaster Street in 1864, and opened a showroom in London.

Scott guns became famous worldwide, especially among live-pigeon shooters. Much of this international success is credited to Scott's older son, William Middleditch Scott (1835-1916), who traveled the Continent and America boosting the guns and establishing a chain of importers. One famous user of Scott guns was Captain A. H. Bogardus, the champion live-pigeon shot who won events worth as much as £1,000 with his specially made Scott gun fitted for both 10- and 12-gauge barrel sets. The prestigious Monte Carlo "Grand Prix" of pigeon shooting was won by Scott guns in 1902, 1905 and 1906 to ensure the company's fame. The company records also show that, in 1882, Charles Macalester of New York won $2000 by killing 178 out of 200 pigeons with a Scott from the 30-yard handicap—and in 1882 that was a tremendous amount of money. Thus, Scott guns were in the midst of things during this Golden Era of scattergunning.

Early Scott breechloaders were made in three letter-designated grades. The highest of these was the A grade, and the Scott "Best" gun consisted of the A-grade nucleus plus the finest workmanship and materials. These Best guns were then known as the Premier Quality doubles. The grades B and C has descending amounts of workmanship. Both hammer and hammerless guns were made, with hammer guns apparently being phased out in the 1920s. The boxlocks seem to have been mainly of the Anson & Deeley design, but the sidelocks had various features and were made in both bar-action and back-action types. Bolting was primarily done by a combination of the Purdey double underbites and a Greener-type crossbolt, which had a square bolt instead of a round one. This square crossbolt was generally fitted under the name Triplex. In 1898, Scott switched to a new bar-action mechanism known as the Rogers principle, in which the cocking levers of hammerless guns are held by screws within the action bar; guns of this sort are recognizable by the pair of visible screws in the water table.

The manufacture of boxlocks began in 1890, but the guns were made only in B and C grades.

A major business change took place in 1897, when W. & C. Scott & Son merged with P. Webley & Son to become Webley & Scott Revolver & Arms Co. Ltd. Initially, each segment was still managed separately, but within a couple years, joint management was instituted. Scott's London showroom was closed; all sales went through the Birmingham offices. Further changes kept occurring. In 1906, the name was cut to Webley & Scott Ltd., and the Webley long-gun work was transferred from the Webley factory to the Scott works on Lancaster Street. From that time, Webley's factory engaged mainly in the manufacture of revolvers, semi-automatic pistols and other military items. World War I buoyed the company, which turned mainly to the production of Webley Mark VI revolvers and signal pistols.

But hard times fell on Webley & Scott after WWI. The 1920s did not roar for them, and the Great Depression of the 1930s forced a closure of the Lancaster Street works in 1935. The remaining Scott shotguns, approximately 150, were sold piecemeal between then and 1950.

World War II prevented a failure of Webley & Scott, which made 38-caliber Mark IV revolvers and other materials from 1940 through 1945.

After the war, the production of doubles was again inaugurated, and production reached about 1000 guns a year by the late 1950s. But now changes in management began occurring rapidly. In 1958, Webley & Scott Ltd. was purchased by R. H. Windsor Ltd., and a new factory was built in Birmingham. Only one year later, however, the company was taken over by Arusha Industries Ltd., and in 1965 W. W. Greener was absorbed by Webley & Scott. Little was gained as a result of this acquisition; in fact, production began falling. The company again changed hands in 1973 when it was purchased by the Harris & Sheldon Group, but the downward trend continued. Less than 300 doubles were being made each year during the late 1970s, these being the Webley & Scott Model 700 series of boxlocks that Harrington & Richardson handled stateside, and in the fall of 1979 the company terminated its shotgun line. Intense competition from Italian, Japanese and Spanish gunmakers was the main cause, along with other international economic factors. For a brief time, Webley & Scott made only air rifles and pistols.

This is when an interesting quirk in modern British gunmaking took place. Rather than let the shotgun segment of its new acquisition die, the Harris & Sheldon Group reshuffled and took an aggressive step. It dropped the former Webley & Scott name, established a new version of the Premier Works on Tame Road,

The rejuvenated W. & C. Scott Company of Birmingham offers this Best Quality sidelock known as the Blenheim.

Witton, in Birmingham, and resurrected the old name of W. & C. Scott to inaugurate a new line of quality doubles. The crew was small, having just 33 people initially, and the first year's output was but 100 guns. That jumped to about 250 guns by 1982 and is probably somewhat higher now.

This modern rebirth of the W. & C. Scott line is based heavily on high-quality boxlocks and a best quality sidelock, all of which are pointed toward export as well as traditional U.K. and Continental markets. They are basically game guns, but half- or full-pistol grips can be ordered, as can a beavertail fore-end. A nonselective single trigger runs $750. The boxlocks are made in 12, 16, 20 and 28 gauges; the fine sidelock, known as the Blenheim, is made in 12 gauge starting at only $15,000. A deluxe version of the Blenheim, which has beautiful exhibition-grade wood and the finest checkering and metal work, starts at $16,500.

The sequence of boxlocks begins with the Kinmount. First offered in 1981, it has the same lines as the former Webley & Scott 700s sold stateside in the 1970s. The receiver has a straight line contact with the stock and is case-colored. Scroll engraving covers about half the action body, leaving the fore-end iron and trigger guard only lightly touched by the engraver's chisel. At this time, the gun is listed at $3500 in 12 gauge, and the price increases to $4400 for the 28 gauge.

Next in line is the Bowood, starting at $4500 in 12 gauge and ascending to $5600 in 28 gauge. The Bowood differs noticeably from the Kinmount, having a rounded action body and a scalloped line that is not only eye-catching but also requires more workmanship to fit. About three quarters of the Bowood body is covered with tight scroll.

The Chatsworth is the new W. & C. Scott's best boxlock, commanding $6500 in 12 gauge and $7700 in 28 gauge. It has a rounded, scalloped action body akin to the Bowood's, but scroll coverage is finer and more lavish, with added attention to the fore-end iron and trigger guard. Checkering is done at an extraordinary 32 lines per inch, as opposed to 20 lines per inch for the Kinmount and 24 lines per inch on the Bowood. The highest grades of French walnut are employed on the Chatsworth. False sideplates with special engraving can be had on either the Bowood or the Chatsworth for approximately $900 to $1000.

In 1981 and 1982, the resurrected W. & C. Scott name took a further step beyond British gunmaking traditions when two side-by-sides were introduced for the American market. One was the Texan, a boxlock dressed up with heavily engraved sideplates and

The classy boxlock being turned out by W. & C. Scott is called the Chatsworth.

complemented by a full pistol grip, fashionable beavertail forearm and single, nonselective trigger.

The other is a plain boxlock known as the Crown. It is based on the same squarish action body as the Kinmount with similar half-coverage engraving. Both the Texan and the Crown have tasteful little teardrops trailing the stocks' cheeks. Prices for these were not available at printing time. The stateside agent for W. & C. Scott guns is John A. Crawford, who operates a business known as British Guns in Corvallis, Oregon. Crawford has, in tandem with Patrick G. Whatley, written a history of W. & C. Scott gunmakers, and it is also available from the Corvallis operation. The book will be especially interesting to collectors, as it helps identify many of the past guns turned out by the company, whatever its name was at the time. Fortunately for shotgun buffs, it isn't the final history; for the new management and business approaches of the Harris & Sheldon Group, along with a revitalized world interest in fine guns and some excellent workmanship by W. & C. Scott, may well ensure a future that is far better than the recent past.

(The saga continues: at press time, we learn that W. & C. Scott has been acquired by Holland & Holland. What this bodes for the future is anyone's guess.)

THE GREAT POWELL GUNS

Another great name in Birmingham gunmaking—perhaps *the* greatest when it comes to finely finished handmade doubles of classic British game-gun persuasion—that isn't giving in to inflation or stiff international competition is William Powell & Son Ltd. Often called "the Purdey of Birmingham," Powell has taken a constructive look into the future and has formulated positive plans. The famous handcrafted sidelocks and boxlocks of Powell's line will remain intact, their assembly being the traditional impeccable methods. Thus, the Powell No. 1 sidelock and No. 3 boxlock are destined to remain among the very finest examples of British handmade doubles.

But the directorship of William Powell & Son Ltd. knows that inflation has hurt the market for, and the profitability of, the traditional handmade long guns, and they have entered a

The William Powell & Son No. 1 sidelock, often called the Purdey of Birmingham. One wonders if beautiful guns of this quality shouldn't leave Purdey the Powell of London!

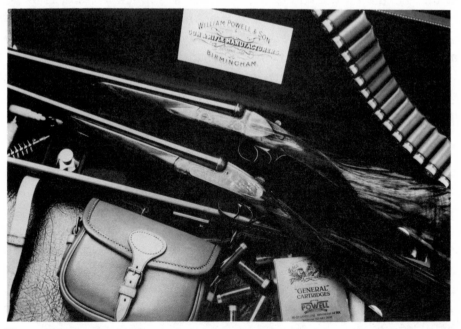

To provide a quality double at a lower price, Powell & Son has undertaken to build the Heritage sidelock, shown here below the No. 3 Powell boxlock.

progressive new program to supply finely finished guns faster and at a lower price. The guns in point will be known as the Heritage Series, and they will not have the same amount of costly hand labor in the roughing stage. Powell has entered into an agreement with a foremost Italian gunmaker (who will remain anonymous for the time being) who will supply barreled actions already roughed to Powell specifications. Powell assemblers and finishers will then finalize the guns, filing and polishing individual components for perfect hand fits (albeit not total hand cutting and shaping from scratch). This will reduce the amount of labor cost while not detracting from the finished product. All that's lost is the snob appeal of having a fully handmade gun. However, given the same fit, finish and balance, the Heritage guns will be difficult to separate from totally handmade guns.

The salvation of Powell is that they pursue an active retail business in connection with gunmaking, handling everything from sporting publications to outdoor clothing (Barbour), shooting and hunting accessories and even fishing tackle. Moreover, Powell distributes periodic catalogs and will sell overseas by post or by phone via a credit card number. Orders are quickly dispatched by return airmail. This retail business not only helps finance the costly operation of building fine guns but also provides sportsmen ready access to the best British books, clothing and shooting accessories. Obviously, a licensed importer would have to handle gun purchases, but Powell has those contacts stateside and will advise the prospective customer accordingly.

Thus, the directorship at William Powell & Son have faced the future squarely and will undoubtedly continue to do so. In October 1984, the sixth generation of the Powell family took his place in the company, this being Robert Powell, son of David Powell and nephew of Peter T. Powell, who currently direct matters.

The difference between London and Birmingham gunmakers is therefore obvious. Whereas the Birmingham gunmakers have taken note of the rest of the world, have altered their methods accordingly, and have begun pursuing business on a wider basis, the London houses continue the rather staid pattern of waiting for business to come along.

On those bases, what is left for the British gunmakers? The

London houses have apparently stabilized after the crazy inflation, and they could have a future as prestigious as their past if they can train and retain skilled and dedicated craftsmen. As long as there will be people to buy Rolls-Royces, there will be people to place orders at Audley House. In fact, even in the worst economic conditions the class of people who buy London Best guns will have money to buy exactly what they want, and the only thing that can destroy the boutique gunmakers could be a fierce wage-price spiral that drives the cost of handmade guns beyond anyone's willingness to pay. Such gunmakers may have to trim their forces and reduce output. It is difficult to envision a significant expansion of the London houses.

Aggressive marketing by the Birmingham houses should, theoretically, broaden their market. But one important question remains: Will they convince people to buy guns in the price range of £2,000 to £4,000? This, it seems, has always been a tricky market, and only history has the answer. Much depends on the advertising, the workmanship and the sincerity that go into the various intermediate models, such as those of the W. & C. Scott line and the Powell Heritage gun. What's left for the British then, is to butt heads with the rest of the world!

Chapter 11

The 12/20 Concept: When Joseph Lang Dared to Be Different

The English government may flip-flop from Whig to Conservative to Socialist or Labour parties, but British gunmakers have had mainly one loyalty: ultra-conservative. Ever since the drop-barrel double reached its form as a slim, trim game gun, nothing much has changed. It's as if the clock had stopped in the United Kingdom, with any variation in gun line or overall concept being rejected as radical. In the first edition of this book, for instance, I traced the difficulties that the late Robert Churchill had in getting his 25-inch-barreled XXV gun accepted.

But every now and then, a British gunmaker would risk the verbal gallows by trying something out of the ordinary. One such man was Joseph Lang, a truly outstanding London gunmaker of the old school and classic period. Lang operated independently from 1821 to 1875, at which time his son joined the business under the banner of Joseph Lang & Son. In 1896, the company became known as Lang & Hussey; and later, in 1901, it gathered other prestigious gunmakers like Stephen Grant, Charles Lancaster and Harrison & Hussey to form Stephen Grant & Joseph Lang Ltd. Later, as post-WWII fates transpired against many gunmakers, the group merged with Churchill to become Churchill, Grant, Atkin, Lang & Watson. All were storied names in classic gunmaking circles but, by the late 1970s, Churchill faded into history, too.

In his heyday, Joseph Lang was reputed to be one of the best gunmakers in that select lineup, and his forte was the classic straight-gripped game gun. In the late 1800s, however, Joseph Lang & Son came up with a radical twist for achieving gun balance. It

116

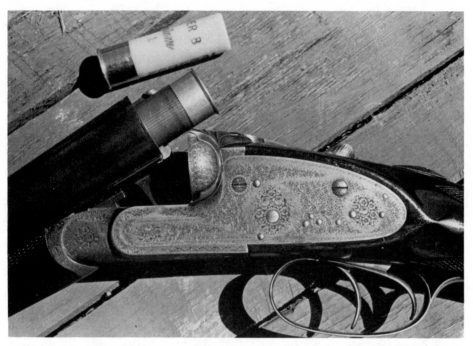

A side view of the Joseph Lang 12/20, the gun with 12-gauge chambers and 20-gauge muzzles. It is finished in the typical bouquet and scroll fine-line pattern.

was initially called the 12/20 concept and was later given the Latin name of *vena contracta,* meaning a narrowed passage. Both epithets fit. It was a 12-gauge gun with barrels that quickly tapered down to 20-gauge bore diameters!

Why reduce the 12 gauge's bore so drastically that wads must swage from 12 gauge to 20 gauge during passage? The answer seems to rest with an attempt to establish an easier balance than normal. To explain, let me back up and state that a classic British side-by-side game gun is expected to have between-the-hands weight concentration; that the half-weight is supposed to be squarely between the shooter's hands while the remaining weight is distributed equally between the muzzles and the butt. Such a weight distribution produces a lively, responsive gun that pivots with only minor physical energy. The only way to achieve this delightful dynamic, of course, is by careful and patient handwork, which means draw-filing the tubes to match butt density. At any time in history, the procedure involved time, and time was money even in the nineteenth century. Thus, the use of quickly tapered barrels appears to have been Lang's experimental way of lightening the muzzles without employing extensive labor.

Some readers, especially engineers, may associate the term *vena contracta* with the venturi principle, causing them to believe that the 12/20's bores were reduced to squeeze added velocity from the load; for with any given flow of fluid, be it water, air or gunpowder gases, the pressure will be heightened as the passageway is narrowed. And since velocity is the product of pressure, the association does have merit: The 12/20 may have experienced slightly increased velocities. However, increased velocity does not seem to have been Lang's reason for employing the concept. No less an authority than Major Sir Gerald Burrard, writing in *The Modern Shotgun,* treats Lang's 12/20 gun merely in terms of balance. Moreover, the British have never focused on high shotgun velocities, having traditionally been content with light shot charges and moderate speeds. Thus, the venturi principle doesn't seem to be the 12/20's raison d'etre.

I have been able to inspect a Lang 12/20 very closely, thanks

The chamber/breech area of the Lang 12/20 was sized to handle the full 12-gauge cartridge, as in the left tube, while the 20-gauge cartridge obviously didn't fit the right chamber.

At the muzzle end it was different, however. Here the 12-gauge shell on the left was bigger than the bore and muzzle diameter, but the 20-gauge round on the right shows how the bores were narrowed to attain trimness and balance.

to Jim Wills of Virginia. This particular specimen is in the tradition of other London sidelocks except for the rapid barrel taper. It is adorned with typical floral bouquets and fine-line scroll, has racy lines created by a splinter fore-end and straight-hand grip, and is activated by double triggers. The bolting utilizes a round doll's head and Purdey-type double underbites. The comb is thin, relatively high as the British like them for overhead shooting of driven game. It scales just 6 pounds 2 ounces, balances perfectly at the hingepin, and moves like a wand.

The radically tapered barrels are 30 inches long and have full-diameter 12-gauge chambers. The interior bore dimensions are apparently intended to swage the ejecta mass gradually, because what serves as a forcing cone is about 6 inches long and has a gentle taper. The narrow bore begins about 6 inches ahead of the chamber, and an interior dial caliper indicates a nominal diameter of just 0.650-inch for both barrels for the majority of their lengths. This tends to split the difference between 16 gauge (0.670-inch) and true 20 gauge (0.615-inch). It is my understanding that the 12/20 concept was made variously, with some tubes drawn closer to 16 gauge than 20 gauge. Theoretically, that would change the designation from

A full-length profile of the Lang 12/20 illustrates the slender barrels coming from the larger 12-gauge action and breech area.

a 12/20 to a 12/16; however, the gunning world seems quite content to apply the 12/20 designation overall. In any case, this particular Lang 12/20 had chokes with a 0.630-inch diameter. The exterior barrel diameters, beginning about 6 inches ahead of the chamber, ran a nominal 0.707-inch from that point to the very muzzle.

The 12/20 concept has no application today and must be viewed as a period piece in gunmaking history. Modern metallurgy has given us strong steels to lighten barrels safely, and the acceptance of shorter barrels by sportsmen has eliminated the need to balance long, 30-inch tube assemblies with relatively lightweight stocks. Moreover, the reduced bore diameter is hardly receptive of plastic wads, which, obviously, swage down less readily than the old card/filler stacks used in shotshells when the *vena contracta* idea was applied to smoothbores. The fact that it undoubtedly threw longer shot strings than a conventional 12 argues against it as well.

As time has proved, the 12/20 concept was not the answer to quick and easy gun building without sacrificing balance. Shooters didn't buy it in any quantity, which is why the 12/20 guns are now rare collectors' gems. Indeed, Lang's idea may not have prevailed, but it has given us a novelty to enjoy.

Chapter 12

Those Boutique Smallbores

There is something delightfully magnetic and extraordinarily appealing about finely made smallbore doubles, meaning those of .410 bore to 20 gauge. Everyone from the most sophisticated connoisseur to the casual visitor at his first gun show is attracted to them. The refined and diminutive smallbores tend to be boutique guns that are displayed proudly but seldom, if ever, used afield.

What is there about smallbore doubles that brings so much joy and pleasure to both owners and viewers? What is the mystique, the magnetism?

There are a couple of explanations for this phenomenon. One pivots on the mundane; the other is purely esthetic. First the mundane . . .

Not everyone in the world of shotguns is a shooter or a hunter. An important segment of that world, especially insofar as truly fine guns are concerned, is an amalgam of traders, collectors and investors who never hunt and wouldn't think of trying to shatter a clay target. They are interested in only one thing: gun value. And, in general, the smallbore shotguns do have more value than the larger gauges of the same basic makes and models; for, historically, fewer small gauges are made. They are what traders and collectors call rare items. Consequently, the bid-and-ask situation is clearly on the side of a trader or a dealer, since the supply/demand factor is in his favor. Scarcity is the only reason why a Parker VH in 410 is now selling for $3000 or more while a 12-gauge VH in identical condition brings no more than $700 to $1000.

The reason for this scarcity of smallbores in now-obsolete brands and models is obvious. People who bought guns in the past were primarily hunters, not investors, and they gravitated toward the larger gauges for field effectiveness. Thus, fewer smallbores were made. The same reason holds true for the current market, although to a lesser degree, because some forward-looking investors are ordering and buying high-quality smallbores to take advantage of the marketing potential years hence. But there's a catch here, too, that will impede any flooding of the market: Many makers of high-quality, handmade doubles either do not want to build smallbores or else they take a tremendously long time doing it. Purdey took years building the .410 over-under made for Bill Jaqua, the famous Findlay, Ohio, gun dealer, and to date it remains the only such 410. Filing all those small parts to fit perfectly is no small chore. Even Famars, the Italian firm that established a line of lesser-gauge over-unders known as "Jorema," needs substantial time to assemble each gun, and they are the cost equivalent of a new, full-sized Cadillac. Thus, due to the greater demand for the larger gauges and to the gunmakers' reluctance to build the tiny .410s and 28s, the scarcity will undoubtedly continue. Smallbores of

A close-up view of the only .410-bore Purdey over-under ever made. Its gold inlays are by Ken Hunt of London. (Photo courtesy of Jaqua's Fine Guns, Findlay, Ohio)

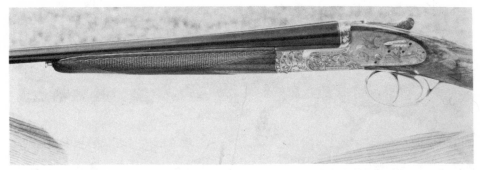

A .410-bore Holland & Holland with quick detachable sideplate and a flushing quail scene done with hammer-and-scriber. (Photo courtesy of Jaqua's Fine Guns, Findlay, Ohio)

classic proportions will remain gems, often being worth significantly more than the same quality and style of gun in 10 or 12 gauge.

But enough of the mundane. Erase the dollar signs and we learn why gun fanciers cherish the smallbores: esthetics, of appreciating line, beauty and elegance, and of admiring the artistry of gunsmithing assemblers and finishers and engravers. It is especially a matter of profile, trimness and size. For as is so true in many other things, smallness becomes appealing. It is something special, something novel, something apart from the gross, the bulky and the ordinary.

The smallbore doubles become truly electric when one has a

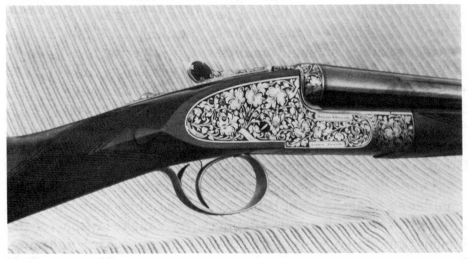

A 28-gauge Holland & Holland with lavish gold inlay set in flowing leaf-and-stem decor. (Photo courtesy of Jaqua's Fine Guns, Findlay, Ohio)

A Westley Richards .410-bore boxlock with a grouse scene and scroll, single trigger and beavertail, and scalloped receiver. (Photo courtesy of Jaqua's Fine Guns, Findlay, Ohio)

chance to handle them and to inspect them at arm's length. Double 410s, 28s and 20s by Purdey, Holland & Holland, Boss, Westley Richards, Merkel, Vouzelaud, Darne, Parker and Winchester are the pinnacles of gunmaking skill. With the exception of the Winchester Model 21 in 410 bore, which has an action body and breech area too large for the gauge, they are not only proportioned to match the specific shotshell and bore diameter but are made with careful attention to details. Famars excels at this creation of spectacular smallbores, both side-by-side and over-under.

Are there any *good* production-grade or semiproduction-grade smallbores that one can buy for less than a king's ransom? The Browning Japanese-made sidelock, retailing at $1500 at this writing, exhibits splendid qualities and is petite in 20 gauge. Winchester has a series of Golden Quail editions of the Model 23 side-by-side, the first of these having been in 28 gauge, with a 20 gauge now available and a .410 indicated. Only 500 of each Golden Quail double will be made, meaning there's a potential for increased value. The same may be true for Winchester's Model 101 Grouse Gun, a neat 20 gauge that is being limited to just 250 pieces.

Some Spanish makers turn out relatively streamline smallbores, a case in point being AyA, which ships many different grades to various stateside suppliers. AyA makes a copy of the famous Churchill XXV gun, and in 28 or 20 gauge it is a lightning-fast upland gun of exceedingly trim proportions. The AyA XXV is made in both boxlock and sidelock versions with various options.

Hunters, collectors and investors can still find some of the early American doubles in 410 bore or 20 gauge, although the price will certainly be higher than for a 12 or 16 gauge in the same breed. This could range anywhere from an Iver Johnson 20 gauge to a Fox Sterlingworth or LeFever Nitro Special. The Fulton line of doubles, made by Hunter Arms Company, which also made L. C. Smith guns, was a boxlock produced in 20 gauge and might interest collectors or hunters who like to carry the old-timers. Moreover, some field-grade L.C. Smiths are still around in .410 and 20 gauge at prices below those of the high-priced Parkers.

The truly refined smallbore doubles, then, are the epitome of line, proportion, grace, elegance, fit, balance and finish. They are at the same time the gunmaker's toughest challenge and his greatest pride. They are also a collector's dream, an investor's hedge and a hunter's joy.

Chapter 13

Datelines: The Continent

Although there seems to be much about gunmaking that is bound by tradition, changes do occur. What is a hobby or a sport to most hunters, shooters and collectors is a serious business to those responsible for the profit and loss statements within the industry, and on the continent of Europe a number of interesting changes have taken place in the last decade. These changes, along with totally new concepts and a review of the tried and true classics, provide the background for this chapter.

SPAIN

It is widely known that Spanish gunmakers have habitually built guns based on the foremost British and European concepts. They have competed mainly by offering their guns at significantly lower prices rather than adding anything innovative or advanced. In side-by-sides, for example, it isn't unusual for Spanish gunmakers to advertise Holland & Holland-type sidelocks with Purdey bolting systems for less than $500. Historically, however, the Spanish bargains have not withstood the test of time. Workmanship comes up short, and gun longevity and field operation have been victimized by poorly hardened components. Some Spanish actions are now being cast rather than machined from forged steel blocks. (Unfortunately, we are led to believe that other nations have bought cheaply cast Spanish actions for use on more expensive guns, something that either has or shall ruin their respective reputations.)

One of the better Spanish gunmakers is Union Armera, now known as Grulla, which makes guns for The Orvis Company and fashioned this bar-action sidelock in the $2000 range.

The engraving on an AyA boxlock XXV/BL.

In Spain, as anywhere else, good guns cannot be made cheaply. The best Iberian horizontal doubles seem to be made by Aguirre and Aranzabal, otherwise known as AyA, and Union Armera, which has recently had its name changed to Grulla. Armas Garbi also rates attention. The AyA line is imported by several American firms, as are the Garbi guns. The famed Yankee supplier of fine fly-fishing tackle, The Orvis Company of Manchester, Vermont, offers custom-made Grulla doubles. The catch is, however, that one must opt for the more expensive AyA, Grulla or Garbi doubles if he wishes good workmanship. As the prices top $2000, these Spanish guns get better. Tooling marks begin to fade, wood-to-metal fit improves, and both the checkering and engraving sharpen noticeably. In the AyA line, the Model 1 and Senior Grand Deluxe have optimum Iberian workmanship, while American upland hunters might be interested in the AyA copies of Churchill's 25-inch-barreled XXV gun, which are made in both boxlock (XXV/BL) and sidelock (XXV/SL). These do not reach the level of the AyA No. 1's workmanship, but they have snappy dynamics. The Grulla Models 219 and Super M-H are top-of-the-line guns with bar-action sidelocks, Purdey bolting, sideclips and English-style fine-line scroll patterns. A variation of the Super M-H is the Super M-P, which is made with a beavertail fore-end and single trigger for live-pigeon competition. Garbi's Model Special and Model 200 retail stateside for about $4000 to $4500 and represent that firm's best in typical side-by-sides.

It is in over-unders where Spanish gunmakers have shown the most promise as innovators since the 1960s. Prior to that time, the only Spanish over-unders were also copies of all-time greats. AyA made a duplicate of the Merkel, calling it the Model 37 Super, and Victor Sarasqueta made a low-profiled replica of the Woodward over-under, neither of which received any international acclaim.

But one Spanish gunmaker has broken from his compatriots to test new ground with an over-under that is not predicated on the concepts of yesteryear. This is Felix Lanber, whose over-under utilizes modern features and assembly techniques. The models being made and distributed are not the fancy, frilly guns that ape traditional game guns but rather are solidly made arms that fit the popular price range, have a pleasing profile, and are apparently made of properly hardened steel to take a pounding from hard-recoiling ammunition. Felix Lanber plunged directly in with a selective single trigger that seems to work perfectly (something not always true for all Spanish single triggers), and he has given the gun screw-in choke tubes, which he has dubbed the Lanberchoke. At least six different Lanber models exist, ranging from field grade to skeet, trap and live pigeon. Each gun has fine-line engraving rolled onto its receiver, and the checkering panels, although certainly not perfectly acquitted, are adequately done for guns in this price range.

I had the fun of using the Lanber over-under for a hunting season, and the gun performed admirably. Its balance point is just a bit forward due to slightly heavier barrels than those found on trim game guns, but that weight distribution wasn't the least distracting. Other over-unders sold stateside have decidedly more weight up front and do not respond as well as the Lanber. The gun rides bifurcated lumps and is bolted by a lateral lug that engages

The Caprinus Sweden is made of stainless steel and has an exceedingly shallow action of just 2.2 inches.

below the lower chamber like the Browning bolt. Made only in 12 gauge at this writing, the Lanber scaled about $7^1/_8$-$7\frac{1}{4}$ pounds. Although it is not an expensive gun, ranging from $500 to $800, the Lanber over-under strikes me as the best thought-out and the strongest shotgun yet to come from Iberia.

SWEDEN

Announced after the first edition of this book was printed is a stylish over-under made by Caprinus AB of Varberg, Sweden. Known as the Caprinus Sweden, it has two claims to fame. One is that it has the trimmest profile of all over-unders, measuring just 2.2 inches through the breech. The second is that all the gun's working parts are made of high-quality stainless steel, the first sporting arm to receive such material throughout. The gun is said to have been test-fired 80,000 times with no measurable wear.

Caprinus Sweden guns weigh from 6¾ pounds in field style to about 7¾ pounds in the trap model. Its trigger is a crisp single selective unit, and its lock mechanism features straight strikers instead of the conventional tumblers. Designed and made to receive screw-in choke tubes, the Caprinus Sweden has a barrel selector lever directly ahead of the trigger. Each gun is delivered in a fitted case covered with Indian water-buffalo hide. Stateside prices begin at $5500. The company maintains an office in Stamford, Connecticut.

FINLAND

Another Scandinavian country with worldwide shotgun ties is Finland, where Valmet guns are made. Considerable mechanical change has taken place here, along with the development of a more aggressive marketing program.

For decades, Valmet over-unders were basically plain hunting arms with a novel squarish U-shaped stirrup acting as a pivot for opening and closing. In the late 1970s, however, Valmet changed to a solid trunnion pivot and added strength to the frame. New machinery permitted the cutting of closely matched barrels and receivers so that assemblies could be readily interchanged, and the company began publicizing over-unders that interchanged from shotgun barrels to rifle barrels or combination (rifle/shotgun) barrels as quickly as a hunter could make the switch. The new design also had an improved trigger group, and about all that remained of the former Valmet over-unders were the top bolt and the slab-sided action body.

An additional step has been taken to improve the Valmet's appearance. In connection with the Ken Hurst Firearms Engraving Company of Rustburg, Virginia, the guns are now being engraved with full scroll or game scenes, and the buyer has his choice of American black walnut or Bastonge walnut. With American black walnut and full scroll, the late-1984 price was $1500 for an over-under shotgun. That rose to $2249 for game scene engraving plus American black walnut, while game scenes and Bastonge walnut rose to $2500. The fancier stocks and fore-ends are turned and checkered by Don Allen in Minnesota. Game scenes can be of American or European species such as the Scandinavian red deer

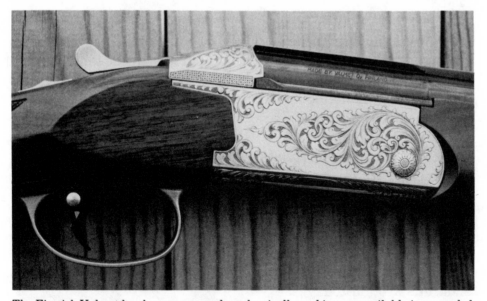

The Finnish Valmet has been revamped mechanically and is now available in upgraded models with American stock dimensions and various engraving designs applied by the Ken Hurst Firearms Engraving Company of Rustburg, Virginia. This is the deep-flowing scroll pattern.

and the capercaille. The finished guns have a very rich appearance
and handle nicely. Valmet handles its own stateside distribution
out of Elmsford, New York, and provides a special order blank for
ordering engraved models.

AUSTRIA

The gunmakers of Ferlach have not become aggressive,
although they maintain stateside outlets. Essentially, they all
make the same types of break-action guns, and the guild system
tends to find them buying barreled actions from the same maker
so that the metallic nucleus is similar for a certain type of gun
regardless of who finishes it. Names that appear most frequently
in the Western Hemisphere are Ludwig Borovnik, Johann Fanzoi,
Josef Hambrusch, Josef Just, Johann Michelitsch, R. Franz Schmid,
Anton Sodia, Benedikt Winkler and Josef Winkler.

ITALY

It was a sad loss for the world of fine guns when Mario Abbiatico
died prematurely of cancer in 1984. A partner in the famous Armi
Famars venture with Remo Salvinelli, Mario Abbiatico was
dedicated to gunmaking and artistic engraving. He wrote two books
about engraving: *Grand Incisioni su Armi d'Oggi*, and *Modern
Firearms Engraving*, both of which, like his guns, will become
collectors' classics. Fortunately, Famars will continue.

Another Italian gunmaking great is Ivo Fabbri, considered to
be the most advanced technician in all of gunmaking. Fabbri
designs most of his own equipment, and his machines cut so close
that little final fitting is necessary. His guns are masterpieces, not
because of the machining but because of their final fit and artistic
finish. A Fabbri live-pigeon gun is one of the most prestigious
shotguns around today.

While Fabbri guns continue to be artistically made, it is
rumored that Ivo himself, once an engineer at Fiat, is busy
designing a new camshaft and an entirely new car. Thus, there

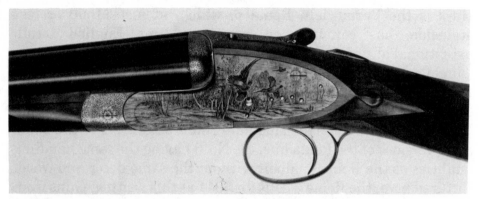

Precise fits and artistic finishes mark all Fabbri guns such as this side-by-side with a mixture of *bulino* driven pheasant scenes and hammer-and-scriber scroll. The engraving is by Angelo Galeazzi, an outstanding Italian gun artist.

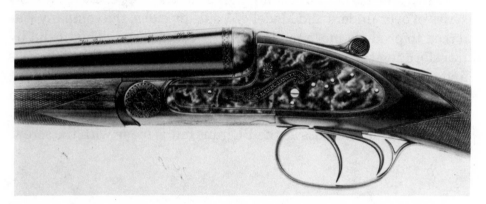

The Bernardelli Roma 3 is a nicely fitted sidelock for those with less than a fortune to spend on a double.

has been nothing new added to the mechanics of the Fabbri doubles. But as one connoisseur put it, how can you improve on perfection? Unfortunately, the Fabbri machinery could cut hundreds, perhaps thousands, more guns each year, but the company chooses to hold production low and quality exceedingly high. This apparently maximizes profit and keeps the demand/supply ratio in the company's favor. It also maintains superb handwork, as the final finishing and engraving are obviously more time-consuming than is the machining.

The name Vincenzo Bernardelli is well known to Americans. For more than 100 years this company has been making a wide range of guns for export, and one of the true bargains in side-by-sides is the Bernardelli Roma 6, which, at just $1500 or less stateside, has coin-finished sideplates, fine English scroll, exceptional bluing, hand-checkered walnut, a hinged front trigger (single trigger optional at just $55), selective ejectors and an English-style stock. Optional beavertail fore-ends run $45. Of all the copies of the British game gun, this Roma 6 and the new Browning Japanese-made sideplate rate huzzah. There are some other versions of the Roma line, the No. 3 having the same handling qualities as the Roma 6, albeit without the same decor and wood. Pictured here, the Roma 3 sells for $944 at this writing. Guns from V. Bernardelli are imported by Quality Arms Inc. of Houston, Texas.

With worldwide inflation driving up the cost of Beretta's SO series of over-unders and Model 451 side-by-sides, the company was forced to produce more moderately priced doubles. This it did by transforming the earlier BL series of over-unders into the 680 series and, at the same time, developing the Model 625 *paralleli.*

Hunters who enjoyed the former BL series of guns will warm immediately to the Model S685L, the L standing for lightweight. It has the same trimness as the BL guns but is made with the screw-

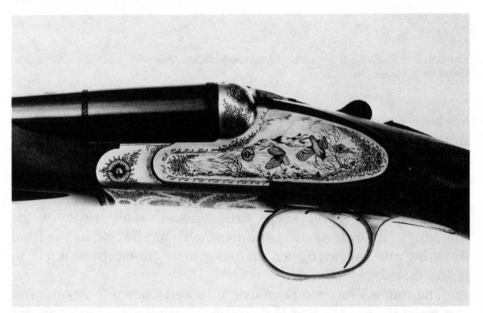

The left lock's scene as found on a relatively new Beretta Model 627EELL. This is a boxlock gun with false sideplates.

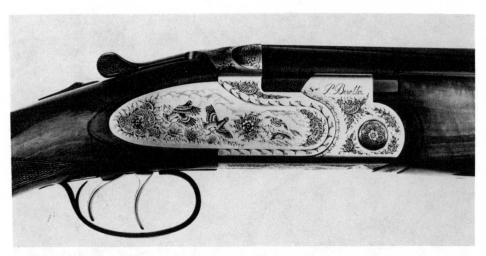

The sideplated Beretta Model S687EELL, a lightweight field gun shown here in its European version with twin triggers.

in Mobilchokes that disappear into the muzzle. The S685L is available in several different engraving patterns, from minor scroll to dog and bird hunting scenes.

The Model 625 side-by-sides have the same classic profile as the $10,000-plus 451; however, the 625s are boxlocks that, in the 627 EELL and 625 EL Sport models, have been given purely cosmetic engraved sideplates. The 627 EL Sport has neat border scroll; the 627 EELL has a floral and scroll design. Interestingly, the 626 E, 627 EELL and 627 EL Sport all have semi-beavertailed forearms, and the entire line has excellent European walnut in ascending quality as per the individual's gun grade. At this writing, the 625s and 685Ls aren't well known stateside, but they should be. Beretta has its own outlet in Accokeek, Maryland.

GERMANY

For many years, the late J. J. Jenkins of Santa Barbara, California, was the main American importer of Merkel guns, and with his passing there was a short period in which Merkels were hard to come by stateside. The trade barriers between East and West have hindered a free flow of guns from the Suhl area of East Germany. However, another American company has recently

The Model 201E Merkel over-under has a typical Germany hunting scene done in relief. It is probably as much hand engraving as one will find on an over-under in its price range.

jumped into the void: Dunn's Inc. of Grand Junction, Tennessee. The guns being offered are in 12, 16, 20 and 28 gauges and .410 bore. They are apparently the basic Merkel 200E and 201E; however, Dunn's catalogs them as the Scroll Engraved Impervious and the Game Scene Engraved Impervious at $2129 and $2684, respectively. The name Impervious is Dunn's, and the catalog description contains the surprising statement that each gun is guaranteed for five years, even with steel shot! Thus, the Merkel is back in the United States, at least on a limited basis, as Dunn's publications advise of a 9- to 12-month lag time.

Krieghoff of Ulm, West Germany, is another gunmaker that deserves special attention. Because the Krieghoff Model 32 and K-80 competition guns have proved so successful, we tend to ignore the other gunmaking segment of Krieghoff. However, the original firm of Sempert & Krieghoff began making hunting guns in 1885, and the current company, known as H. Krieghoff, *Jagdund Sportwaffenfabrik,* continues to do so. The target guns became a part of the line only after acquiring the rights to Remington's Model 32 over-under following WWII.

Originally from Suhl, which is now part of East Germany, the Krieghoff family packed up after WWII and moved to Ulm rather than succumbing to the communist mode. A new plant was set up there, and the American distribution center is often listed as Guns of Ulm rather than as Krieghoff. In Ulm, the new K-80 line, which is a revision of the earlier Model 32, is only part of the production. European-style break-action hunting guns are also made, including side-by-side shotguns and rifles, over-under shotguns and rifles, and drillings and combination guns. These are magnificent examples of German gunmaking skill and artistry. The Krieghoff TECK is a boxlock over-under; the Model ULM is a sidelocked over-under. Both can be finished according to the customer's requests, and the sky's the limit on price. The boxlock TECK has an action body design and bolting akin to the Merkel, while the sidelock ULM has secondary intercepting sears.

Krieghoff also sells fashionable side-by-sides, which, to my eyes, have features that are more Italian than German. Known as the KS-2, the Krieghoff side-by-side is a sidelock with V-springs and the general Holland & Holland bar-action construction. Unlike the German penchant for scriber and chaser engraving, however, the KS-2's sideplates are adorned with scenes done in *bulino* and have game-bird arrangements much like those found on Italian plates. There is no scroll on the sideplates, although surrounding metal components have fine scroll tastefully done. A trim semi-beavertail, not unlike that seen on Beretta guns, is also featured on the KS-2, which can be had in any popular gauge plus .410 bore. The starting price is around $4,000, and exhibition-grade English walnut and a single, nonselective trigger is included. The KS-2s are beautifully finished and elegant in every respect, and each one comes in its own leather-covered case.

Thus, while Krieghoff K-80s win important skeet and trap tournaments, there are splendid hunting models coming from the same company, and, as fine field-style guns go, they may not be receiving adequate attention. Dieter Krieghoff maintains an office in Ringoes, New Jersey (P.O. Box L), under the style of Shotgun of Ulm. Catalogs of the conventional hunting guns are available.

BELGIUM

As nations go, Belgium has always been one of the most competitive in the field of gunmaking. And although the name Browning, intertwined with Fabrique Nationale (FN), is the most widely known, there are a number of other small gunmaking establishments in the Liege-Herstal area who, on a low-volume basis, steal much of the thunder from the necessarily production-oriented FN operation. The important ones today are Lebeau-Courally, Le Forgeron and Ernest Dumoulin. All of these are relatively small shops that employ traditional hand fitting and finishing, and they still work with forged actions and components, not castings, which is no longer true of some other names in Belgian gunmaking. I will sidestep those companies that have been suspected of using cast action bodies and/or Spanish-made actions.

Lebeau-Courally was established in 1865 and supplied such famous figures as Czar Nicholas II and Alphonse XIII, King of Spain, and other royal houses. At Lebeau-Courally, extreme care and attention is put into every gun. While there are basic models, each gun is considered a custom order, and an estimated 400-600 hours go into every one. The company has an interesting way of backing its workmanship: It is ready to repurchase guns at prices higher than the customer paid for them!

Lebeau-Courally makes Anson & Deeley boxlocks, sideplated boxlocks, and full sidelocks of side-by-side persuasion. It also builds an over-under sidelock that is a direct copy of the British boss. This over-under is called the Boss-Verrees in memory of Joseph Verrees who, from 1956 to 1982, assembled the gunsmithing team that so carefully turned out great guns at Lebeau-Courally. In keeping with the low-profile concept, the Boss-Verrees has an action depth of just 2.44 inches (61mm) in 12 gauge.

In side-by-sides, the first grade Lebeau-Courally boxlock is known as the Grand Russe. It is fitted with chopper lump barrels and Purdey triple bolting. A sideplated boxlock of equal quality is called the Sologne. Among the sidelocks, the Prince Koudacheff grade is made exactly like the famous British game guns with fine scroll and a Holland & Holland self-opener. Two other sidelocks of exceptionally high quality are the Comte de Paris and the Wiesbaden. Lebeau-Courally also makes a magnum sidelock with a sturdier action and slightly more weight for live-pigeon and trapshooting competitions.

Le Forgeron is also a well-established Liege house with high quality and low volume. Its future hangs in the balance. Forgeron himself is nearing retirement, and since he has no sons, it is a question as to whether the firm will continue and, if it does, what the quality will be. At this writing, however, Forgeron guns are among the very best in the world. Sticking mainly with side-by-sides, Forgeron builds boxlocks, sideplated boxlocks and full sidelocks, which, on the American new-gun market, range anywhere from $4500 to $12,000.

The name of Dumoulin has been common to Belgian gunmaking, but it has now become a question of *which* Dumoulin. At one time it was Henri Dumoulin who attracted attention, but he has retired and his personal operation has ceased. Henri's son, Ernest Dumoulin, is now considered to be the most innovative, successful and demanding gunmaker among the various Belgian houses. He is working from his shop, which was established well before Henri retired, and he carries on independently from his father's practices and business philosophies.

One of the finest gunmakers of Belgium is Le Forgeron, who created this British-type classic with detachable sideplate and oak leafs in relief on the fences.

Versatility and innovation are keys to the success and mounting reputation of Ernest Dumoulin. The company not only makes boxlocks, sideplated boxlocks and full sidelocks of the game-gun variety but is also beginning to build its version of the British Boss over-under. Forged actions are available in the Belgian guild, and the Dumoulin Boss guns will follow the trim profile and refined features applied to such pieces. Along with developing the Boss gun, Ernest Dumoulin has created a new, fast-acting back-action sidelock and an improved system for the chopper lump concept. This latter pair of developments will probably be more important to the line of horizontal double rifles than to the shotgun, but their presence does indicate the dedication that seems to prevail here.

What should interest fanciers of fine guns is a joint venture that will have Ernest Dumoulin finishing Browning-style FN actions and FN side-by-sides. Stateside shooters and collectors have always equated FN with the Browning over-under, but the fact is that the company also made side-by-side guns mainly for European distribution. Moreover, some cheapening has gone on in the FN plant in the Browning over-under action, and many of the former high-quality Browning-FN Superposed models are no longer available. Back in the early 1970s, for example, it was found that the original Browning Superposed action, considered by many authorities to have been the best ever made, was becoming too expensive to produce. Known as the B-25 action, it was modified drastically in 1972 as the B-27 and sold as the Liege Model. The experiment was not a great success; observant gun critics knew a cheapened action when they saw it. However, hunters and shooters who don't follow gun trends have failed to discern a difference, and they've become willing to pay considerable sums simply for the Browning-FN epithet on over-unders without taking a discriminating look at the nucleus. Unless a Browning over-under has the actual B-25 action, it isn't the original Browning design.

Along with decelerated use of the expensive B-25 action, FN reduced the output of, or dropped entirely the production of, smallbore Superposed guns. The last .410-bore Superposed was made in 1976 with a serial number of 414J76. In 1984, however, a special series of 200 410s was made from remaining parts and shipped to the United States with serial numbers of 415J83 to

614J83. The FN plant, of course, is busy with other production, ranging from military guns and hardware to diesel engines. One gets the feeling that FN would sooner not bother with the low-volume assembly of high-quality sporting arms but would rather seek profits elsewhere.

Whatever the motivation at FN, it appears that (based on behind-the-scenes information) Ernest Dumoulin will work in connection with FN in finishing high-grade FN actions, namely, the B-25 and the remaining side-by-side actions virtually unknown stateside. Ernest Dumoulin already receives Browning 20-gauge over-under actions on which he builds double rifles and shotguns. By the time this book is printed, the Dumoulin-FN connection should be established. Guns that come from this tandem of gunmakers will be handled in the United States by Antoine Falise, who operates Midwest Gun Sport/Belgian Headquarters, 1942 Oakwood View Drive, Verona, WI 53593 (608/845-7447).

Thus, although one tends to equate Old World craftsmanship with tradition, there are changes taking place in European gunmaking. Some of them are for the better, such as those of Ernest Dumoulin of Belgium, Felix Lanber of Spain, Valmet of Finland, and Manufrance of France. Where traditions hold sway, as at Vouzelaud of France and Le Forgeron and Lebeau-Courally of Belgium, the guns are carefully fit and finished to retain their levels of prestige. But where backsliding is noticed, as with the Browning-FN B-27 action and the cast Spanish action, the change is lamentable. The point is that there are still excellent, dedicated, trustworthy gunmakers on the Continent—but there are others, too.

Chapter 14

French Connections

The sporting world has long praised the gunmaking greats of England, Scotland, Belgium, Germany and Italy, but the French have largely gone unsung. One reason for this is that the production of fine French guns has always been a calm, quiet, careful, low-volume affair, and the European market has always absorbed most of the guns so that the rest of the world knew little about them. But the foremost French gunmakers do indeed build doubles that can be either mechanically innovative or conventionally exquisite, as connoisseurs of the Western Hemisphere are about to learn because some venturesome and discriminating American entrepreneurs have finally established long-overdue connections with those hitherto ignored craftsmen. The flow of such guns won't reach floodlike proportions; however, on a dollar-value and quality basis, they will be difficult to beat.

RETURN OF THE DARNE

Shortly after the first edition of this book was published, the French Darne fell from sight. The Darne, as many shotgun buffs know, has a novel sliding breech rather than the conventional drop-barrel design. The gun is longitudinally rigid. Loading and unloading are done by means of a sliding breech that is operated toggle-style via earlike appendages located directly behind the fences. The mechanism gives more camming power than the normal drop-barrel system for chambering shells, a feature that was vastly more important in the days of paper hulls than it is with today's

142

nonswelling, self-lubricating plastic cases. To that extent, the Darne's breech mechanism can be regarded as an anachronism. However, it is still a viable field design, and the gun's overall weight and balance made it greased lightning afield. A 12-gauge Darne scales only 6-6¼ pounds depending on barrel length, and the elegant 20- and 28-gauge Darnes are like fairy wands.

Features aside, the Darne operation fell into troubled financial waters about the time my earlier tome went to press. It seems that one of the upper management people slithered away with a considerable stock of company francs, and the family that owned the enterprise, being somewhat detached from it all, decided against refinancing it. For several years it appeared that the novel Darne had passed into history.

But the Darne is back. It isn't being called the Darne anymore, although, conceptually speaking, it is the same gun. If anything, the quality seems a tad better.

The revitalized venture is headed by Paul Bruchet, a former Darne employee, who struck up a deal for the original Darne machinery and equipment but couldn't afford to buy rights to the renowned name. Thus, the new generation of Darnes will be known by the name Bruchet, which will be engraved somewhere on them. The American side of this French connection will be handled by Loren Thomas Ltd. of Dallas, Texas.

The former grades of Darne guns have been dropped in favor of new designations. The prior line included six basic numbers, some of which also had names. They differed mainly in the amount of engraving, checkering and the grade of wood. The Model V was mainly a full custom order. The Model R11 was the lowest number and was followed in this fashion: R11 Bird Hunter, R15 Pheasant Hunter, R16 Magnum, V19 Quail Hunter, V22, and V *Hors Série* No. 1.

At the present time, only two models will be available stateside. The Model A will have bold scroll and, at this writing, starts at $1800; the Model B will have finer scroll, added bird or hunting scenes, fancier wood and finer checkering for $5000. Options will be offered in gauge, barrel length and grip style. The popular bore sizes from .410 through 12 gauge are obtainable, and the European brochure lists the 24 gauge as well. Barrel lengths are generally kept below 28 inches on these feathery guns, with 25-26 inches

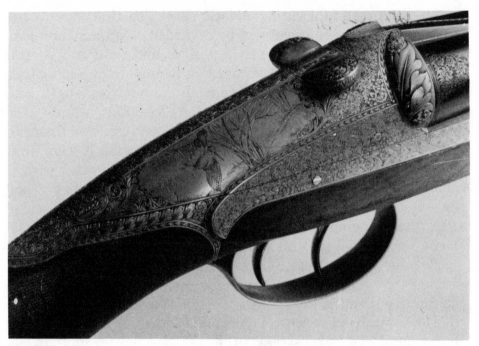

A close-up of the engraving now being put on the Model B Bruchet-Darne. This is a 28 gauge with scroll, a woodcock scene, and deeply chiseled fences. It was made in 1984.

being normal. Grip possibilities include the half-pistol and the racy English straight handle. Only double triggers are made. Splinter fore-ends are standard, but a semi-beavertail can be fashioned at extra cost.

Thus, after an unfortunate interlude, the Darne—whoops, Bruchet—is back, perhaps better than ever. For the time being, production is expected to run about 150 guns annually, so there will be a demand. The novel, elegantly made gun deserves it.

VOUZELAUD

Although St. Etienne is the gunmaking center of France, an updating of American-French relations makes this a shotgunner's tale of two cities. For a very prestigious French gunmaking family operates instead out of Brou, which is about a 90-minute drive southwest of Paris. These are the Vouzelauds, who have given their family name to the business. Privately owned since 1888, the company and the family have a storied past. The parents of the current managers, who are Hubert and Alan Vouzelaud, were cited for valor by President Roosevelt, General de Gaulle, Prime Minister Attlee and other notables for their role in the French underground during WWII. Primarily, the Vouzelauds rescued and hid downed Allied airmen and helped them escape to England.

Vouzelaud is a somewhat more active operation than are the other French gunmakers, turning out Vouzelaud shotshells and having a shooting school with five full-time instructors as well. The shooting school has Olympic skeet and trap plus two 30-meter trap towers to simulate driven game. One tower has an elevator trap for variable heights and target angles.

The gunmaking portion of Vouzelaud pivoted on 14 gunsmiths at the time of this writing. The guns are boxlocks, but the higher grades carry false sideplates that fool even the sharpest expert. The false sideplates have dummy axle and screw heads perfectly positioned and finished, some of them gold-plated. Locks are typical Anson & Deeley, carefully adjusted for crisp pulls. It would be difficult to find a sidelock with better triggers.

Vouzelaud doubles are traditional side-by-side game guns with all the features that made the type famous. They are given straight hand grips with the classic long tang extending well back from the trigger guard. Fore-ends are splinters with front-mounted plunger-type releases, and both stock and fore-end are finished in hand-rubbed oil. It was my pleasure to have a pair of Vouzelaud doubles on trial, and they proved to be magnificent examples of the French gunmaker's art. Moreover, their handling qualities were equal to practically any other side-by-side available, and the engraving was immaculate.

Vouzelaud guns are being handled stateside by Waverly Arms of Columbia, South Carolina. The line involved three obvious boxlocks and two bearing false sideplates. The boxlocks and their prices are:

Model 315-E	$2900
Model 315-EL	$3500
Model 315-EL Special	$4900

The Models 315-E and 315-EL are made in 12, 16 and 20 gauges

The sideplated Vouzelaud Model 315-EGL looks exactly like a fine sidelock, but the axle and screw heads in the sideplate are false. The gun is a sideplated Anson & Deeley boxlock elegantly done with British floral-and-scroll fine-line engraving.

A close-up of the Vouzeland Model 315-EL boxlock showing its scalloped action body and fine-line British-type engraving on a coin-finished background.

only. The Model 315-EL Special is a dainty smallbore in either 28 gauge or .410 bore. One of my trial guns was a 28-gauge 315-EL Special, and it was just that—something special.

Vouzelaud doubles sporting false sideplates are:

Model 315-EGL	$4900
Model 315-EGL Special	$5900 up

These are 12-, 16- and 20-gauge guns, and they have silver satin sideplate and action body finishes. The Model 315-EGL receives English-style engraving of the floral bouquet and fine scroll variety, while the Model 315-EGL Special is given chiseled hunting and game scenes plus adorning scroll. It also has a long, painstakingly fitted fore-end tip.

Vouzelaud guns are made in matching pairs with the numbers 1 and 2 inletted. The price for matching guns so closely is an added 10 percent.

In general, the Vouzelaud guns emphasize the fact that boxlocks can indeed be made to rival the elegance, quality and effectiveness of any sidelock.

GEORGES GRANGER

Returning to St. Etienne from Brou, we find the equally small company of Georges Granger. It was started in 1902 by Aime Coeur Tyrode, who in 1913 filed a patent for his sidelock similar to the Holland & Holland with double sears. Tyrode was followed in 1933 by Henri Guichard, who built up a considerable clientele by winning a gold medal at the Universal Exposition of 1937 in Paris.

For 20 years, Guichard's journeyman was Georges Granger. In his dedicated career, Granger has been nominated for several prestigious French awards: Best French Worker (1968), Master Craftsman (1978) and Laureate of Artistic Professions (1979). He now owns the business, continuing its fine traditions.

Granger guns are handmade. The craftsmen begin with heat-treated steels; the "team" as it is called in Granger literature, makes lock plates, trigger guards and receivers in the same artisanal methods practiced in St. Etienne since the sixteenth century. Stocks are handmade according to the individual customer. Engravings range from English scroll to some surprising rococo endeavors that rival the most flamboyant Italian endeavors.

Granger guns are solely side-by-sides of the game-gun pattern, stressing straight grips and splinter fore-ends. However, variations are possible if the customer is willing to pay. All interior parts are glass polished, and every Granger gun has removable lock plates. Prices vary, as the company seems to have no set models but works on a gun-to-gun basis instead.

THE BRETTON

One of the most novel over-unders, if not *the* most novel stackbarrel, is the Baby Bretton with its pull-apart action. This flush, vertical, full-length fit of breech to receiver leaves no action bar to be affected by the bending forces of recoil, and the gun can consequently be made very light. French figures put the 12 gauge

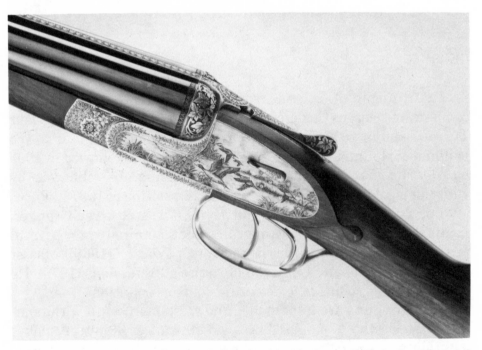

A view of engravings on a G. Granger double. On this side shot, note the leaf motif carried out on the fences, opening lever and fore-end iron.

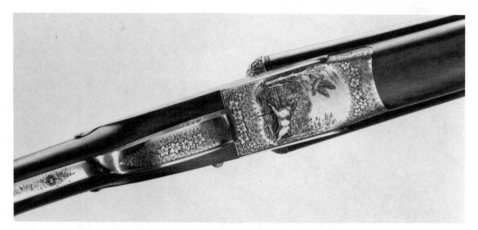

A floorplate photo of the same Granger with the scroll-and-leaf carried through, plus a lifelike woodcock and springer scene.

at 2.2 kilograms, or just 4.8 pounds! The Bretton is operated by an opening lever on the action's right side, and the barrel and butt sections slide apart on a pair of hardened rods. The barrels are all 27 inches long, and interchangeable choke tubes are part of the package. Baby Brettons are handled in the United States by Quality Arms Inc. of Houston, Texas, which offers three grades: the Standard, the Elite and the Baby Luxe. Made in both 12 and 16 gauges, the Luxe edition retails for just $795. If you're looking for a conversation piece as well as an easy-carrying walking stick, the Baby Bretton is it!

MANUFRANCE

The largest maker of shotguns in France is Manufrance, which turns out both over-under and side-by-side models. These are mainly production-grade guns, although they are excellent examples.

The side-by-sides from Manufrance are known as the Robust Series. They have been made since 1902, and there are approximately 800,000 already in circulation. They begin with the economy Model 221, a nonejector, and range through the Model 245 DeLuxe with its high grade of French walnut, automatic ejectors and a nickel-chromium steel action with what appears to be etched scroll. Bolting is done by an underlug plus crossbolts that

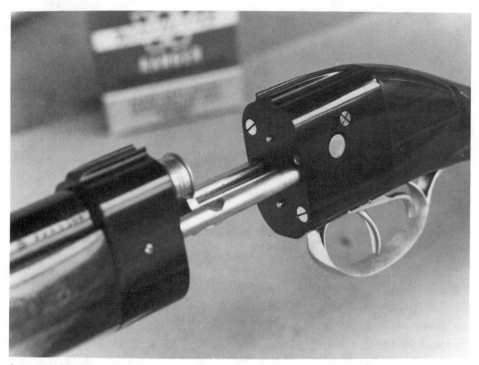

The Baby Bretton has a novel pull-apart action and is very light.

fit a lengthy barrel extension. The fore-end being used on Model 245s shipped to these shores is a fashionable beavertail, but like so many European doubles, a sling hanger extends from the barrels' underside. The DeLuxe Robust sells for just $760 from Armsource Inc. of Orinda, California.

For the European market, the Robust gun is carried to a very high degree of refinement in the Ideal Luxe and the Prestige models, which run thousands of dollars. They have hand-engraved scroll and fancy walnut, plus articulated front triggers. Neither gun is listed by Armsource for the American market.

Manufrance has also revamped its over-under, the Falcor. In many respects, the mechanical changes seem to follow those of the new Valmet guns. Falcor over-unders have the same top bolt and trunnion system as the Valmet, and their action bodies are equally flat. Both Valmet and Falcor changeovers came at about the same time. In Europe, Falcor guns run through a sequence of grades and styles, beginning with a plain Model 1958 and running to the hand-finished Falcor Luxe with its hand engraving, fine walnut and

The Robust Model 245 from Manufrance, a sturdy side-by-side with semi-fancy walnut and scroll coverage.

The Falcor Model 1977 Pheasant Grade over-under, also from Manufrance, with stylishly tight pistol grip and sharp schnobble fore-end plus scroll coverage.

hinged front trigger. In the United States, however, the only field-grade Falcor listed by Armsource is known as the Pheasant Gun, although skeet and trap guns are available. The Pheasant Gun is an eye-catcher, beginning with its bold fore-end schnobble and continuing to its tight pistol grip reminiscent of the Etchen grip. With a flat rib and silvery receiver covered with scroll, it looks very sleek. The European version of the Pheasant Gun is known as the Sporting Falcor 1977. It retails stateside at $940 complete with single trigger and ejectors.

CHAPIUS

Relatively new to the Western Hemisphere, if not the entire world, Chapius doubles include the Progress and Progress Artisan side-by-sides and the Odegaard Chapius over-under. They are made essentially as double-triggered hunting arms with weight and handling qualities like spirited game guns. The basic Chapius Progress is a boxlock with a straight receiver, while the Progress Artisan has a scalloped action body. As one would conclude from its name, the Artisan has a finer finish and more elaborate engraving and checkering than the Progress. Both guns have the traditional hingepin rotational system, but the barrel assembly's engagement lugs are split so the cocking mechanism can fit between them for centralized power.

The over-under is a boxlock with engraved sideplates and twin triggers. It scales about 6½ pounds in 12 gauge. Both the side-by-sides and the over-under have streamline appearances, especially the horizontal Progress guns. Those who must hunt their big game with shotgun slugs will be interested to know that Chapius guns are regularly made with special slug barrels of 22 inches. Additional marketing information is difficult to obtain on these guns; a pair of letters to the American-based importer in Austin, Texas, produced no replies. A letter to the home office at 42380 Bonnet-le-Chateau, France, brought only a catalog with no price listings.

Despite our lack of familiarity with French guns, and despite the difficulty in finding most of them, we must admire the work of leading French gunmakers.

Chapter 15

A New World Classic:
The Winchester Model 21

A bird gun's design and construction are heavily influenced by its time and place. But if it is a solid concept handled by knowledgeable gunmakers, it is refined through an evolutionary process that gradually utilizes the best ideas that science, theory and gun artists can offer. The British hammerless game gun is an obvious example. Beginning as a revamped flintlock in the early days of percussion ignition, the game gun's lines and mechanisms went through tubelock, pinfire and underlever stages before, eventually, reaching its ultimate form and features in the early 1900s. Thus when the British had their golden age of gunmaking, the classics they created were the end result of nearly 100 years of constant tinkering with theoretical and mechanical considerations.

Winchester's Model 21 side-by-side has a similar history, having progressed from a high-quality, production-grade gun to an

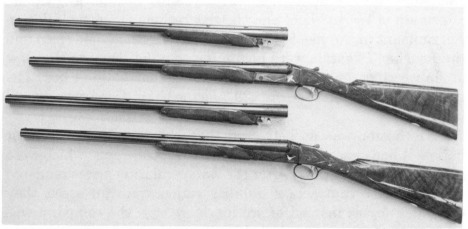

A pair of matched, custom-made, straight-gripped Model 21 Grand Americans.

outstanding custom double that has been mechanically and conceptually refined to satisfy the Western Hemisphere's wing-gunning habits and tastes. In other words, it is wrong to judge the Model 21 by equating it with the British/Continental game gun in every respect. Indeed, if Winchester fashioned the Model 21 after a classic Purdey with straight grip, splinter fore-end and twin triggers, nobody would buy it! American and Canadian gunners use more powerful ammunition and heavier shot charges than do their overseas counterparts, they face different hunting conditions, many are more active shooters on clay targets during the off season, and those who order custom doubles are generally influenced by the style of stock and fore-end configurations found on skeet and trap models. Consequently, the American double is commonly heavier than the traditional game gun to offset greater recoil forces and is, more often than not, ordered with some form of pistol grip and beavertail fore-end. The Model 21, then, in answering these New World demands, must be judged by itself within the framework of New World conditions and demands. Unfortunately, the critic's eye is frequently jaundiced in favor of the Old World classics, and he fails to appreciate the influences that affect and dictate Yankee approaches to the fine double. This chapter will trace the Model 21's course with emphasis on those forces that have shaped it into a uniquely New World expression of fine gunmaking.

The Model 21 was developed during the late 1920s, a time of financial chaos for both the world in general and Winchester in particular. International monetary systems were failing in the aftermath of World War I and the reparations schemes; inflation ran rampant in Europe. In the United States, prices had risen and the Roaring Twenties were beginning to quiet down to that low groan which accompanies a hangover. The party didn't last. The stock market would crash in 1929, and the Great Depression would begin.

Winchester was no better off than the rest of the world or nation. It had expanded rapidly to meet war contracts, which were of the fixed-price variety. After the war, escalating prices rendered the fixed-price contracts a liability rather than an asset; they generated losses instead of profits. Moreover, the company was unable to organize its expanded facilities effectively, and its entry into markets other than firearms—such as hardware and roller skates—didn't help. Winchester teetered on the brink of bankruptcy for years, finally falling into receivership in 1931. The excesses of the Roaring Twenties had once carried Winchester common stock to $2500 a share, but in these bleak times the issue became a leader on the downside, plunging to virtual worthlessness.

And yet, with financial systems and even societies crumbling about them, the Winchester development group set about designing a high-quality double. It was an extraordinary move, to say the least. Some would later argue that it was a legitimate move, justified by what then appeared to be a surge away from market hunting and toward sport hunting. The argument seems valid. Intellectual history indicates that American tastes did turn toward the finer things in life during the 1920s. There was a ready market for the finer Parker, L. C. Smith, LeFever, Ithaca and A. H. Fox guns, so why shouldn't a mainline gunmaker like Winchester try its hand, too? Indeed, nobody knew for certain that the economy wouldn't recover, and, optimistically, Winchester looked ahead. The Model 21 thus became a reality, the initial shipment being made to dealers in 1930.

The original Winchester Model 21 was designed to be a high-quality, production-grade gun. It was not then a hand-crafted, custom-made item. The idea was to compete broadly. The guns were machined to tight tolerances so that an excellent overall fit could be achieved. Added care was given during assembly by selected gunsmithing finishers. Winchester did not have a custom shop at the time, but the Model 21s were fitted and assembled in a special crib where only a few appointed workers could venture. In other words, it was not a production-line job even though the gun was regarded as a production-grade item. Special attention was given to the fitting and assembling, as selected gunsmithing assemblers either selected or matched components or made minor filing adjustments.

The original Model 21s had splinter-type fore-ends with double triggers, a pistol grip and either plain or selective ejectors. They were considered field guns and could be had in the standard choke combinations—such as improved cylinder and modified, modified and full, and full and full—with barrel assemblies of 26, 28, 30 and

31 inches. Each set of barrels carried a raised matted rib. The wood, checkering and finish were a stride beyond the norm for field guns of that day, but they hardly reached the full fancy level of today's Model 21. That was how Winchester intended it, of course. They were supposed to be *better* doubles, not London-grade Best guns, and they reached that goal while laying a solid foundation for future refinements. Indeed, these first Model 21s were as good as or better than the remaining American doubles in their price range.

The Model 21 was not given a top fastener, a fact that was lamented by another generation of writers who were used to seeing Greener crossbolts and doll's heads. But the designers were not oblivious to the trio of potentially destructive forces that work against a double's frame and bolts. A sizable knuckle pin held against axial forces; a single but sturdy underlug held against rotational movement and was set high enough so that, when properly fitted, it could help take some sting out of the bending force's thrust. In the main, however, the single underlug's purpose was supplying hold-down pressure.

Winchester's development team took two additional steps to offset the impact of bending forces. Each side of the frame was given a shapely panel, or "boss," to strengthen the angle. Likewise, the Model 21 was given an action bar longer than that found on other side-by-sides, thereby improving the single underlug's effectiveness by invoking Westley Richards' old dictum that the most efficient bolts are those placed the farthest from the knuckle. Added distance between the knuckle and the underlug moved the Model 21's fulcrum forward, reducing the leverage that can be applied by a downward-thrusting barrel and, in turn, lessening the strain placed on the angle of the frame. These design features, along with the selected use of 4140 chrome vanadium and 4140 chrome molybdenum steel in the action body and barrel assembly, produced an action nucleus that was both sound and sturdy despite being mechanically simple. Even hard-kicking shotshells with heavy payloads have not prompted frame cracking or early looseness.

Extensive shooting can wear the knuckle pin of a Model 21, of course. A readjustment is then made by installing a new and larger pin, and the gun is designed to accommodate a series of these larger-diameter pins, if necessary. The first knuckle pin starts at roughly a .360-inch diameter, with .380-inch being the largest that can comfortably be fitted. However, the .020-inch leeway gives the Model 21 a tremendous lifespan. Lug wear can also be adjusted by installing a new one or by building up the old lug and filing to fit. Thus, the design anticipated normal wear and provided relatively easy solutions for continued usage.

The Winchester Model 21 has always been a boxlock. Its hammer and sear assembly is much like that of the Anson & Deeley, and the M21's action body shows a pair of transverse holes to handle the hammer and sear axles like any other A&D double. But the Model 21 uses powerful coil springs on the hammers instead of the V-springs common to Anson & Deeley actions. The coil-type mainspring of each individual Model 21 lock entwines itself about a connecting (cocking) rod that runs through the action bar and hooks directly into a notch on the tumbler's upper surface. Whenever the Model 21 is opened, a cocking cam at the knuckle is influenced by the fore-end iron to shove the connecting rod backward, cocking the hammer and compressing the mainspring. With the hammer/sear assembly reset and the gun closed, a void now exists between the connecting rod's foremost extremity and the cocking cam; and when the trigger is pulled, freeing the hammer to pivot about its axle, the compressed mainspring is also freed to regain its normal length. It drives forward, filling the former void, and in doing so yanks the hammer about its axle to fire the chambered load. The system has proved quite successful, giving consistent and positive ignition with virtually trouble-free operation.

Except for a timing-type single trigger that came along in April of 1931, the innards of the Model 21 have seen little or no change. However, exterior alterations began taking place even while it was still considered a production-grade gun. A raised ventilated rib became available as an option during the 1930s, and that necessitated the addition of two new action bodies. Hitherto, the Model 21 had employed two frames to blend with the lower-sitting standard rib; one was the 12-gauge frame, the other a scaled-down unit for 16- and 20-gauge barrels. But the ventilated rib design for the Model 21 was a lofty arrangement, and a high ramp was needed between the shoulders of the standing breech to effect a smooth transition from frame to rib. This brought to four the number of Model 21 frames, a count that remains today.

Clay-target shooting had its impact on the Winchester Model 21's evolution. Skeet, which was in its infancy as a competitive game during the 1930s, seems to have influenced the Model 21's stocking more than trap. Skeet then was shot with the gun held at a lowered position until after the target was released, and a premium was put on fast, accurate alignment. The Model 21 skeet grade took this into account with a streamlined beavertail fore-end that provided an effective grip away from the hot barrels while still offering an excellent hand-to-barrel relationship. Teamed with the Model 21's pistol grip, the skeet-style beavertail also established a good hands-in-line arrangement to facilitate natural pointing. But when skeet rules were modified to permit a fully mounted gun prior to target emergence, this advantage was lost.

But natural pointing qualities are still the heart and soul of a great bird gun. And the trim, slender, upward-tapered, field-style beavertail of the Model 21 gives a secure feel to the leading hand while also providing excellent hand-to-barrel relationship. It is the perfect companion for a straight-gripped Model 21, creating an ideal hands-in-line situation in the best game-gun traditions. It would be difficult to find anything better for American upland hunting— from far-flushing sharptails through pass shooting on doves to bobwhite over pointers—than a 16-gauge Model 21 with straight grip and field-style beavertail, in my opinion.

Trap has never taken kindly to the side-by-side, for optical reasons. Most serious tournament shooters hold a high gun, and the broad barrels obscure the clay as it emerges. Even binocular vision doesn't improve this to a significant degree. However, the Model 21's trap-style beavertail is long and graceful.

Custom-built Winchester Model 21s were available in the 1950s, as were the production grades. But labor costs were mounting, and in 1959 it was decided that the production grade would be dropped and the Model 21 retained solely as a custom gun at increased prices. The Model 21 was offered in three custom

grades—the Custom, the Pigeon Grade and the Grand American—
with an extensive list of options.

When Winchester's custom shop went into business in 1960,
only the most talented craftsmen were selected because the custom-
grade Model 21 now demanded more handwork to justify the price
and the grade designations. It was not a matter of rubber-stamping
an old product with a new label. Each stock was carefully fitted
to its individual action according to the customer's orders. Barrels
were polished to mirrorlike smoothness by hand prior to bluing,
each stoke being made longitudinally with the emery cloth. Lock
and trigger components were polished and carefully fitted for
positive operation; machining and tool marks were mainly
removed, which was not the case on production-grade guns. Barrels
were then blued by the browning process. All engraving was done
after the guns had been fitted and test-fired in the white. The metal
was therefore hard, and to cut sharply, the engravers made their
own tools by grinding them from rifling broaches.

Although the above steps smack of finishing a Model 21, careful
handworkmanship was equally important in the early stages.
Barrel/body units were fitted in the white. The barrel face had to
fit perfectly against the standing breech. It was held in that position
by a fixture to receive a proper knuckle pin, after which the unit
was proof-tested. The action body was then given its final shaping
by hand to blend its lines with those of the barrels.

The Model 21's barrels are not brazed in the normal manner.
They are coupled by a vertical dovetail and pinned. The patterns
from a field or trap gun must have a common point of impact at
40 yards; those from skeet guns are adjusted for a 25-yard
convergence. A barrel assembly's individual vibration
characteristics can affect point of impact, and it has been found
that the longer barrels, especially 30-inch tubes supplied with the
3-inch 20-gauge magnum, need an upward "influence" to deliver
their patterns level with the sighting plane. Otherwise the patterns
print low. Apparently the long barrels dip farther and/or recover
more slowly from their initial downward thrust than do shorter
tubes, and the shot charges therefore exit before the bore axes
rebound. This slight upward influence isn't noticeable on long-

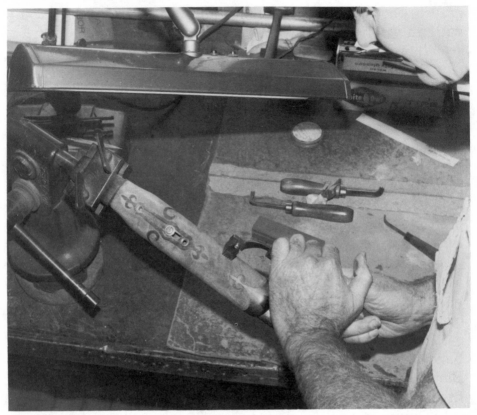

Carving, checkering, and cleaning up the fleur-de-lis pattern of a Grand American is roughly a one-week job even for a master craftsman.

barreled guns in any gauge unless one looks very, very closely. Thus regulating each unit by hand ensures accurate pattern placement without destroying the cosmetics.

The Model 21's lumps are machined integrally with the barrel. This is the best and strongest method, superior to brazed and dovetailed couplings, and is known in the trade as a "chopper" lump.

Except for the skeet No. 1 boring, choke tapers in the Model 21 are cut with a 17-foot radius and have parallel flats between the point of tightest constriction and the muzzle. Cylindrical in form, the flats vary in length according to the choke. The more open chokes have shorter flats, or "margins," than do the tighter tubes. Each barrel is checked to make certain it is delivering its designated percentages.

The Model 21's frame was modified in 1960 when the gun

All custom-grade Model 21s are fitted and shaped "in the white." Dave Carlson, who has recently retired after having been with the custom shop since its creation, shows a barrel action nucleus ready for mating. The 21's long action bar and sizable lump notch are readily apparent. The underlump is machined integrally with the barrels.

reached custom status. The arrow-shaped side panels were removed, giving the gun a long bar uncluttered by lines and contours. It also gave the engraver a broad working surface without sacrificing any strength. The story behind the change is interesting.

In the late 1940s, Winchester executives attended the national skeet championships where they saw what was, in all probability, the first .410 Model 21. It had been made by Ernie Simmons Sr., the gee-whiz shotgun tinkerer of his day. Simmons had cut off the barrels of a 20-gauge Model 21 and, in monoblock fashion, had attached the barrels from a pair of 410-bore Winchester Model 37 single-shots. The gun was poorly balanced and had a rather ugly appearance because .410 barrels don't harmonize with a 20-gauge frame. But it was a novelty, and Winchester executives asked Dave

Model 21 barrels are joined by a vertical dovetail and pinned rather than being brazed in the usual manner.

Carlson, who was then production supervisor at the New Haven plant, to make one. Having seen the Simmons conversion, Carlson was less than enthusiastic about the project. However, one does not argue very long with his bosses in modern corporations (even if they are wrong), and he soon had the first .410-bore Model 21 assembled on the small frame.

The first Winchester-made Model 21 .410 announced to the world that it was *not* going to be a great gun. Like the Simmons, it had horrible balance and an unsightly appearance. A huge, squarish breech segment was used on the barrels to fit the angle of the frame, and this brought the gun's weight heavily to the rear. Controlling the whippy barrels was difficult, if not impossible. Virtually nobody shot it well even with the appropriate tender touch required on lightweight shotguns. One is inclined to wish that Dave Carlson had succeeded in sidetracking the project. It is the only blemish on the Model 21's record.

The .410 Model 21 was eventually mentioned in a Winchester catalog, and about 60 or 70 were eventually made.

Developing the .410 Winchester brought about a change in the

Model 21's frame. Because the .410 Model 21 had such poor weight distribution, Carlson lightened the action body by milling and drilling at strategic points where the presence of metal and the absence of direct bending pressure allowed. Part of the weight-reduction scheme included the removal of the arrow-shaped side panels, since it was believed that the bending force of .410 shot-shells didn't require as much rigidity at the angle of the frame. None of this really improved the .410's balance or shooting qualities; what it needed was a scaled-down action body.

While testing the lightened 20-gauge frame for safety, however, it was found to be exceedingly strong despite the cuts and trimmed action bar. Checks were then run with 16- and 20-gauge barrels on similar lightened frames, and they stood up, too. Thus, while the .410-bore Model 21 hadn't been saved by these modifications, Winchester had learned that the Model 21 didn't need side panels running along the action bar to strengthen the angle of the frame. And when the Model 21 went to full custom status in 1960, the frame was revamped to eliminate the arrow-shaped panels. The interior cuts had been restricted only to the .410, of course, but individual experimenters have milled strategic areas to bring the Model 21 closer to game-gun weight without experiencing any damage. Long action bars and sturdy steels have made the Model 21's action as strong as any ever designed and produced.

Unfortunately, the change from production to custom status has confused the picture. Many average hunters and clay-target dusters don't realize that the post-1960 custom grades have been upgraded by additional hand craftsmanship. Some equate all Model 21s with what they see in the older production grades, not knowing that the custom pieces now receive vastly more individual attention from specialists. That is why the prices are higher and why the delivery time is longer.

Likewise, people who mistakenly believe that all Model 21s are alike are continually being fleeced by gun traders who have blown their prices out of proportion, carrying the price of used production-grade guns to the level of current custom jobs. I hope this chapter will alert the uninitiated to the fact that all Model 21s *aren't* alike. Unless the gun has "Custom Built by Winchester for . . ." engraved on the rib, it is probably a production-grade gun from the pre-1960

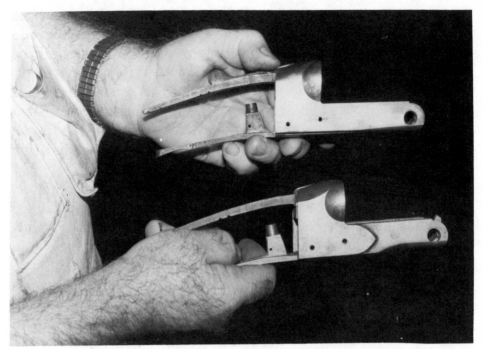

The original Model 21 action body had a shapely reinforcing panel, or "boss," to strengthen the angle of the frame. When experiments proved the reinforcement wasn't necessary, the action body was given a new, flat-sided shape which serves as a better surface for engraving.

era, and one cannot expect the same detailed workmanship as that which now goes into the Model 21 custom grades. This is not to say that the older 21s weren't excellent guns, of course. As I wrote earlier, they were indeed fitted and finished with greater care than other production-grade doubles. But some traders will cleverly take advantage of any situation. *Caveat emptor!*

Thus, the Model 21 is not a true British Best gun. It was never intended to be one and probably would have failed if the company had stubbornly held to overseas traditions. Instead, the Model 21 evolved according to American needs. And because of Winchester's continued upgrading, it has narrowed the gap considerably between itself and the prestigious British and European pieces, becoming the sole American-inspired double that we can now appreciate for its quality, apply to our specialized usage, and afford—which is why the Model 21 is a New World classic.

More handwork goes into a current Model 21 than is imagined. This 16-gauge Grand American shows extensive and expert engraving, gold inlay, and carefully fitted and finished lock parts. Note that the body for a ventilated rib has a ramplike effect missing on the solid-rib models.

A NEW ERA

As has been its history, Winchester again fell into financial distress in the late 1970s. It was mainly the profits from ammunition that buoyed the Winchester Group of Olin, and critical observers opine that stale and staid management led to the downturn in gun sales and profits. The parent Olin Corporation thereupon divested itself of the former stateside gunmaking plant in New Haven, Connecticut, retaining for Olin the profitable ammunition line (which is produced in East Alton, Illinois) and the line of imported doubles from Japan. The New Haven works were sold to a group of investors who incorporated under the name of U.S. Repeating Arms Company, and they obtained the manufacturing rights to all American-made Winchester guns and were also licensed to use the Winchester name and horse-and-rider logo.

Since the Model 21 was made entirely in the New Haven custom shop, its future hung in the balance. Would the powers-that-be at U.S. Repeating Arms Company drop it? If they were solely interested in returning to profitability as rapidly as possible, the situation was indeed ripe for such a deletion; for the low volume, extensive costs and sometimes narrow margins involved in building fine guns have always been risks. Early in the 1980s, however, the gun world was happy to hear that the Model 21 would be continued, albeit with some model and price changes. The executives at U.S. Repeating Arms Company apparently felt that retaining the prestigious Model 21 would enhance their company, which it definitely does.

Whereas the former Olin/Winchester Model 21s were offered in three grades, the 1985 catalog deletes the Pigeon Grade and lists instead these three grades: Custom Built, Custom Grade and Grand American. The Custom Built is a plain gun sans any engraving, with a base price of $7500. The Custom Grade appears to be the Custom Built gun with a modicum of scroll. The Grand American, starting at $21,060, is still made with two barrel sets, rather lavish scroll and a bird or dog scene tucked into the lower rear of the action body. All grades, of course, are subject to customer options at added cost, and each Grand American comes with its own baize-lined, leather-covered wood case made in trunk style.

Engraving changes have taken place. Upon the retirement of former Winchester engravers, the powers-that-be at U.S. Repeating Arms Company decided not to employ any in-house engravers. All work is being done outside the shop on a contract basis. Critics and management feel this has not hurt the Model 21's quality one bit, and that it may have improved the esthetics by permitting the use of engravers who can handle certain specialties better.

In an interesting move, U.S.R.A.C. has begun advertising .410-bore and 28-gauge Model 21s, something not done in recent decades by prior management. These sizes, according to my latest information, are available only in the Grand American grade at $32,400 if the two barrel sets are of the same bore; the price rises to $37,800 if one barrel set is 410 and the other 28 gauge.

As this manuscript is being prepared, U.S.R.A.C. is executing a smallbore promotion known as the One of Eight, in which eight sets of Grand Americans will be made with three interchangeable barrel sets—one each in .410 bore, 28 gauge and 20 gauge—for $54,648. The barrels are 26 inches long, and the buyer's name will be inscribed in the top rib. This move is akin to the Wildfowler and Wader collection made by Holland & Holland, and if U.S.R.A.C. can continue to reach new heights of quality and artistry with the

Model 21, such projects can enhance the reputation of an already respected gun.

With the constant escalation in fine gun prices, the various used Model 21s tend to be outstanding bargains that should gain considerably in value. The used-gun lists as of late 1984 showed excellent to like-new Model 21s ranging from $2400 to $3000 for the equivalent of the new Custom Built (unengraved) guns. The hunter who likes an exceptional boxlock for American sport will do no better than a Model 21, and he could probably hunt all his life with one and not lose much, if any, money. Investors or collectors looking to the future may find no better hedge than used Model 21s. They are still within the budget of many people, and it's a cinch that they'll not lose appreciable value in our lifetimes.

Chapter 16

American Collectibles and the Parker Mystique

Dictionaries tell us that the word *mystique* means "a framework of doctrines, ideas or beliefs constructed around a person or an object endowing it with enhanced values." Given that, there is indeed a mystique surrounding Parker guns. How else could one explain the current fascination that permits collectors and investors, along with typical hunters, to spend hundreds of dollars for a Parker Trojan, which was once an economy-grade knockabout gun, or a thousand or more for the lowest letter-grade Parker, the VH?

The purpose of this chapter is not to rap Parker guns. They were, and are, an excellent example of Americana. But the prices of Parkers have soared so far out of proportion to those of other equally excellent Yankee doubles that one must step back to gain a new perspective. Could it be that the marketplace has run rampant, that Parkers are overvalued?

When it comes to the guns themselves as shooters and mechanical objects, some good arguments can be ventured against the high prices. Gunsmiths have reported finding soft original parts in them. Moreover, although Parkers in general are praised for their handling and pointing qualities, most have very low combs that don't jibe with today's lean-into-it wingshooting style, and they kick hard. I have hunted with three different Parkers, and I cannot say that any one of them flowed to the target the way my Merkel over-under, Neumann (Belgian) 24-gauge side-by-side or even a Remington M1100 autoloader does. That may sound sacrilegious, but so be it. I know when a gun fits my technique, and the Parker brings nothing special, generally speaking, when it comes with the original stock. And with any but the lightest loads, the front trigger

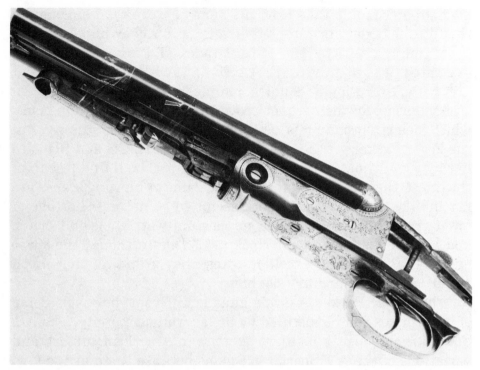

The ironwork of a Parker GHE. Could Parkers be overrated and overprided in the lower grades?

of a Parker invariably stings the finger when one operates the rear appendage.

As to field functioning, a Parker performs no better than an equally adjusted LeFever, A. H. Fox or Winchester Model 21. Of all the early American doubles I've owned, in fact, the Syracuse LeFever impresses me the most for both field handling and smoothness of operation. Were I to enter the market for an old-time "shooter," my search would begin for a LeFever letter-grade gun. The locks of those false-sideplated LeFevers may have been somewhat rococo, but they worked well, as did the other features of the guns.

For various reasons, however, the world has put an emphasis on Parkers, creating a demand that has sent Parker prices skyrocketing. We are at the point where the so-called "greater fool" theory comes into play in Parker buying and trading: If somebody buys a Parker at an outlandish price, will he be able to find an even greater fool to take it off his hands for even more money in the future? Sooner or later, the traffic won't bear higher prices.

In many respects, the lower grades of Parkers have been overrated. It is mainly AHE, AAHE and A-1 Special grades that are truly exceptional doubles manifesting the very finest in craftsmanship for their era. Moreover, very few of them were made, which means a premium is justifiable because of their scarcity. But the lower Parker grades—the VH, PH, GH, DH, CH and BH—are hardly the ultimate. If one assesses their art, he'll find less than the finest; the scroll is scanty, and the game or hunting scenes are not lifelike. Furthermore, there seems to be no real shortage of lower-grade Parkers; they show up constantly at sizable gun shows, and some dealers have them stockpiled. Thus, although the lower grades of Parkers are excellent guns, they aren't all that much better than contemporary doubles.

The trio of Parker A-grade guns is different, however. Some of their prices can be justified by art as well as scarcity. The A-1 Special is obviously a brilliant exercise in American gun art, and variations of the A-1 Special are gems because there are so few. Most A-1 Specials, for example, had fine scroll flowing over the action body and furniture, and the only break from scroll tended to be a smallish game bird inlaid or just engraved into the lower rear corner of the body. But variations have surfaced. An accompanying photo shows an A-1 Special with a far bolder scroll than normal, and it is indeed a rare and precious item. But no 12-gauge VH Parker with its case colors gone and checkering worn flat is worth the money being asked for it these days!

The same is basically true for all other makes of early American doubles: The valuable guns are those of high grade in which outstanding workmanship was applied. Traders may be asking huge sums for the lower grades, but, in many instances, they aren't worth it. Indeed, try to sell an L. C. Smith field grade to a trader at *his* price and you'll be chased away. In the L. C. Smith line, for example, there were only 33 Deluxe grades ever made, followed by 30 Premier grades and 281 Monogram models. At Parker, on the other hand, slightly more than 300 A-1 Specials were made. Hence, on the basis of scarcity, the L. C. Smith Deluxe is a greater find and should, theoretically, demand a higher price. This isn't

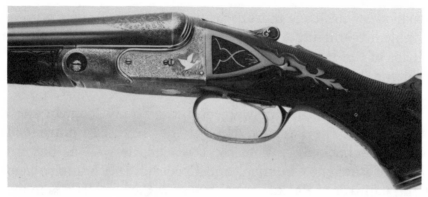

This is the more normal appearance of a Parker A-1 Special with flowing scroll of the fine-line variety and only a small bird as added decor, in this case inlaid in gold. (Photo courtesy of Herschel Chadick)

Parker A-1 Specials with a deep, bold scroll such as this are extremely rare, however, and justifiably command a premium. (Photo courtesy of Herschel Chadick)

always so, however, because the name Parker stamped on a double is currently magic.

The Parker mystique seems to have started back in the early 1960s when Peter H. Johnson published a book titled *Parker: America's Finest Shotgun* and set in motion a belief that has gained tremendous momentum.

A PARKER PRETENDER

There is one lingering question about Parkers: Are people honestly and knowledgeably interested in the shooting qualities of Parkers, or are they merely drawn by the gun's potential as a profitable investment? And if they praise the handling and shooting qualities of the Parkers, would they buy a newly made replica of the old guns? Or would they hold out for one of the originals because it has the name Parker on it?

We do not have the answer yet, but we may soon. In 1983, a perfect copy of the Parker DHE hit the American market. The venture was backed by Tom Skeuse who, as well as being the founder of Reagent Chemical and Research Inc. has also been a lifelong admirer of Parker guns. His new Parker DHE is made in Japan by a joint association of the Parker Gun Division of Reagent Chemical and Winchester's Asian operation, Olin-Kodensha. Using modern technology, the new Winchester-Parkers are a perfect copy of the former guns; parts will interchange between the originals and the new replicas. The first ones were made in 20 gauge only, but a 28-gauge on the 00 frame is indicated for 1985.

The Parker reproductions are faithful copies of the originals, then, and several options are available. The customer has his choice of a straight grip or pistol grip, a single or double trigger, and of the famous dog's head buttplate or a skeleton buttplate. The engraving is a dead-ringer for the true Parker's scroll and scenes, as are the checkering patterns and overall weight distribution and balance. Thus, a brilliant Parker reproduction is now available, albeit at $2800 at this writing.

Will people buy the replica? Perhaps. But I have a hunch that few people today really want a Parker for hunting and shooting. They want an original Parker purely to make money on the resale. And since some original Parkers are still available at less than $2800, they'll opt for the originals, even if they are below B grade, because the investment indicates a future profit whereas the replica Parkers will certainly not possess the same value enhancement. The original may not have screaming colors, but it *is* original and therein lies the difference.

We will know the answer to the Parker question in a few years. If the new Parker Gun Division of Reagent Chemical and Research prospers, it is indeed the gun and its features that are in demand. If the venture fails, the big play in Parkers is for profit on resale.

OTHER YANKEE COLLECTIBLES AND SHOOTERS

There is obviously no set pricing for older doubles. The seller takes what the traffic will bear, and today it appears that the market will bear a lot. If one peruses the prices in *Shotgun News*, the tabloid for gun traders, he discovers that the guns are often outlandishly priced. Yet, there must be enough buyers around to keep the dealers happy, as the prices continue to edge upward. It is difficult to believe that one can buy at current prices as a hedge against inflation; many dealers already ask inflated sums. Moreover, a buyer must be aware of the specimens being offered, as many advertised items are upgraded in print; guns in fair to good condition are advertised as being in excellent condition. Many such misrepresented guns are nowhere near the value put on them by sellers, a situation that could be corrected if prospective buyers simply held off for a couple years while traders had to sit with investments earning no return. Do not jump at the asking price on any old double; always make a counter offer. Remember that gun trading is generally based on give-and-take negotiations.

Although the L. C. Smith is often praised as an American sidelock, its lock works are terribly simple and possess only the single sear, not a secondary safety sear as is the case on most British and European sidelocks.

What are some interesting plays? I must profess to being prejudiced against the L. C. Smith guns for the field, never having found them to be smooth and trouble-free. The Smith (Lard patent) single-trigger is an abomination, and any amount of shooting generally finds the stock cracking at a point where the tail of the sideplate contacts the inletting of the jaws. The cranklike cocking mechanism doesn't always make for easy opening, either. And while people often look with pride on the Smith's sidelock feature, it is the simplest sidelock ever conjured up and doesn't possess the safety sear mechanism used extensively abroad. Even the Baker sidelock is a better design. However, the rotary bolt of an L. C. Smith is exemplary, and the guns do have good handling qualities. Twelve-gauge field-grade Smiths are very common, but the Featherweight models are desirable, as are all small-gauge models. Tables at gun shows are often awash with field-grade Smiths priced too high.

In the A. H. Fox line, the HE grade is gaining collector attention. The HE, sometimes called the Super Fox, is a magnum-grade double chambered for the 3-inch hull. It is said to have been specially bored for tight patterns with the then-new 3-inch load, the boring being an oversized bore that may have run to a 0.740-inch diameter instead of the normal 0.725- to 0.730-inch diameter for a modern 12. Whether all HEs were overbored is not known. This overboring was publicized by Nash Buckingham, the once-popular outdoor scribe who used a pair of custom-made Fox guns so overbored with $1^3/_8$-ounce 3-inch loads. The only rap against A. H. Fox guns is that they did not have rebounding hammers, and guns could fall out of adjustment and remain striker-bound. Those who buy old A. H. Fox doubles may well find that, upon the first firing, it will be terribly hard to open the action. Shoot no more; have a gunsmith readjust the locks.

Ithaca doubles have never excited collectors, and only the very highest grades have any real value. The lack of demand makes this a buyer's market, as traders holding Ithacas may be stuck and open to bids well below their asking prices.

LeFever doubles have not commanded much attention, either, but it is possible that they have been sadly overlooked. The locks and cocking mechanism may be somewhat on the gross side, what

Despite the current fascination collectors have for Parkers, doubles like this B-grade Ansley H. Fox were also well made and, all things being equal, may well have handled and operated afield better than some Parkers.

Although some might consider the massive cocking hook of a LeFever to be gross, it gave a mechanical advantage that made operation easy.

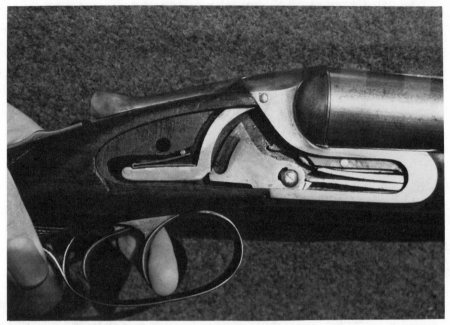

Although a sideplated gun, the Syracuse LeFever was a boxlock with an innovative design, featuring a long, suspended sear that ran from the trigger blade to the hammer bent in a straight line and then proceeding over the hammer in an arc to pivot on a pin set directly behind the fences. The gun is shown here in its cocked attitude . . .

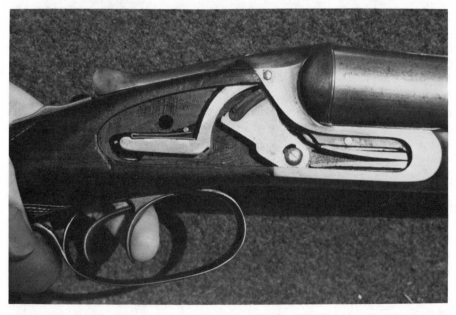

and here is the same LeFever after the trigger has been pulled to release the hammer, which, in its rotation, sweeps inside the lengthy sear's arc.

with the ultra-long sear and the massive cocking hook jutting up from the action flat, but the concepts seem to provide mechanical advantages for smooth, easy, dependable operation. Indeed, the simplicity of the Syracuse LeFever's design apparently did much to frustrate Murphy's Law. Few high-grade LeFevers were ever made, and they—the Thousand Dollar Grade, the Optimus and the AA Grade—are dear due to their scarcity. But guns like the FE and GE, which once sold for about $80 and $57, respectively, are excellent collectible shooters. And did you know that the Olympic gold medal in trapshooting was won by a shooter using a LeFever in the London games of 1912? I have a hunch that once active shooters begin to rediscover the old Syracuse LeFevers, the market may turn brisk.

Although the early Charles Daly doubles were not made in America, they are definitely a part of our culture. Imported by the grand New York firm of Schoverling, Daly and Gales, the Daly guns—especially those made in Prussia—have the reputation of being first-class guns that are often the equivalent of a British Best gun of the same era. Not all Daly guns came from Prussia, however.

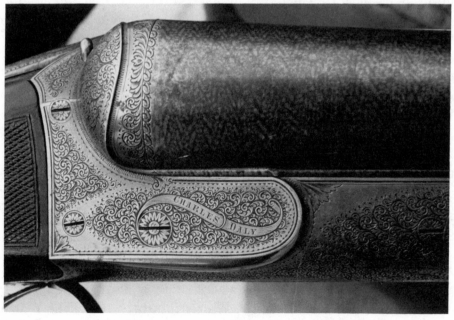

A Charles Daly Diamond Quality Prussian double with Damascus barrels. Many Prussian Dalys were as finely made as anything the British were doing at the same time.

The identifying mark on valuable Dalys: the word PRUSSIA stamped into the action flat.

Some of the first ones were apparently made by J. & W. Tolley of Birmingham, England, between 1870 and some time in the 1880s. Then the scene shifted to Belgium, where Neumann Freres et Cie made some Daly doubles. Next Daly changed to the gunmakers of Suhl, Germany, where Sauer, Schiller and Lindner made truly fine doubles. This period, while Schoverling, Daly and Gales were at 302-304 Broadway in New York City, may well have been the Golden Age of Daly guns. There were four grades, beginning with the lightly engraved Superior Quality and ascending through the Empire Quality, Diamond Quality and Regent Diamond Quality guns. The line seems to have lingered until the early 1930s, and can often be detected by the word "PRUSSIA" stamped on the action flat. Some Merkel-like over-unders were also made under the Daly name in Suhl, but some other over-unders known as the Model 100 and Model 200 Commander were also made in Liege, Belgium, by Masquelier between the world wars.

The original Charles Daly was no longer with the company when the Belgium over-unders came in. Immediately after WWI, Schoverling, Daly and Gales was sold to a man named Henry Modell, who in turn sold it to the Walzer family in 1927. The Walzer family operated it as two different businesses, the Charles Daly

& Company Division, and Sloan's Sporting Goods. It seems that this was the tag end of the great Prussian guns, with imports from Heym, Sauer, Beretta, Bernardelli and Armi Garbi beginning to play a dominant role in the Sloan's offerings. Then, after WWII, the Walzer family pioneered in the sale of Japanese-made (Miroku) shotguns, which continued to use the former name-grade designations of Superior, Empire, Diamond and Regent Diamond. These guns were introduced to Americans in 1963 and were available until about 1973. The Walzer family eventually sold rights to the Charles Daly name to Outdoor Sports of Dayton, Ohio, in 1976, and Outdoor Sports is trying to resurrect the name with Italian-made over-unders also tagged Superior and Diamond grades.

Although there are more different Daly Diamond grades than one can shake a cleaning rod at, there is only one of any significant value: the Prussian. It can be found with Damascus or fluid steel barrels, but in either case the workmanship is superb and, in most instances, equivalent to any in the world. Thus, the great Daly Prussian doubles may not have been made stateside, but they were made especially for the U.S. market and can be considered premium artifacts.

Finally, collectors and hunters with limited finances may have some fun with the economy boxlocks, namely, the Fox Sterlingworth, LeFever Nitro Special and Stevens Model 530 or Fulton by Hunter Arms. There were reasonably well made, although often with low combs, and could be made up into usable field guns. But caution is the key word in shopping, as many such older economy grades were hunted hard by their original owners and, in published ads, are frequently misrepresented as being in better shape than they actually are. There is a lot of scrap iron being passed off to gullible buyers as "fine old guns."

The market for older American guns and special imports, then, has been hyped to the extent that there is much overpricing. The guns were good, but not *that* good. Be a frugal, patient, careful and critical shopper!

Chapter 17

The Stateside Scene

Aside from the Winchester Model 21, there is currently very little in the way of fine shotgun building in the United States. The gun artistry here pivots mainly on independent engravers and stockers who upgrade existing sporting arms. The engravers rank with the world's best, but very few stockers have a classical approach to the double, a situation that may stem from the fact that many stockers began by working on rifles. One American who has mastered both is Winston Churchill of Proctorsville, Vermont. The sideplated Browning B-25 shown here was brought to the United States as a barreled action in-the-white, and Churchill took it from there, finishing with a custom-made carrying case and engraved accessories. Other engravers like Howard V. Grant of Lac du Flambeau, Wisconsin; E. C. Prudhomme of Shreveport, Louisiana; Robert E. Maki of North Brook, Illinois; Lynton McKenzie of Tucson, Arizona; and Angelo Bee of Chatsworth, California, can do exceptional jobs. For further information about American engravers, one can write to Robert Evans, Secretary, Firearms Engravers Guild of America, 332 Vine Street, Oregon City, OR 97045.

Luxury-grade sidelocks are fully made by only two small firms on this side of the Atlantic. One is the K. Genecco Gun Works of Stockton, California. This company is making Holland & Holland-type bar-action sidelocks in 12 and 16 gauges with either single or double triggers. The receivers are drop forgings, not castings, and the barrel assemblies have the forged chopper lumps so desirable among Europe's foremost gunmakers. These are totally custom-made and can range from 6½ to 8 pounds. The base price

180

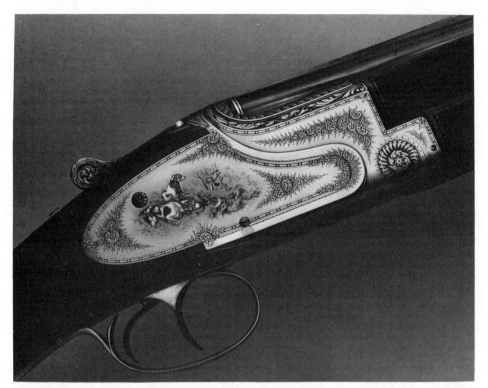

This Browning B-25 was brought to the United States in-the-white as a barreled action, and engraved and stocked by American gun artist Winston Churchill of Proctorsville. Vermont.

is advertised at $5500 at this writing. To date, I have not seen a Genecco-built double, but an illustrated catalog is available for $2. The company's address is in the directory in the back of this book.

The second stateside company to make fine shotguns is Barnett International Inc., which is based in Odessa, Florida. Oddly enough, Barnett International has a reputation for being the world's largest manufacturer of crossbows, and it had no position in the sporting firearms world until the early 1980s when it acquired Frank E. Malin & Son (Gunmakers) Ltd. of Melbourne, Ontario, Canada. Since then a Florida-based offshoot known as the Boswell line has also emerged to go with the Malin guns, but they are apparently both made in the same Ontario shop.

The Malin gunmaking venture can rightly be termed a transplant. It is a Canadian business developed and operated mainly by craftsmen from England. Born in 1943 in England,

Frank E. Malin followed his father's footsteps into the gunmaking trade and spent 17 years in the major houses of England. When economic conditions caused radical changes and closures among the formerly prestigious British gunmakers, Malin sallied forth to Canada. He enticed other skilled workers to join him, including world-class engraver Ron Collins. The small Ontario shop centered upon sidelocked game guns that incorporated the classic features. In fact, Malin actions and chopper lump barrel assemblies are forged in Birmingham and shipped to Canada, where they are hand-fitted, polished and finished. All stock making is done in Canada of high-grade English or European walnut.

A boxlock has also been added to the Malin line. It is built around the Anson & Deeley action and can be had in 12, 20 and 28 gauge. Malin guns displayed at the 1983 SHOT Show were nicely finished and exhibited attention to detail. Since then, this author has not seen any further Malin guns and has never seen a Boswell, so a further report on continuing quality cannot be made. Letters to Barnett International requesting photos and recent prices were met with silence. In general, however, the guns appear to start around $7000.

The only other American-made doubles fall well below fine gun levels. They are the Ruger Red Label over-under, which employs a cast receiver and relatively heavy barrels that send the 20 gauge's weight to 7-7¼ pounds; the Stevens Model 311, a low-priced knockabout that is crudely finished; and the Savage-Fox Model B, which, like the Stevens Model 311, is a mass-produced side-by-side lacking any attention to detail. In past months, however, some new Savage-Fox Model Bs have been seen with an improved finish, and one can only hope that the company can improve its image by upgrading its doubles, which have been noted for breakdowns and heavy, spongy triggers.

OF SHOGUNS AND SHOTGUNS

The stateside scene is otherwise dominated by Japanese-made doubles. Although this may upset the United States' balance of trade, it is a boon to hunters who want as much quality as possible for their dollar. The Japanese work ethic dotes on attention to detail, and that puts quality into moderately priced doubles.

The sales sensation of 1983-1984 has been Weatherby's new line of Japanese-built over-unders, the boxlock Orion and the sideplated Athena, behind which there is a story: When I was writing the first edition of this book, the SKB doubles were attracting much attention. SKB side-by-sides were especially attractive, as were the straight-gripped over-unders. And their prices put them within reach of typical wage earners. However, the original stateside marketing group that handled SKB guns made serious mistakes and folded. For a time the excellent SKB line was missing from American gunshop shelves.

Into this void stepped Roy Weatherby, the famous riflemaker. An earlier shotgun venture by Weatherby, which had given us the trim Regency over-under, had failed when the Italian maker (Zoli) lowered his quality. The Weatherby people approached SKB and offered to buy machine time for the production of over-unders made to a new Weatherby design. When the guns went into production, Weatherby had no idea how the market would greet the products, and the contracted machine time was conservatively set. When the resulting Orion and Athena came to these shores, however, a tremendous demand arose, and many orders went unfilled, as may still be the case.

The Weatherby/SKB over-unders are attractive doubles, especially the sideplated Athena. Its silvery sideplates have just a modicum of scroll, but it is tastefully arranged. Moreover, both guns have the usual Weatherby fancy Claro wood to set them off from other guns in their price range. As usual, the pistol grips are long and capped, and whiteline spaces are clearly in evidence. Both grades, the Orion and the Athena, are made in field, skeet and trap models, and as of 1985, the 12- and 20-gauge field grades will both have screw-in chokes. I was privileged to do some duck shooting with the prototype 20-gauge Orion with Multi-Choke tubes, and it handled very well. Patterns with 3-inch magnum reloads were super.

What is especially interesting about the Weatherby Athena is the way hunters are drawn to this thousand-dollar-class double. Thus, the Weatherby/SKB connection has definitely enlivened

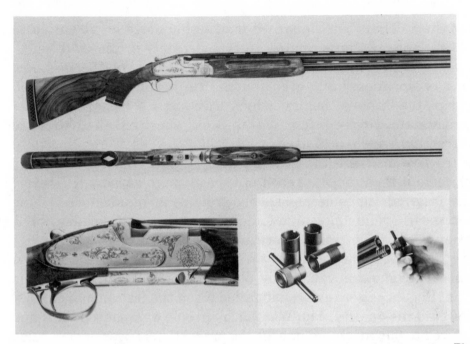

The Weatherby/SKB over-unders have been a sales sensation since their inception. The Athena is a sideplated boxlock stylishly outfitted with excellent field-handling qualities and the Multi-Choke feature.

stateside shotgunning, and the guns are deservedly popular. We can only hope that someday Weatherby will return the SKB side-by-sides to the Yankee market.

When the Winchester Group of the Olin Corporation divested itself of certain holdings in the early 1980s, it retained the line of Japanese-made doubles made as a joint venture known as Olin-Kodensha. The guns are the Model 101 over-under and the Model 23 side-by-side, and they have been brought to very appealing proportions and appearances, both as standard and commemorative models. This wasn't always so, of course, because the Model 101 spent nearly 10 years looking the same regardless of its grade or gauge. Whether it was a 12-gauge magnum or a .410-bore skeet gun, the first 101s always had the same straight-grain stocks and fore-ends, the same engraving patterns and the same basic profiles. It wasn't until about 1975 that things began to change with the introduction of a Pigeon Grade Model 101 that did indeed differ from the basic design. The Pigeon Grade was a study in color contrast: The wood was very dark with minor swirls, while the receiver was a sparkly silver as a result of brush polishing. It wore etched engraving, had a round-knob pistol grip, and a flat rib instead of an elevated rib. I was at the Winchester new-product seminar that announced the Pigeon Grade M101, and the gun handled nicely on the pheasants and quail we hunted at the Armwell Hunting Preserve.

Since then, the Pigeon Grade Model 101 has gone into various models, both standard and commemorative, and has been joined by a stylish side-by-side, the Model 23, which is also made in various standard grades and limited-edition commemoratives. With its proportions and ramp-type rib design, the Model 23 is one of the fastest-pointing doubles on the American market. Its locks are a flattened version of the giant-headed sear-lifter found on the Model 101.

Along with the pistol-gripped models, both the M101 and M23 are made in straight-gripped fashion with 25½-inch barrels. These

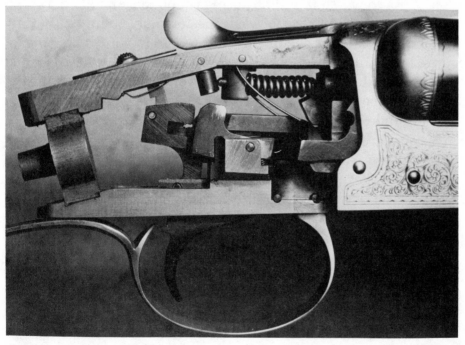

The locks of Winchester's Model 23 side-by-side are a flattened version of those found on the Model 101.

are designated as Lightweight models, and they can be had in 12 and 20 gauges. Lightweight M101s and M23s have fancy walnut, trim recoil pads, silvery action bodies with elegant fine-line roll-on engraving, and generous panels of hand-cut checkering done about as well as one can expect on production or semi-production guns. Quite frankly, the Winchester Lightweights deserve more attention than they are getting from Yankee uplanders. Not only do they handle well but, despite being less than handmade guns, they are fitted excellently.

The Model 101 is made in a 32-inch-barreled Waterfowl model that has a blued receiver, full-sized recoil pad and screw-in choke tubes from modified through extra-full. Both the Model 101 and Model 23 standard field grades have their barrels tapped for the Winchoke feature, I believe the M23 being the first side-by-side commercially available with that feature.

Because Olin-Kodensha has developed an improved method of roll-on engraving, both the M101 and the M23 are given various game scenes and/or equally fine scroll suited to the grade of gun and the use to which it will be put. Perhaps some hand engraving is done here or there on various Winchester doubles, but it is mainly done mechanically or chemically. That is no insult to the guns, of course, as they are tastefully attired, and the only alternative would be expensive hand engraving which would, in turn, run up the stateside price considerably. As it is now, Model 101s and M23s start around $800 and range to nearly $2000.

Special limited editions of both guns have been made. There was a 500-gun run of Model 23 Heavy Duck Guns with 30-inch barrels, and there is currently an ongoing sequence of Model 23s known as the Golden Quail editions that will range from 28 gauge to the 12 gauge. In the Model 101, some interesting limited runs

A limited edition run by Winchester is this Ruffed Grouse Model 101 20 gauge, of which 225 guns will be made.

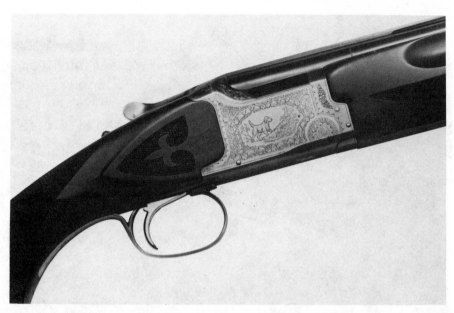

The close-up of the Ruffed Grouse Model 101 shows a grouse scene applied by Winchester's fine roll-on method.

have also been made, the most recent being a 225-gun lot of 20 gauges called the Grouse Gun. Another set of 25 Grouse Guns will be made matching 12- and 20-gauge guns. The Grouse Gun has fleur de lis checkering layout on the cheeks of the stock, a round-knob pistol grip and a full beavertail plus flat rib. The wood is full-fancy American walnut with a satin finish and 24-lines-per-inch checkering. The engraving pattern applied grouse hunting scenes and a mixture of elaborate and fine scroll. The guns will no doubt have collector status one day.

This, then, is the trend in Winchester's line of doubles. They are better-than-average guns, something reflected in their prices, but give the hunter a stylish, nice-handling field gun.

The current stateside Browning line is a mixture of Japanese- and Belgian-made doubles, with the Japanese items taking on major market proportions because they are less expensive than the Belgian Superposed guns, which, comprising the Presentation Series, are considerably more costly. There are really two different series of high-grade Superposed guns in the current Browning stateside catalog: One is the number-graded Presentation line; the other is the limited edition series dedicated to various species of

Browning Belgian-made Superposed guns are now high-grade models, such as this limited edition waterfowl series celebrating the black duck.

waterfowl. The Presentation Series has four grades, the first three of which are boxlocks with varying degrees of engraving and gold inlay. The Presentation IV has false sideplates for added decor. Prices start at $4560.

The waterfowl series carries gold inlays of the duck to which it is dedicated. Thus far, the mallard, pintail and black duck have been honored at about $8000 for each piece of a 500-gun edition.

For 1986, a special Classic Superposed has already been announced. It will be a 20 gauge built on the Superlight concept, with schnobble fore-end, straight grip and an engraved profile of John M. Browning plus upland scenes wrapped in bold scroll on a silvery gray action body. The gun will apparently be made in Classic and Gold Classic models, meaning the same Classic pattern will be used with gold inlays in the Gold Classic.

Essentially, the popular Browning guns today are the Japanese-made Citori and B-S/S lines, which Browning has continually upgraded. The side-by-side B-S/S guns, for example, are obtainable in pistol-gripped field models, straight-gripped upland styles known as the Sporter, and now a true sidelock with the profile of a British game gun. This Sidelock B-S/S is a bargain in every sense, although its twin triggers will not appeal to many Yankee hunters. As an example of what appears to be a semiproduction-grade double, however, the Sidelock B-S/S is super. At roughtly $1500, it gives one substantial gun: high-grade French walnut, plunger-type fore-end release, cocking indicator, checkered butt, long trigger-guard tang, and acceptable checkering and scroll engraving with rosette-and-scroll patterns. The gun is made in 12 and 20 gauges, and the 20 is a wand.

Citori over-unders started out as bulky field guns with thickly combed stocks and massive beavertail fore-ends, and the standard grades are still that way. However, Browning was sensible enough to trim the Citori and make it into a slender Superlight version with a straight grip and thin, schnobble-tipped forearm. For 1984, the Superlight Citori had its barrels bobbed to 24 inches for fast handling, whereupon it was called the Citori Upland Special. The Invector choke system is employed universally on the Upland Special.

The Citori line has been taken to an artistic level by the inclusion of Grade V, Grade VI and Sideplate models. Both the Grades V and VI have the same basic scenes and scroll, but the manner in which they're finished sets them apart. The Grade V Citori has a silver-gray action body, while the Grade VI has a blued body with the game birds plated in gold. Both grades are delightful, and the engraving is akin to that applied on Belgian Superposed guns at significantly higher prices. The Sideplate Citori is again the normal boxlock with a false sideplate festooned with etched scroll and hunting scenes. For whatever reason, the Sideplate Citori is made only in 20 gauge as I write this.

THE REST OF THE STORY

The United States is now receiving doubles from nations not traditionally associated with sporting arms. One of these is the Gamekeeper over-under imported from the People's Republic of China by Clayco Sports Ltd. of Clay Center, Kansas. The gun is

The complete range of Browning Citori over-unders, beginning with the scroll-engraved standard grades on top and ending with the Grade VI and Sideplate guns on the bottom. The lower three guns—the Grade V, Grade VI and the Sideplate—offer as much or more quality and artistry than any other guns in their price range.

made by China North Industries Corporation, and is one of the least expensive doubles of the decade, having a suggested retail of about $299.95 but being discounted widely at about $169.95.

The Gamekeeper is a high-framed gun measuring 2.745 inches at its highest point, which is more than a half-inch taller than the ultra-low-profiled Caprinus Sweden. It is currently made in 12 gauge only with 28-inch barrels and an overall weight of about 8 pounds. One interesting aspect about the Gamekeeper is that it does not employ the conventional knuckle pin or bifurcated lumps. Its barrels rotate on a novel, movable hinge-pin block that fits a recess machined into the underside of the monoblock. Assembly and disassembly are also different: The barrel assembly is set or lifted straight upward or directly down into the action body, not rotated into place. The triggers tend to be heavy, about 8- to 9-pound pulls on those I have handled. The metal is generally finished in a semi-gloss blue. The wood, being an Asian hardwood, has a pronounced schnobble at the fore-end tip, 16-lines-per-inch checkering, and a finish that clogs the checkering to minimize gripping potential. The muzzle hangers give the lower tube a chance to move longitudinally as heating occurs. Workmanship is purely production grade, and the comb tends to be a bit low for current Yankee tastes. Some economy-minded hunters, however, will find the Gamekeeper's profile tempting.

Brazil is also sending two shotgun lines to the United States: the Rossi and the I.G.A. I have no personal experience with any Rossi double and therefore cannot comment on them. The I.G.A. offerings being handled by Stoeger Industries include both a side-by-side and an over-under, which, at this writing, are selling for about $190 and $250, respectively. The I.G.A. doubles I have handled could use higher combs and lighter trigger pulls; otherwise, given their very crude innards, they could serve as knockabouts.

As one observes the American market, then, he begins to realize that it is difficult to find a truly good double of current manufacture for less than $500. Dependability, style and handling qualities begin somewhere between $500 and $1000 these days. The inflated cost of labor, along with the other overhead expenses of gunmaking, have again driven doubles upward in price. A hunter, shooter or gun buff of any sophistication will wisely spend another year or two saving added coins rather than plunging into a dubious deal.

Chapter 18

Fine Boxlocks Are a Bargain!

Bird hunters and other shotgun fanciers who acquire any degree of sophistication soon become enamored with sidelock doubles. To them, the sidelock is the *piece de resistance* of gunmaking, the absolute ultimate in gun artistry.

This is not to say that sidelocks aren't great guns, of course. No one in his right mind would turn one down. But anyone who has priced the truly outstanding sidelocks knows that they aren't for everyone even in the best of financial times. At this writing, for example, new Purdeys cost more than $15,000, and used ones command $10,000 or more. Perazzi makes a neat .410 sidelock, the DHO Extra, for $56,700! If you're satisfied with a plain ol' 12-gauge sidelock, Perazzi will put together a DHO Gold for only $24,500. Beretta's Model 451EELL side-by-side costs more than $13,000, and the sidelocked Beretta SO3EELL tops $10,000 if you want a single trigger. You don't have $16,000 to spare? Then don't bother asking about the exceptional Italian-made Piotti King EELL. To finish this off, we'll point also to the Westley Richards Best Quality sidelock, which costs $13,000 with double triggers and no options.

Figures such as those may squelch the enthusiasm with which some hunters and gun fanciers approach fine guns, but that needn't deter them from dreaming on—or from realizing that dream to own a personal, custom-made double of extremely high quality. For sidelocks aren't the only game in town. Given the same amount of craftsmanship and attention to detail, a boxlock from one of the world's great gunmakers can be equally satisfying and prestigious. No gun ever handled better or hit more targets simply because it had a sidelock mechanism. The boxlock has simply been

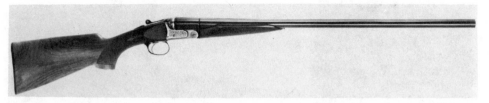

The Beretta Model 626-E is a light, fast-handling boxlock made to sell at a price slightly higher than an ordinary gun.

discriminated against by sheer snobbery. The fact is that boxlocks from premier gunmakers are the biggest bargains in the field of fine guns. The Westley Richards 1984 price list, which lists the Best Quality sidelock at $13,000, for instance, has the 12-gauge Connaught boxlock at just $4250, the 20 gauge at $4376 and the 28 gauge at $4500. Powell's best boxlock is slightly higher at $6250. Thus, it can cost anywhere from $6000 to $16,000 *less* for a premium maker's best basic boxlock than for his sidelock sans options and accessories. To some people, even a price tag of $5000 may seem extraordinary for a fowling piece; however, it is a better investment than, say, a bassboat, which, often costing more than $5000, depreciates significantly on the first outing.

Why are boxlocks from premium gunmakers such bargains? It isn't simply because boxlocks require fewer hours of labor, although that certainly enters the picture; for the careful metal-to-metal and wood-to-metal fits, along with the hand polishing of fitted components, do indeed magnify the production costs of sidelocks.

What seems to be more important in the pricing structure of boxlocks versus sidelocks, however, is international competition. The world's truly great gunmakers are probably not setting boxlock prices as high as they would like to because that reduces volume. The same type of international competition apparently does not exist in the sidelock market, as people who can afford sidelocks are generally indifferent to price.

Putting one's finger on the exact nature of boxlock competition is difficult, but it seems to pivot most heavily on British sales *vis-à-vis* the Belgian manufacturers who, by the late 1800s, had become aggressive gun peddlers. A certain amount of the British

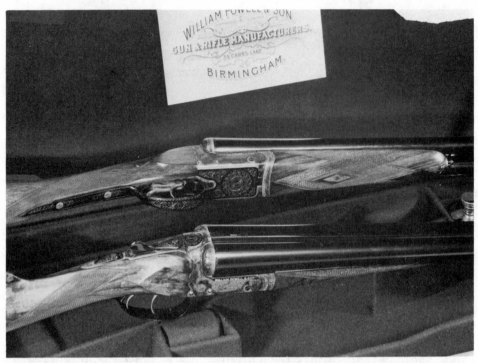

A most prestigious pair of matched boxlocks, the Powell No. 3, which receives as much attention to detail as does the same firm's No. 1 sidelock. To be competitive, however, the boxlocks are priced considerably below a comparable sidelock.

The Powell No. 6 boxlock, at just £1,500, has classical trimness and attention to detail, plus the handling qualities of the most famous game guns.

dilemma may also have derived from their own Parliament's restrictive trade measures, which, on both a home and colonial basis, made the British gunmakers weak at a time when the Belgians were strengthening and operating without their government hindering them. This subject of home and colonial legislation adversely affecting the British gun trade is covered at length in a 1907 publication, *The Causes of Decay in a British Industry*. Written by "Artifex" and "Opifex," who were reputedly the sons of W. W. Greener, *Causes* leaves no doubt in one's mind about the surge of Belgian gunmaking nor about the loss of trade suffered by the Birmingham gunworks because they could not compete favorably against the Belgians. Of course, there was more to the competition than merely sporting guns versus sporting guns; much of the controversy aired by Artifex and Opifex rested upon the production of military arms and cheaper guns formerly absorbed by the colonies. The manufacture of fine guns was just a small portion of that market, then as now. But the book and the situation argue that the production of relatively cheap boxlock doubles by the Belgians did in fact influence the pricing of even top-grade boxlocks to be lower, worldwide, than it might have been without the fierce competition from Belgium's many small makers.

The competition that started around the turn of the century continues today. Beautiful, handcrafted boxlock doubles by premium gunmakers can still be had at a fraction of the price of the same maker's sidelocks.

Fine-line engraving on a Winchester Model 21 Pigeon Grade gives the gun an exquisite look. An enduring boxlock, the Model 21 still sells for less than half the price of a British sidelock.

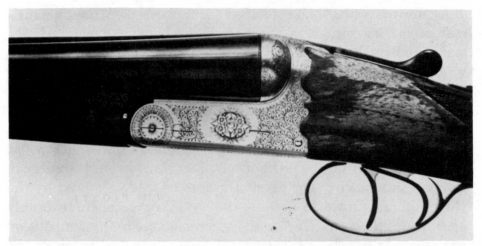

A Piotti boxlock showing the scalloped action frame that requires careful hand-fitting. The Piotti is little known stateside but is a prestigious gun in Europe where it is made by a low-volume, high-quality shop in Brescia, Italy.

As implied above, then, one need not swallow his pride to own a boxlock double. The Vouzelaud guns from France are truly great guns in their own right. The same is true for the Westley Richards Connaught and the Powell No. 3. Piotti's Puma is a prestigious gun, and the newest W. & C. Scott boxlocks, the Bowood Deluxe and the Chatsworth, are indeed worthy numbers. It would be difficult to find anything wrong with the boxlock Krieghoff TECK over-under, the Chapius or the freshly resurrected Darnes. The famous Belgian-made Browning B-25 Superposed guns were all boxlocks, as is the Winchester Model 21. And if boxlocks are so inferior, why are people willing to pay exorbitant sums for American Parkers?

It would seem, therefore, that the gun fancier's preoccupation with sidelocks is unwarranted. A magnificent obsession it may be, but the spell can be broken by stark financial reality: Beautifully made boxlock doubles, both side-by-sides and over-unders, can be bought for considerably less than otherwise equally excellent sidelocks. The market is extensive. The prices are right. Indeed, high-class boxlocks by prestigious gunmakers are the biggest bargain in the world of doubles.

Chapter 19

Target-Grade Guns and Influences

There can be no doubt that the interest in fine doubles is greater now than it has ever been. A considerable portion of this interest and activity is due to the current widespread use of expensive, high-grade doubles in skeet, trap and live-pigeon shooting. For although break-action doubles have always been seen at shotgun tournaments, their popularity was relatively minor before their ascendency of the late 1960s. About the only place where fine doubles dominated was in live-pigeon shooting, which until just recently was mainly a Mexican and a European sport; hence, the guns chosen by box-pigeon shooters hardly influenced American gun-buying trends. Only a wealthy few could afford the time and travel involved in "flyer" shooting.

Stateside skeet and trap didn't generate a rampaging demand for fine doubles, either, during those pre-1970 years. Skeet shooters, for example, primarily opted for Cutts Compensator-equipped pumpguns and autoloaders to mitigate against the recoil for which doubles were, and still are, noted. The single sighting plane was also a factor in the horizontal double's failure in clay-target shooting. That is why so few skeet-grade side-by-sides exist today, and this scarcity has driven up their value. Skeet was extremely popular in the 1930s and 1940s, but L. C. Smith still only sold 770 of their Skeet Special model between 1939 and 1945; and when the Premier Skeet gun was made by L. C. Smith, it was only produced for about one year (1949-1950) due to low sales. Records say that just 507 Premier Skeet guns were turned out. There is no public record of the number of Skeet guns made by Parker, but the number is equally small. Ditto for A. H. Fox guns.

Trapshooters have gone heavily into the over-under for doubles, as the design gives reliability and fast second shots.

About the only American-made doubles to gain any following in skeet were the Winchester Model 21 and the Remington Model 32, which was an over-under. Richard Shaughnessy won the National 12-gauge Skeet Championship in 1936 by breaking 248 out of 250 with a 16-gauge Winchester Model 21, a very commendable performance at that time. Alex Kerr, a frequent National champion, used a Model 32 Remington for much of his career, employing it for both American-style skeet and low-gun international events. The Model 32 is still a viable clay-target gun, but the Winchester Model 21 is never seen at tournaments. Side-by-sides were never known as winners on the skeet circuit.

However, there is still a brisk demand for used Winchester Model 21 skeet guns, especially in 16 and 20 gauges. The chokes and handling qualities of Model 21 skeet guns play into the hands of upland hunters. Generally bored Skeet No. 1 in the right barrel and Skeet No. 2 in the left, the Model 21s gave a wide pattern from the right tube and closed down to a weak modified from the left. The Skeet No. 2 choke had a reputation for throwing evenly distributed patterns despite its greater density, which is perfect for a second shot on pheasants or grouse. Moreover, the 16- and 20-gauge Model 21s are easier carrying and faster handling than the heavier, bulkier, harder-kicking 12 gauge. With their trim beavertail forearms, excellent stock dimensions and excellent single triggers, 16- and 20-gauge Model 21s with skeet-bored 26-inch barrels may be the greatest Yankee-built side-by-side ever to cover the uplands.

Trapshooters did not seem to generate a tremendous demand for quality doubles during the first half of the twentieth century, either. They used break-action guns, but many of them were single barrels like the Ithaca E Series, the Parker S line, the L. C. Smith (Hunter) single, the Baker, plus imports like the single from Charles Daly's Prussian contingent.

Finally, although trapshooting does have a doubles vent, in which a pair of clays is airborne at the same time, many shooters never entered the event. Even today the trap doubles entry is well below that of 16-yard and handicap singles; consequently, there was no need for a typical trapman to own a double-barreled gun. And most typical trapshooters of said era often bought a pumpgun and used it for the few doubles events they entered.

Thus, trap-grade side-by-sides are somewhat scarce. Gunmakers who offered a specific trap grade in side-by-side arrangement were frequently frustrated with the sales. The L. C. Smith Trap Grade horizontal double went into the company's catalog in 1913, for example, and it only sold 3355 copies before it was dropped in 1939, which averages out to 129 per year. Likewise, the A. H. Fox Model XE, a high-combed gun made expressly for trap, sold poorly and is today a scarce item among collectors. High-combed Parker doubles are also somewhat rare. Remington's sales from Model 32 trap guns were apparently so disappointing that, after WWII, the company sold manufacturing rights to Krieghoff. Winchester's trap grade Model 21 certainly didn't set the trapshooting world ablaze.

If there was one exception to the above discussion of doubles in skeet and trap, it was the Browning Superposed. The gun kicked like a mule, but shooters still bought it and won with it. For years, the Superposed was a standard for trap doubles; if single-shot or pumpgun users wanted a second gun for twin clays, they almost invariably bought a Belgian Browning with the now-obsolete B-25 action. But although the B-25 was a fine gun, the Brownings did not propel us into the double-gun craze that has swept tournament shooting and carried over into an expanded market for all high-quality doubles. That developed differently. . . .

THE TOURNAMENT GUN REVOLUTION

For many generations, American clay-target shooters shopped for the cheapest guns they could find; pumps and autoloaders dominated. But the improved economy of the 1960s helped change all that. Tournaments became crowded; some days at the Grand American trapshoot turned out nearly 4000 gunners. Even local shoots were taxed to the limit, and many of them added new fields.

Along with more shooting came the urge for a better gun. It is almost axiomatic that as a shooter improves, he foresakes the equipment that brought him to greater levels in favor of a fancier piece. But which gun to buy? Many typical shooters had their minds made up by the consistent winners and all-Americans, who were using a new generation of break-action guns. The higher prices of these guns didn't deter Mr. Average; the rose-colored glasses he wore for shooting told him that economic good times would continue to roll. Thus, people who just a couple of years earlier would have shuddered at the thought of spending $300 on a double suddenly began spending $3000 for a higher-quality break-action like the champions were shooting. In that manner, then, a breakthrough was scored. And once acquainted with fine doubles, the public has retained its interest.

There were two target-grade break-actions that inspired this revolution. The first of these was the Ljutic Mono Gun; the next was the Perazzi.

LJUTIC

Ljutic's Mono Gun was the first departure from what had become a staid line of trap models. It was hardly a frilly creation like a London or Birmingham Best-grade game gun in .410 bore. Developed in the 1960s by Al Ljutic, a talented trapshooter and

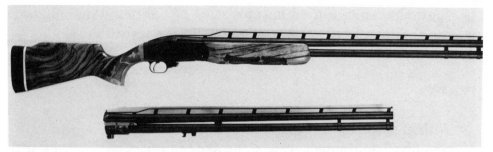

Ljutic guns were among the first to entice shooters into the high-priced, custom-gun field. Although they have appearances all their own, Ljutic guns are winners on the tournament trail.

a skilled machinist whose shop was near Harold's Gun Club north of Reno, Nevada, the Mono Gun was a highly specialized trap gun. A break-action single shot at its inception, the gun was a classic example of design concepts in which the final form followed the function for which the gun was intended. It was bulkier than the Ithaca E Series of single shots, had a deeper receiver, a higher rib placement so the shooter could stand with his head in a more natural upright posture, and opened via a push-button mechanism that was located just ahead of the trigger guard. The gun had only eight parts in the entire firing operation, and each barrel was custom honed for concentricity and custom choked. The Mono Gun was popularized by Dan Orlich, who used it to win national championships and to break some of the first perfect scores of 100 straight from the maximum handicap distance of 27 yards. Shooters began buying the Mono Gun even though it cost more than $1000 at a time when trap-grade pumps could still be had for $200.

Al Ljutic carried his Mono Gun concepts into an over-under called the BiGun. It is a target-grade gun available in skeet, trap and live-bird styles with lofted Olympic ribs. A totally custom order, the BiGun's barrels are adjusted for the point of impact specified by each customer. An upgraded BiGun with exhibition-quality English or American walnut, fine-line checkering and double recess choking for shorter shot strings is being made in very limited numbers as the LTD O/U. The 1984 Ljutic price for the single-shot Mono Gun was $3495; the BiGun started at $7995; and the enhanced LTD O/U, with its finer finish plus custom performance features, listed at $9984. Also in 1984, the guns wooden accoutrements were trimmed to produce lightweight models.

Ljutic has since moved his operation to Yakima, Washington, where his line of innovative guns has continued to grow.

PERAZZI

Although the Ljutic guns introduced shooters to the advantages of specialized equipment, it was the added impact of Perazzi guns that finalized the revolution from ordinary guns to high-grade, high-priced target models. Beginning as an unheralded gunmaker among all the other famous houses in Brescia, Italy, Daniele Perazzi's guns leaped forward prominently when one of them was used by Ennio Mattarelli in winning the 1964 Olympic gold medal in trapshooting. The gun was basically the model we have come to know as the Mirage, a low-profiled over-under with flat rib, trigger-plate action, and a strong, heavy action body with Holland & Holland side lugs. For the 1968 Olympics, the same basic gun was given a higher rib to combat the heat waves of Mexico City, and this variant of the Perazzi over-under became known as the MX-8.

Ithaca Gun Company was the first American firm to import Perazzis, and it was through their efforts that the line received extensive publicity. Yankee trapmen did not plunge into the Perazzi market immediately, but when certain champions began winning consistently with them, the parade was on. Initially, then, the Mirage and MX-8 got their start via bandwagon psychology.

Perazzi guns didn't win on the clay-target circuit by flukes, however. They have exceptional dynamics. In some respects, they have a weight distribution that, although being heavier than a trim British game gun, does indeed follow the concept of concentrating the weight between one's hands while leaving the extremities lighter for responsiveness. For along with having a stout, massive action body and breech area, thanks in part to the side lugs, the Perazzis have somewhat lighter barrels than those found on most shotguns. The result is fast starts as the extremities pivot easily around the compact body.

Perazzi guns also have fast locks and crisp triggers. Many of the current models have higher-than-normal ventilated ribs for

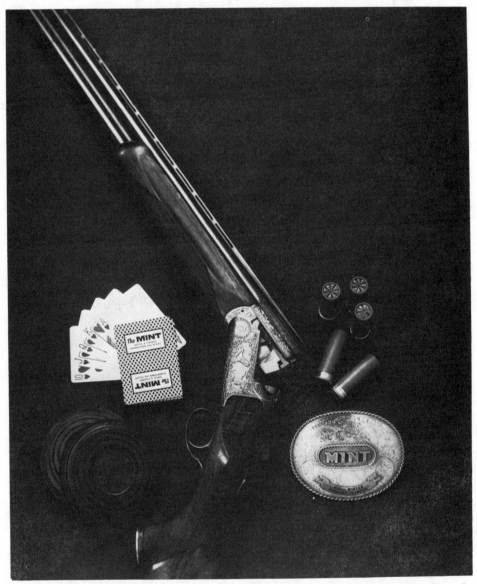

This Perazzi Mirage with deep-relief engraving exemplifies the trend toward high-grade guns for tournament shooting. One big win at an important trap or live-pigeon tournament will more than pay for the gun.

improved target visibility, heat-wave dissipation and a more upright shooting posture.

Because the price of production has increased the retail cost of the Mirage/MX-8 designs, Perazzi has focused on a less expensive model known as the MX-3, and an MX-4 is rumored. It remains to be seen if the MX-3 excites shooters the way the Mirage and MX-8 did. But whatever the future holds in store for Perazzis, any history of sporting arms must reflect their importance in changing the gun-buying habits of typical or average shotgunners.

KRIEGHOFF

Krieghoff is another name associated with the sudden rise in stateside sales of high-quality target guns. Its position is attributable to Remington's decision to drop the Model 32 over-under and its own willingness to push and improve the line. The Krieghoff Model 32, which got Krieghoff's foot into the American shooting door, was simply the Remington Model 32 as made in Ulm, West Germany. Remington sold those rights after WWII. Since then, the Krieghoff Model 32 has gone on to become the most popular 4-barrel skeet set, and it shone in Olympic glory when American Don Haldeman used one to take the 1976 gold medal in trapshooting at Montreal.

But the people at Krieghoff have not sat back. The Model 32 is no longer cataloged, having been replaced by an upbeat variant known as the K-80 after 1976. Essentially, the K-80 is a slightly altered and refined edition of the Model 32, including both standard and lightweight models. It retains the same basic profile of the Model 32, has the sliding top bolt, and continues to utilize separated barrels. The K-80, however, has an adjustable trigger position that allows each shooter to move it backward or forward according to his or her hand size, finger length and comfort. It also has palm swells on both sides of the full pistol grip, and release triggers are available. When it comes to the action nucleus, only minor changes were made; about 90 percent of the original Model 32's parts will still fit the K-80. In standard weight, the K-80 has caught on significantly among trapshooters, and this model was popular at the 1984 Grand American. One feature that appeals to trapshooters is the possibility of adjusting the K-80's underbarrel's point of impact by switching muzzle-end hangers.

The K-80 Lightweight is a special model intended primarily for skeet. The weight has been trimmed via a lighter receiver that takes about 1½ pounds off the gun. The reason for trimming the K-80's overall weight stems from the current popularity of full-length smallbore inserts among tournament skeet shooters. The inserts convert a 12-gauge over-under to a 20 or 28 gauge or .410 bore simply by slipping a pair of tubes machined for the specific barrel. Such tube sets are deemed an advantage by serious skeet shooters because they put "more gun" into a competitor's hands for small-gauge events, thereby eliminating the whippiness inherent in scaled-down .410s, 28s and 20s. The sole flaw in this use of full-length inserts was that many 12-gauge tournament guns were already so heavy that adding inserts made them inert masses. Hence, by reducing the K-80's weight to about 7½ pounds for the Lightweight 12-gauge skeet gun, Krieghoff made it possible to employ the inserts while maintaining a more reasonable gun weight.

The standard K-80 has a silver-satin receiver with the K-80 designation machined into it. Lightweight skeet models have a very modest scroll pattern. Advanced grades are available, beginning with a Bavarian Grade, which has moderate scroll around a game scene. Next is the Danube Grade with British-style bouquet and scroll, followed by the Gold Target Grade, which is covered with bold scroll and has a novel shattered clay target inlaid in gold on the sliding top bolt. The Crown Grade is Krieghoff's highest catalog grade per se and is covered with engraved hunting scenes, gold inlays and scroll.

Krieghoff has not yet followed Perazzi's lead in making a lower-cost gun for widened public consumption. The switch from the Krieghoff Model 32 to the K-80 was not the same as from the MX-8 to the MX-3. At this writing, standard K-80s are priced around $3500, whereas dealers are selling the MX-3s at less than $2300.

ROTTWEIL

The Rottweil line of dynamic clay-target guns first flashed across the firearms firmament when Konrad Wirnhier of West Germany used one to win the 1972 Olympic gold medal in skeet at Munich. The guns themselves are made in Italy by Fratelli

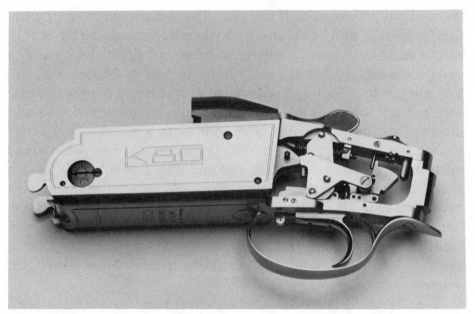

A Krieghoff K-80 action. This is a revamped version of the old Remington Model 32 over-under, and it has caught on well with American skeet and trap shooters.

Gamba, but they are distributed by Dynamit Nobel of West Germany and are named after the city in which Dynamit Nobel is headquartered, Rottweil. After the Munich Olympics, the line of Rottweil guns became known as the Rottweil '72 shotguns to commemorate Wirnhier's victory.

The current line includes guns specially designed for international skeet, American skeet, trapshooting, live pigeons and field gunning. The International-style skeet gun, called the Olympia '72, was the first to draw attention. It has a moderate Monte Carlo to bring the comb into contact with the cheekbone more quickly for this fast game in which the shooter starts with a lowered gun. It also has the Tula Choke, which the British sometimes refer to as the Retro Choke. Whatever its name, the Tula Choke involves a radical expansion of the bore near the muzzle, causing a bulbous appearance up front. This choke concept derives its name from the city of Tula, which is the gunmaking capital of Russia, and it has been described as a Cutts Compensator swaged directly into the barrel. Its purpose is to promote even

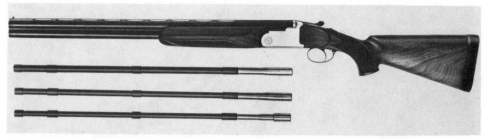

A Rottweil American skeet gun showing full-length smallbore tubes that are slipped into the lightweight barrels for use in the .410-bore, 28- and 20-gauge events. Note the high, straight comb that is becoming more common on American-style skeet guns.

distribution for close-range shooting and, some people believe, to lengthen the shot string somewhat.

Rottweill's American-style skeet gun is made specifically for stateside skeet, which permits a fully mounted gun prior to the target's appearance and allows the use of four gauges. It has a very compact, albeit impressively strong, action body; and it is fitted with relatively thin-walled barrels to keep the muzzle weight down when inserts are employed. On an overall basis, it is somewhat lighter and faster starting than the K-80 with smallbore inserts aboard. Stocks for the American-style skeet gun follow the current trend toward high combs. The gun has a flat rib rather than a lofted one.

Rottweil's trap-grade over-under has a rib like that of Perazzi's MX-8 and is a responsive gun with 30-inch barrels. It has, unfortunately, been grossly overlooked by shooters. When a single-barrel assembly is included in combo sets, the single barrel has a sliding muzzle feature that permits one to adjust the pattern's point of impact.

The top grades of Rottweil guns have unique trigger-plate actions. Unlike many European doubles that have flat or V-spring power, they utilize stout coil springs that are shrouded in tubular housings. The entire lockplate is nicely damascened. Those Rottweil models that do not have the removable trigger plates are labeled the 720s instead of the 72s. At this writing, the Model 72s sans engraving run between $2000 and $3000.

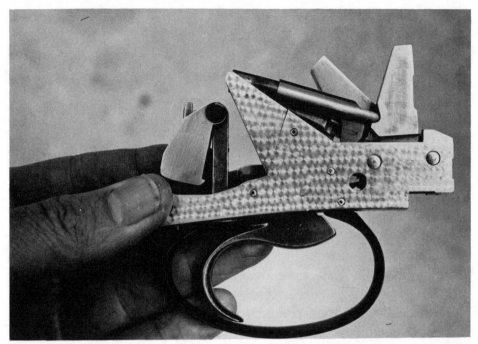

The Rottweil trigger-plate assembly is engine turned, polished and has the coil springs fitted inside tubular housings to keep them on a straight line for maximum power at a very efficient angle.

ARMI MAROCCHI

An Italian gunmaker just emerging as a crafter of fine competition guns is Armi Marocchi, also of Gardone, Val Trompia. This company came into being in 1922 but is virtually unknown outside the Continent.

Marocchi action bodies closely resemble those of the Perazzi line. The main line of clay-target guns is called the Contrast Series, in which there are two levels: the Contrast Cup line, consisting of basic guns without engraving; and the Contrast Prestige Cup line, including engraved guns with fancier wood and finer checkering. In general, the Contrast Series includes a flat rib like that of the Perazzi Mirage.

There is one trap and live-pigeon design that makes a concession to the changing scene. The America grade has a high rib, tighter pistol grip curve, and a hint of a schnobble at the fore-end tip. All other guns remain loyal to conservative European concepts.

Current information indicates that the Marocchi guns do not have removable trigger groups. Both the America and the Contrast models are available in combo sets. The company apparently enjoys making engraved models and, to date, has made no attempt to attract the same market that Perazzi does. A price of $2000 is the base for Contrast Cups and the America gun. The American importer, who operates out of Bedford Park, Illinois, did not provide photos.

BERETTA

The Beretta SO series of sidelock over-unders has won many important tournaments involving clay and feathered targets. It was, in fact, the first over-under to gain any acceptance among box-pigeon competitors, and the gun has more than proved itself on Olympic trap ranges.

However, the ravages of inflated production costs have run the SO guns out of sight for the mass market, and Beretta has had to create an entirely new generation of lower-priced competition guns to retain a broad base. The former BL series of over-unders fell by the wayside, but its action nucleus was retained and upgraded for an entirely new family of target-grade models designated the 680 Series. This starts with the plain 680 skeet and trap guns, but rises quickly to the better-than-average 682, 685 and 687 models, which have finer finishes, varying amounts of engraving and added competition features. The S 682 guns take on added significance, with their fancier stocks and fore-ends, optional high ventilated rib on the trap grade, and 3-position adjustable trigger. The S 682 is also available as a trap combo outfit, and the S 682 DL over-unders have a tasteful clay-target motif engraved on the receiver walls, with the left side marked "Pull" and the right side engraved "Mark." A 4-barreled skeet version of the 682 is scheduled for 1985.

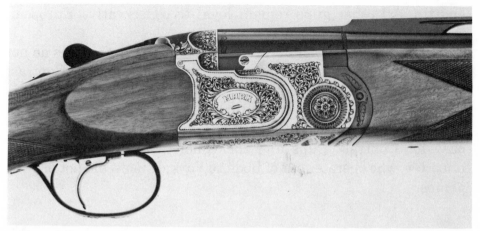

The new line of Beretta 682 clay-target guns has a 3-position trigger adjustment and a clay-target motif.

REMINGTON

Matt Dryke of the United States shot a Remington Model 3200 to win the gold medal in skeet shooting at the Los Angeles Olympics. The gun was a favorite of those who, like Dryke, preferred a heavy gun. However, the limited market didn't justify continuation of the M3200, which has now been dropped. One important feature on the M3200 was its lock time, claimed to be the fastest of any production-grade gun.

The Competition Grade M3200 had fancier wood than the standard grade, and some skeet sets were made with 4-barrel assemblies. Limited editions of engraved 3200s, known as the One of 1000 Series, were sold in both skeet and trap models, and these may one day take on some collector value. To my knowledge, only eight F-grade Model 3200s were ever made, those for the Du Pont Board of Directors.

BROWNING

Although the Browning/FN Superposed guns have won widely in all shotgunning disciplines, their fame has been overtaken by the current Browning line of Japanese-made competition guns,

The now-obsolete Remington Model 3200 in Competition Grade had fancy wood. It is shown here in the 4-barrel skeet set.

The Remington Model 3200s that may have collector appeal some day are those of the limited One of 1000 Series, which were made in skeet and trap grades.

especially the BT-99. A single-barrel break-action, the BT-99 has gained tremendous fame for American-style trapshooting. Its companion, the Citori over-under, is popular with trap-doubles shooters who want the lowest-priced double that can be considered reliable, but the Citori has not yet gained fame as a tournament gun. A 4-barrel skeet set is made for the 12-gauge Citori frame.

Designed for serious skeet shooters, the new Winchester Diamond Grade 4-barrel skeet set is the first over-and-under set ever offered by Winchester. Barrels in 12, 20 and 28 gauge and .410 bore all weigh the same, giving the shooter the same "feel" regardless of gauge mounted. Suggested retail price is $3950 each.

WINCHESTER

Winchester's original Model 101s never cut a wide swath in tournament circles. Most shooters thought they were too light, especially through the barrels. After Winchester had handled the Perazzi line for a short time, the Model 101s began to change, and we now have the fashionable Diamond and International Grades. Both have relatively good triggers and different dynamics than the original 101s. The guns are more controllable. The Diamond Grade has a high rib in all skeet and trap models, is made in all four skeet gauges, and can be had as a trap combo set. The International guns have flat ribs, a higher grade of wood and a finer engraving pattern. However, all engraving work appears to have been done by mechanical and/or chemical means. Prices hover between $1000 and $2000.

The current interest in high-quality guns is keyed to the impact of advanced-grade tournament guns. When shooters broke through the mental and financial barriers that had kept them from buying better guns, the overall market came to life. For the latest in high-grade competition doubles, the shooter's mecca is Jaqua's Fine Guns of Findlay, Ohio. Bill Jaqua will have the latest in stock when the items in this book are obsolete.

Chapter 20

Live-Pigeon Guns

Of all the target-grade doubles, live-pigeon guns are the most prestigious. Despite the popular belief that such shooting has been outlawed, live-pigeon contests, commonly referred to as "box pigeon," are making a strong comeback in certain areas; and many top trap and skeet competitors are visiting the pigeon rings more frequently, if for no other reason than the fact that there's far more prize money in box pigeon than either of the clay-target games.

The essence of live-pigeon shooting is easily comprehended. A series of five to nine traps is set on a straight line ahead of the shooter, who can have his gun mounted before calling "Pull!" On the shooter's command, any one of the traps will pop open and hurl a pigeon skyward. The exact trap is unknown to the shooter, who then has two shots to drop it cleanly inside a fenced ring. If the bird makes it over the low fence, even if it falls dead, it is scored a lost bird. If the shooter drops the bird inside the ring so that attendants can retrieve it, it is a dead bird. A normal daily event involves 25 pigeons per shooter, although major championships may run for several days and require 100 birds per entrant.

The popularity of box-pigeon shooting stems from the unpredictable nature of the target. Trap-ejected pigeons do not fly known routes like clay targets, and it is almost impossible for anyone to become a grooved shooter. Reactions, timing, coordination and swing speed are vital to consistency, although luck does play a role.

Shooters fire from a handicap walk that runs from 25 to 35 yards away from the trap, depending on the nation and the shoot management's decisions. American clubs tend to use longer ranges

Modern live-pigeon guns are generally built to place their first-barrel patterns high for a built-in vertical lead on fast-rising birds that are still under the impelling influence of the trap.

than do European and Mexican clubs. Because of this range factor, modified choke is about the most open choke selected. Many shooters select improved-modified for the first barrel and either full or extra-full for the second. They emphasize accurate pointing and tight patterns for positive kills rather than relying on more open patterns to pick up an extra bird or two with the fringe; for pigeons are tough birds that can shrug off light hits and still make it out of the ring. In Europe, certain species of small, leathery, hard-flying pigeons are specially bred for the sport, and a pellet or two from the edge of a wide pattern doesn't stop them. Thus, tight chokes prevail, and it is possible that extra-full choke boring is more common in live-pigeon guns than anywhere else in the spectrum of wing-gunning.

Live-pigeon loads are universally standard-length 12-gauge cartridges with 3¼ drams equivalent of powder under 1¼ ounces of shot for about 1220 f.p.s. at the muzzle of a 30-inch barrel. At one time, No. 7 shot was popular among flyer shooters, but since that size has been dropped stateside, No. 7½s and 8s dominate. Where legal, nickel-plated shot is used by money shooters who want every advantage.

The true live-pigeon gun is itself a specialized model, differing subtly from skeet, trap and field guns. It has nothing in common with a skeet gun but instead combines some of the features found on trap and field guns. In general, a live-pigeon gun is somewhat more lively and responsive than a long, heavy trap gun; it needs this dynamic quality because the erratic, unpredictable nature of pigeon flights requires swifter gun manipulation than does a grooved clay target. However, live-pigeon guns are also stocked to deliver a variously high pattern element à la the trap gun; for a bird's flight is most predictable when it is propelled upward by the trap, and practically all shooters fire their first barrel while the target is still rising in a relatively straight line. A high-patterning piece not only provides some built-in vertical lead for this kind of rising shot, but it also permits one to center his bird while watching it over the barrels instead of having to blot it out.

At one time, the comb dimensions of a live-pigeon gun were only slightly higher than those of a field gun. However, in recent times the emphasis has been on increasingly faster first shots, and modern live-pigeon guns are being groomed for considerably higher patterning. Many live-pigeon guns now equal or exceed the comb heights of trap guns. Perazzi has carried the high-shooting concept to an extreme in live-bird guns. The company not only leans toward very high combs—which, in effect, are like elevating the rear sight of a rifle—but it has also switched the firing sequence of over-unders to fire the top barrel first, thereby taking advantage of the natural jump of the top tube for added pattern elevation. The second shot from the lower tube isn't as high because the underbarrel doesn't generate the same jump; hence, the shooter has a flatter-shooting condition for the bird's level or jinxing flight.

There have been some other major changes in both the live-pigeon guns and the attitudes with which competitors approach them. Initially, the twin-triggered side-by-side was *the* live-pigeon gun. The barrels were normally 30 inches long, the second tube being choked to within an inch of its life. Such guns had the responsiveness of game guns, which is one reason why they found so much favor on those helter-skelter targets. Too, twin triggers were deemed essential for absolute reliability, as single triggers hadn't yet been perfected when box pigeon was about the only shotgun contest in town. The unfortunate thing is that generations of live-pigeon shooters wouldn't accept progress. They ignored the single trigger even though it was perfected in the 20th century.

All of that has changed, of course. A double-triggered side-by-side is seldom seen at flyer events these days. The over-under has taken charge, perhaps because its narrower sighting plane is less inclined to cover up rising, erratic-flying targets. The twin-trigger mechanism is also passé; single-trigger groups perform flawlessly. And although 30-inch barrels are still viable, if not favorites, shooters have not hesitated to deviate. European makers have turned out live-bird guns with barrels as short as 27½ inches for exceedingly fast first shots, and some major championships have been taken by gunners using 32-inch barrels for optimum pointing accuracy, smooth swings and a positive follow-through. Thus, there is a more scientific and individualistic approach to live pigeon guns nowadays, and when there is a showdown between the traditional double-triggered side-by-side and the newer over-under, it is generally the over-under that wins.

While Perazzi has made some outstanding innovations to the evolution of live-bird guns, other modern gunmakers have also contributed. Until Remington dropped the Model 3200, for instance, it was made in a live-pigeon model with 28-inch barrels and a comb that about split the difference between a field grade and a trap grade. The M3200 live-pigeon gun never sold very well, and it will one day be a collector's item. However, some distributors still have M3200 live-pigeon guns in inventory at what may be one of the lowest prices for such a specialized model.

Winchester's Model 101 line does not have a live-pigeon gun per se, but the Grand European trap or the Diamond Grade trap will do nicely, especially with the 30-inch barrel assemblies. The Grand European has a flat rib, gentle schnobble on the fore-end, and a deeply curved competition-type trigger leading to snappy

Winchester's Grand European trap gun can serve admirably as a live-pigeon piece.

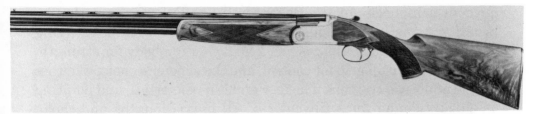

The Rottweil live-pigeon gun is based on said firm's Model 72 Field Supreme.

locks. The Diamond Grade differs mainly by way of a much higher rib. In either Model 101 styling, the barrels are light enough for responsiveness on pigeons.

A good live-pigeon gun coming to these shores is Dynamit Nobel's Rottweil, which is a takeoff on the '72 Field Supreme with a slightly higher comb. Beretta's 680 Series has no pigeon gun, but the famous Beretta series of SO vertical doubles can be had in live-bird styling. The same holds true for custom Brownings of Belgian persuasion.

Krieghoff makes a handsome live-pigeon gun that has nothing in common with the K-80 except that both are over-unders. This is the Model U.L.M.-P, a true sidelock with hand-detachable convenience. The gun itself is a high-framed type with an action body height and profile closely akin to that of the Merkel. It is also bolted like the Model 304 Merkels, meaning Purdey double underbites, the Kersten crossbolt and a full knuckle pin plus a bottom lug that fits in the floorplate. The U.L.M.-P's sidelock is quite novel. It does not have the conventional flat springs but instead derives its energy from a pair of short, strong coil springs. There is a safety catch on the sears, and the trigger is a single, nonselective unit. Engraving patterns are optional, and the wood is select English walnut. Reflecting the trends toward high patterning, the standard U.L.M.-P has a drop of $1^3/_8$ inches at both comb and heel. The workmanship is superb.

Practically any of the Ferlach, Austria, gunmakers can build a live-pigeon gun of side-by-side or over-under configuration, customizing the stock. The same is true for Winchester's custom shop, which can turn out a Model 21 for live pigeons given the customer's choice of barrel lengths, chokes and stock dimensions.

Those interested in a side-by-side specifically designed for live pigeons can check out the Bernardelli Las Palomas imported by Quality Arms Inc. of Houston. A trim boxlock with beautifying sideplates, the Las Palomas has a heavy action body for strength, a palm-swell pistol grip for control, and the shooter's choice of either single or double triggers. The fore-end is a beavertail, and pointing is quickly done over a file-cut rib. All barrel lengths and choke combinations are available. With automatic ejectors and modest fine scroll geometrically applied to the borders, the gun was priced just below $2000 at this writing.

Perhaps the most artistically finished live-pigeon guns, both vertical and horizontal doubles, are made by Fabbri and Famars. Most of their guns are custom-made pieces costing more than a new automobile, but they are magnificent in every respect.

Does all this talk of fancy guns, high combs, innovations and lofty prices mean that live-pigeon shooting is beyond the means of the average shooter? No. The first box-pigeon shoot I ever attended was won by a fellow using an SKB field-grade over-under bored modified and full!

Chapter 21

The Space Age Doubles

There can be no doubt that the classic doubles of our day will remain treasured sporting guns and valuable investments in the foreseeable future. And to those who follow us, the dynamics and elegance of trim doubles will be judged an art form. But will distant generations appreciate the pride and dedication that went into building and owning them? Or will they view them as primitive because, despite cosmetic artistry and form-functional designs, they have gone virtually unchanged in an era when scientific advances have carried all other mechanical concepts forward at record speeds? In other words, are those of us who admire double shotguns so steeped in nostalgia that we can't accept change?

There is at least one man who has taken a futuristic look at the double. This is Al Ljutic. For several years, he has made and sold a revolutionary single-shot trap gun that looks more like a lean walking stick than a shotgun. Known as the Space Gun, it has nothing traditional about it except that it throws pellets. However, the Space Gun can't be shrugged off; it has turned in some tremendous scores, especially in long-yardage trap handicap. You simply can't argue with success!

And now Ljutic has brought the Space Gun concept into the world of doubles. To be known as the Side-by-Side Space Gun, it is a solid-frame, in-line design with only 11 moving parts in the entire mechanism. The walking-stick profile remains, with the butt-pad attached perpendicular to the in-line geometry and with a full pistol grip tied to the trigger-guard system. The pad is cast off at the toe for better anatomical fit. The trigger/grip group is readily detachable for changing and maintenance. Opening and

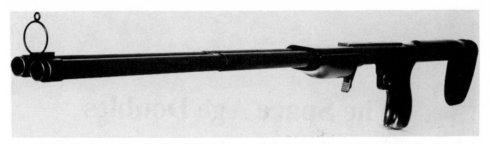

The prototype of Al Ljutic's futuristic Side-By-Side Space Gun, which was scheduled to go into production in the spring of 1985.

closing are done via a lever placed slightly ahead of the trigger guard. A sizable ring-type pointing device, shaped like a figure eight with a substantial lower lobe, pops Buck Rogers-style above the muzzles.

What is the Side-By-Side Space Gun all about? Its primary consideration is greatly reduced recoil, which is accomplished by an internal 2½-pound, spring-loaded thrust hammer that slams forward when the gun is fired. This system is akin to that of an open-bolt firing machine gun, and it invokes the concept of opposing kinetic energies. Perhaps the best equation to apply is the one for conservation of momentum: $M_1V_1 = M_2V_2$, wherein the subscript 1 represents the energy of the thrust hammer and the subscript 2 represents the recoil energy as generated by the action-reaction principle. That the thrust hammer does indeed reduce recoil is known to all who have shot the single-barreled Space Gun; therefore, although the twin-tubed Space Gun is only in its prototype form at this writing and won't be available until spring of 1985 (meaning I haven't shot it), there is no reason to doubt the low recoil level promised for it.

Ljutic's further explanation for the Side-By-Side Space Gun may reverse the current trend of thinking relative to the pointing/sighting qualities of the horizontal double versus the vertical double. For it has been held almost universally that the narrow plane of an over-under lends greater accuracy to shotgun pointing, whereas the initial literature coming my way suggests that, "the side-by-side design gives both the left and the right eye equal tracking capacity for better judging of distance and perspective to the target." The purposes of the lofty figure-eight front sight was not explained, but one surmises that it is to concentrate the gunner's gaze.

Thus, although shooters won't argue the value of a thrust hammer for lower recoil in the side-by-side, there may be some theoretically based discussions forthcoming about the merits of the old side-by-side's pointing qualities. Does the Ljutic concept provide easier, more accurate alignment than the narrow plane of an over-under? The Space Gun's profile in itself will spark some controversy, at least until it starts winning at trap doubles, Olympic trap and skeet, as well as dropping geese from 75-80 yards without the brutal recoil of magnum loads. Then sideways glances will be cast by disbelievers who, as stated earlier, find it difficult to argue with success.

Whether Al Ljutic's Side-By-Side Space Gun will dominate Intergalactic trapshooting in the late 21st century isn't yet known. Nor do we know for sure how it will handle on those running, far-flushing, spiral-flying quail of Mars or the supersonic, polka-dotted geese of Saturn. What we do know is that Al Ljutic has taken the side-by-side farther into the future than other designers, hunters, shooters, and collectors ever dreamed.

Directory

Armsource Inc.
6 Donald Drive
Orinda, CA 94563
{Manufrance doubles)

Beretta U.S.A.
17601 Indian Head Highway
Accokeek, MD 20607

Ludwig Borovnik
Dolligchagasse 14, A-9100
Ferlach, Austria

British Guns
P.O. Box 1924
Corvallis, OR 97339
(W. & C. Scott Guns)

Browning
Morgan, Utah 84050

Caprinus U.S.A. Inc.
100 Prospect Street
Stamford, CT 06901
(Caprinus Sweden over-under)

Chadick Ltd.
P.O. Box 100
Terrell, TX 75160
(Fine double shotguns double rifles.
Sole U.S. importer of Chapuis
double rifles.)

Winston Churchill
RFD Box 29B
Proctorsville, VT 05153
(Engraver)

Donald L. Criswell
P.O. Box 277
Yorba Linda, CA 92686
(Dealer in fine doubles)

Dunn's Inc.
Highway 57E, Box 449
Grand Junction, TN 38039
(Merkel importer)

K. Genecco Gun Works
8825 Thornton Road
Stockton, CA 95209
(American-made sidelocks
and fine gun restoration)

Georges Granger
66, Cours Fauriel
42 St. Etienne
France

Holland & Holland Ltd.
31-33 Bruton Street
London W1X 8JS
United Kingdom

Jaqua's Fine Guns
900 E. Bigelow Avenue
Findlay, OH 45840
(High-grade competition guns;
American and European doubles)

Shotguns of Ulm
P.O. Box "L"
Ringoes, NJ 08551
(Krieghoff guns)

Ljutic Industries
732 N. 16th Avenue #22
Yakima, WA 98902
(Ljutic-design shotguns)

Loren Thomas Ltd.
P.O. Box 18425
Dallas, TX 75218
(New Darne and Granger guns)

Robert E. Maki
P.O. Box 947
Northbrook, IL 60062
(Custom engraving)

Marocchi U.S.A. Inc.
5939 W. 66th Street
Bedford Park, IL 60638
(Marocchi over-unders)

William L. Moore & Co.
31360 Via Collinas, Suite 109
Westlake Village, CA 91360
(Italian Piotti and various
Spanish doubles)

New England Arms Co.
Lawrence Lane, Box 278
Kittery Pt, ME 03905
(Fine modern and antique doubles)

R. Painter Co.
2901 Oakhurst Avenue
Austin, TX 78703
(Chapius doubles)

William Powell & Son Ltd.
35-37 Carrs Lane
Birmingham, B4 7SX
England

Puccinelli Design
114 Gazania Court
Novato, CA 94947
(High-grade Italian doubles,
Fabbri over-unders)

James Purdey & Sons Ltd.
Audley House
57-58 South Audley Street
London W1Y 6ED

Quality Arms Inc.
P.O. Box 19477
Houston, TX 77224
(Fine shotguns: Arrieta, Merkol,
Beretta, Aya)

Westley Richards & Co. Ltd.
40, Grane Road, Bournbrook
Birmingham B29 6AR
England

John F. Rowe, Gunmaker
Champlin Firearms Inc.
P.O. Box 3191
Enid, OK 73702
(Fine gun repair and refinishing)

Thad Scott
P.O. Box 412
Indianola, MS 38751
(Dealer in fine guns)

U.S. Repeating Arms Co.
275 Winchester Ave.
P.O. Box 30-300
New Haven, CT 06511
(Winchester Model 21 maker)

Waverly Arms Inc.
P.O. Box 42062
Columbia, SC 29240

James Wayne
2608 N. Laurent Street
Victoria, TX 77901
(Dealer in fine used doubles)

Theodore C. Wood
1032 Bogtown Road
Salem, NY 12865
(Dealer in fine used doubles)

NOTE TO READER

Prices listed 1985 and 1998 printings were estimated at time when written. Reader should check with dealers for the current suggested prices.

Index

(Boldface numbers refer to illustrations)

A

Abbiatico, Mario, 132
Action bar, 64, 156
Action body, 40, 95-96
Action flat, 64
Action frame, 64
Action size, 65
Actions, compensating, 40-50
Advantages of double shotguns, 12-21,
   21; action nucleus and, 21; balance,
   16-20; hand-to-barrel relationship
   and, 13-16, **14, 15**; hand-to-eye coordination and, 12-13; over-unders,
   13-15; pointability and, 13; side-by-
   sides, 15-16
Aguirre and Aranzabal; *see* AyA
Aiming, 2-3; *see also* Wingshooting
American engravers, 180
American gunmakers, 70-71, 76, 82,
   168-179, 180-191; Fox, 90-92, 125,
   174, **175,** 179, 197, 199; Ithaca, 174,
   199, 202; L. C. Smith, 45, **61,** 62, 92,
   125, 173-174, **173,** 197, 199; LeFever,
   92, 125, 169, 174-177, **175, 176,** 177,
   179; Parker, **42,** 66-67, **68,** 71, **89,**
   90-92, **92,** 121, 124, 125, 168-179,
   169, 171, 175, 196, 197, 199, 224;
   Remington, 50, 82-85, 103, 168, 198,
   199, 204, **206,** 210, **211,** 216; Ruger,
   76, 81, 82, 182; Winchester, 48, 50,
   103, 124, 184-187, **185, 186, 187,**
   212, **212, 216,** 217
American Parker; *see* Parker guns
American Rifleman, 102
Angle of the frame, 64
Anson, William, 41
Anson & Deeley, xi-xiii, 41-43, **42, 43,**
   45, 106-107, 108, 157
Armi Fabbri; *see* Fabbri guns
Armi Famars; *see* Famars guns
Armi Garbi; *see* Garbi guns
Armi Marocchi; *see* Marocchi guns
Armsource Inc., 222

Art, gun, 86-99
Artifex, 195
Arusha Industries Ltd., 109
Atkin, 100
Audley House, 102, 224
Austrian gunmakers, 132; Fanzoi, 132;
   Ferlach, 14, 93, 132, 217; Franz
   Sodia, 14-15, **15**
Automatic hammerless, xi, 153
Axial forces in bolting system, 63, **64**
AyA, 124-125, **127,** 128, 224

B

Baker guns, 45, 199
Balance, 16-20; balance point and,
   18-20; weight distribution and, 19-20
Bank-note engraving, 90, 93-94
Bar, 64
Barnett International Inc., 181
Beavertailed fore-ends, 16, **23,** 24, **26,**
   28, 30
Bee, Angelo, 180
Belgian Brownings, 17, 46-47, **47,** 79,
   138, 140, 187-188, **188,** 189, 196,
   199-200, 217
Belgian gunmakers, 138-141, 193-195;
   Fabrique Nationale, 138, 140-141;
   Francotte, 222; Masquelier, 178;
   Neumann, **43,** 52, 168, 178
Bending forces in bolting system, 63,
   64, 65, 156
Beretta, 15, 45-46, **46,** 76, 82, **83,**
   134-135, **134, 135,** 179, 192, **193,**
   209-210, **210,** 217, 222
Bernardelli, Vincenzo, 133-134
Bernardelli guns, 133-134, **133,** 179,
   218, 224
Bifurcated lumps, 80
Bird gun; *see* Winchester Model 21
Birmingham, England gunmakers, 87,
   100-102, 106-115, 195; Greener, xi,
   100, 106; Powell, 100, 112-115, **113,**
   193, **194,** 196, 224; Webley & Scott,

100, 107, 108-109; Westley Richards, xi-xiii, 41, 62, 66, 70, **71**, 80, 100, 106, 124, **124**, 192, 193, 196, 224; *see also* British gunmakers; London, England gunmakers
Birmingham Small Arms (BSA) operation, 106
Blitz, 50
Blued action body, 95, 96
Bogardus, Captain A. H., 108
Bolting system on over-unders, xv, 75-85; high-profiled, 76, 77, 79; low-profiled, 75-76, 80; shallow-profiled, 76, 79-80; with side lugs, 81-82
Bolting system on side-by-sides, xv, 63-74; action size and, 65; axial force and, 63, **64**; bending force and, 63, **64**, 65; and cracking, 65; crossbolts, 67-72; doll's head, 70-72, **71**, **73**; dynamic action and, 72-74; lifter bar and, 66, **68**; radial force and, 63, **64**; sideclips and, **71**, 74; static action and, 72-74; underbolts, 66-67
Bolts, 40-50
Borovnik, Ludwig, 132, 222
Boss, 13-14, 24-25, 56, 79, 80, **81**, 100, 124
Boss-Verrees, 138
Boswell line, 181
Boxlock, 41-43, **42**, **43**, 157, 192-196; safety and, 45
Box-pigeon shooting, 213-218, **214, 216, 217**
Brazil, 191
Breechloader, x
Breechloading percussion gun, xi
Bretton, 148-149, **150**, 224
British Association for Shooting and Conservation, 104-106
British gunmakers, 24, 67, 79, 100-115, 193-195, 222; *see also* Birmingham, England gunmakers; London, England gunmakers
British, bolting system, field-style shooting, 33-39
British method of shooting, 33-39; compared with American, 33; footwork, 33, 36-38; overhead shot, **37**, 38; stance, 34-35, **35**, 36-38
Browning, John M., 188
Browning guns, 17-18, 77, 103, 124, 141, 180, **181**, 199-200, 210-211, 222; Belgian-made, 17, 46-47, **47**, 79, 138, 140, 187-188, **188**, 189, 196, 199-200, 217; Japanese, 46-47, 134, 187-189, **190**, 210-211

Bruchet, Paul, 143
Bruchet guns, 143
Buckingham, Nash, 174
Bulino, 93-94, **94**, 133
Burrard, Major Sir Gerald, 118

C
Caprinus Sweden guns, **129**, 130, 190, 222
Carlson, Dave, 161-162
Case-hardening of action body, 96
Causes of Decay in a British Industry, The, 195
Chadick Ltd., 222
Chapius, 151-152, 196, 224
Chasing, 93, **94**
Checkering, **98**, 99
China North Industries Corporation, 190
Choke boring, xi
Churchill, Robert, 116
Churchill, Winston, 180, **181**
Churchill guns, 100, **101**, 116, 125, 128
Citori, 188-189, **190**, 211
Claybough, 100
Clay-target shooting, 158
Cogswell & Harrison, 100
Collins, Ron, 182
Cracking, 65
Crawford, John A., 112
Criswell, Donald L., 222
Crossbolts, 67-72; Greener, 45, 69-70, **70**, 77, **78**; Kersten, 77-79, **78**

D
Daly, Charles, 77, 177-179, **177**, 199
Daly guns, 177-179, **177, 178**, 199
Daly/Miroku guns, 179
Damascus barrels, xiii
Darne, 124, 142-144, **144**, 196, 223
Deeley, John, 41; *see also* Anson & Deeley
Deep-relief engraving, 90, 93
Dickson, John, 48-49
Dickson's round action, 49-50
Doll's head, 70-72, **71, 73**
Double triggers, 51-53, **53, 54;** recoil and, 52, **53**
Dryke, Matt, 210
Dunn's Inc., 222
Dumoulin guns, 138, 139, 223
Dumoulin, Ernest, 138, 139-141
Dumoulin, Henri, 139
Dynamic action in bolting system, 72-74

Dynamit Nobel, 206, 217, 222

E

Engravers, American, 180
Engravings, 88-95, **89**; bank-note, 90,
    93-94; bulino, 93-94, **94**; chasing, 93,
    94; deep-relief, 90, 93; fine-line,
    90-93; graver, 93-94; hammer-and-
    chisel, 90, 93; hand methods, 90-95;
    punta e martello, 90; roll-on method,
    90; scriber, 90; scriber and hammer,
    90; scroll, **91, 92,** 93; shader for, 92
European gunmakers, 67, 76, 77,
    126-141; Austrian, *see* Austrian gun-
    makers; Belgian, *see* Belgian gun-
    makers; British, *see* British gun-
    makers; Finnish, 130-132, **131**;
    French, *see* French gunmakers; Ger-
    man, *see* German gunmakers;
    Spanish, *see* Spanish gunmakers
Evans, 100
Evans, Robert, 180
Evolution of double shotgun, ix-xvi, **ix,
    xii**
Exel Arms of America, 222

F

Fabbri guns, 132-133, **133**, 218, 224
Fabbri, Ivo, 132-133
Fabrique Nationale, 138, 140-141
Face-the-shot shooting method, 33-36
Falise, Antoine, 141
False sideplates, 46-47
Famars guns, **44, 94,** 122, 124, 132,
    218
Fanzoi, Johann, 132
Faskell, Bernard, **42**
Fences, 69
Ferlach gunsmiths, 14, 93, 132, 217
Field-style shooting; American com-
    pared with British, 33; British,
    33-39; footwork, 33, 36-38
Fine-line engraving, 90-93
Finnish gunmakers, 130-132, **131**
Firearms Engravers Guild of America,
    180
FN; *see* Fabrique Nationale
Fore-ends, 13-16, **15, 23**; finishing of,
    96-99; full beavertailed, 16, **23,** 24,
    26, 28, 30; and grips, 22-25; semi-
    beavertail, **23,** 24, 25; splinter, 16,
    23, 24, **25, 26,** 28-30, **29**
Forsyth, Reverend Alexander James,
    xiii
Forsyth Gun Company, 102
Fox, Ansley H., 157, 169

Fox guns, 90-92, 125, 174, **175,** 179,
    197, 199
Frame, 40
Franchi guns, **49,** 50
Francotte, 222
Frank E. Malin & Son (Gunmakers)
    Ltd., 181-182
Franz Sodia, 14-15, **15**
Fratelli Gamba, 205-206
French gunmakers, 142-152; Bretton,
    148-149, **150,** 224; Darne, 124,
    142-144, **144,** 196, 223; Granger, **97,**
    147-148, **148, 149,** 223; LeFaucheux,
    x, xiv, 66
Fulton, 125

G

Galeazzi, Angelo, **133**
Game guns, xv, 4, **101**
Garbi guns, 128, 179, 224
Gebruder Adamy, 17
Genecco, 180-181, 223
German gunmakers, 50, 93, 135-137;
    Gebruder Adamy, 17; Krieghoff, **84,
    98,** 136-137, 196, 204-205, **206,** 217,
    223; Merkel, 14-15, **15,** 17, 50, 77-79,
    78, 96, 124, 128, 135, 136, **136,** 168,
    178, 217, 222; Sauer, 178, 179
Grand Incisioni su Armi d'Oggi, 132
Granger, Georges, **97,** 147-148, **148,
    149,** 223
Grant, 100
Grant, Howard V., 180
Grant, Stephen, 116
Grayed action body, 95, 96
Greener, W., x-xi
Greener, William W., xi, 58, 95, 109,
    195
Greener crossbolt, 45, 69-70, **70,**
    77, **78**
Greener guns, xi, 100, 106
Grips, 22-32; British and European
    side-by-sides, 24-25; and fore-ends,
    22-25; full pistol, **26,** 27, **28;** hand
    pressure and, 31-32; hand-to-barrel,
    13-16, 22-25; semi-pistol, 25-27, **26,**
    31; straight (English), 24, 25-27, **26,**
    27-28, 31
Grouse Gun, 187
Grulla, **127,** 128
Guichard, Henri, 147
Gun artistry, 86-99
Gun fit, 4
Gunmakers; *see* under individual coun-
    tries or makers

H

Haldeman, Don, 204
Hambrusch, Josef, 132
Hammer-and-chisel engraving, 90, 93
Hammerless doubles, xi, 153
Hand burnished action body, 95-96
Hand methods of engraving, 90-95
Hand work, 86-88
Hand-to-eye coordination, wingshooting
   and, 1-4, **2, 3,** 9
Harris & Sheldon Group, 109
Harrison & Hussey, 116
Hawker, Colonel Peter, ix-x
Heym, 179
Holland, Henry W., 56, 57
Holland & Holland, 43, 45, 56, 79, 80,
   81-82, 100, 104, **105,** 123, **123,** 124,
   147, 180, 223
Hooking principle, 62
Hunter Arms Company, 125
Hunter One Trigger, 62

I

Inletting cuts, 98
Ithaca Gun Company, 174, 199, 202
Italian gunmakers, 76, 82, 90, 93, 94,
   132-135, 205-206; Beretta, 15, 45-46,
   46, 76, 82, **83,** 134-135, **134, 135,**
   179, 192, **193,** 209-210, **210,** 217,
   222; Bernardelli, 133-134, **133,** 179,
   218, 224; Fabbri, 132-133, **133,** 218,
   224; Famars, **44, 94,** 122, 124, 132,
   218; Perazzi, **48,** 50, **60,** 96, 192,
   202-204, **203,** 205, 207, 215, 216,
   224; Piotti, 192, 196, **196,** 223; Zoli,
   76
Iver, 125

J

J. & W. Tolley, 178
James Purdey & Sons Ltd., 224
Japanese gunmakers, 76, 90, 182-183,
   184-187; and Browning, 46-47, 134,
   187-189, **190,** 210-211; Daly/Miroku,
   179
Jaqua, Bill, 122, 212, 223
Jeffery, 100
Jenkins, J. J., 135
John Dickson and Sons Ltd., 49
Joseph Lang & Son, 116-117
Just, Josef, 132

K

Ken Hurst Firearms Engraving Company, 131, **131,** 223
Kerr, Alex, 198

Kersten, Gustav, 78
Kersten crossbolt, 77-79, **78**
Krieghoff, **84, 98,** 136-137, 196,
   204-205, **206,** 217, 223
Kusmeth, Nick, **91**

L

L. C. Smith, 45, **61,** 62, 92, 125,
   173-174, **173,** 197, 199
Lanber, Felix, 128-130, 141
Lanber guns, 222
Lanberchoke, 129-130
Lancaster, Charles, x, 116
Lancaster guns, 100
Lang, Joseph, x, 116-120
Lang guns, 100, 116-120, **117, 118,**
   119, 120
Lang & Hussey, 116
Lard, 174
Lard trigger, 62
Laurona, 222
Le Forgeron, 138, 139, **139,** 141, 223
Lebeau-Courally, 138-139, 141, 223
LeFaucheux, x, xiv, 66
LeFever, Dan, 70-71
LeFever guns, 92, 125, 169, 174-177,
   175, 176, 177, 179
Lifter bar, 66, **68**
Live-pigeon shooting, 197, 213-218
Ljutic, Al, 200-202, 219-220, **220**
Ljutic guns, 200-202, **201,** 223
Locks, 40-50, 51; boxlock, *see* Boxlock;
   false sideplates, 46-47; safety and,
   45; sidelock, *see* Sidelock; sideplate,
   43-44; trigger-plate action, 41, 47-50,
   48, 49
London, England gunmakers, 100-102,
   102-106, 116-120; Boss, 13-14, 24-25,
   56, 79, 80, **81,** 100, 124; Cogswell &
   Harrison, 100; Churchill, 100, **101,**
   116, 125, 128; Holland & Holland,
   43, 45, 56, 79, 80, 81-82, 100, 104,
   105, 123, **123,** 124, 147, 180, 223;
   Jeffery, 100; Lancaster, 100; Lang,
   100, 116-120, **117, 118, 119, 120;**
   Manton, xiii, 102; Purdey, 24, **25,** 67,
   67, 100, 102, **103, 104, 113,** 122, **122,**
   124, 192, 224; Rigby, xiii, 100; Woodward, 56, 58, 79, 128; *see also* Birmingham, London gunmakers; British
   gunmakers
Long tangs, 97-98
Loren Thomas Ltd., 223

M

MacNaughten, James, 48-49

Maki, Robert E., 180, 223
Malin guns, 181-182, 223
Manton, Joseph, xiii, 102
Manufrance, 141, 149-151, **151**, 222
Marocchi guns, 208-209, 223
Masquelier, 178
Mattarelli, Ennio, 202
McKenzie, Lynton, 180
Merkel, 14-15, **15**, 17, 50, 77-79, **78**,
    96, 124, 128, 135, 136, **136**, 168, 178,
    217, 222
Metal-to-metal fit, 88
Michelitsch, Johann, 132
Miroku guns, 179
Modell, Henry, 178
Modern Firearms Engraving, 132
Modern Shotgun, The, 118
Moore, William L., 223
Mottled action body, 95-96
Murcott, xi
Murcott's mouse trap, xi

N
Needham, xiii
Needlefire paper cartridges, xiii-xiv
Neumann, **43**, 52, 168, 178
New England Arms Company, 223

O
Olin-Kodessha, 184-187
Opifex, 195
Orlich, Dan, 201
Orvis Company, The, **127**, 128
Over-unders, bolting system; *see*
    Bolting system on over-unders; *see*
    also individual guns

P
Pape, xi
Parker: America's Finest Shotgun, 171
Parker guns, **42**, 66-67, **68**, 71, **89**,
    90-92, **92**, 121, 124, 125, 168-179,
    169, 171, 175, 196, 197, 199, 224
People's Republic of China, 189-191
Perazzi, Daniele, 202
Perazzi guns, **48**, 50, **60**, 96, 192,
    202-204, **203**, 205, 207, 215, 216, 224
Percussion ignition, xiii
Piotti, 192, 196, **196**, 223
Pointing, 2-3
Powell guns, 100, 112-115, **113**, 193,
    194, 196, 224
Prudhomme, E. C., 180
Prussiate of potash, 96
Punta e martello, 90
Purdey, James, 102

Purdey guns, 24, **25**, 67, **67**, 100, 102,
    103, 104, 113, 122, **122,** 124, 192,
    224
Push-out technique, 4

Q
Quality Arms Inc., 224

R
R. Painter Co., 224
Radial forces in bolting system, 63, **64**
Rahn, L. Joseph, 224
Regency, 183
Remington guns, 50, 82-85, 103, 168,
    198, 199, 204, **206**, 210, **211**, 216
Repeaters, **21**
Retro Choke, 206
Richards, Westley; *see* Westley
    Richards
Rigby, xiii, 100
Roll-on method of engraving, 90
Rottweil, 205-208, **207, 208,** 217, **217,**
    222
Round action, Dickson's, 49-50
Rowe, John F., 224
Ruger, 76, 81, 82, 182

S
Sakaba guns; *see* SKB
Salvinelli, Remo, 132
Sarasqueta, Victor, 128
Sauer, 178, 179
Savage-Fox, 182
Schmid, R. Franz, 132
Schoverling, Daly and Gales, 178
Scott, Thad, 224
Scott, William, 107, 108
Scroll, **91, 92,** 93
Semi-beavertail fore-ends, **23,** 24, 25
Sempert & Krieghoff, 136
Shaughnessy, Richard, 198
Shooting; *see* Field-style shooting;
    Wingshooting
Shotgun News, 173
Shouldering, 10
Side-by-Side Space Gun, 219-220, **220**
Side-by-sides, bolting system on; *see*
    Bolting system on side-by-sides
Sideclips, **71,** 74
Sidelock, 41, 43-46; American-made,
    45; back-action, 44-45, **44;** bar-action,
    44, 45; overseas, 45; safety and, 45
Simmons, Ernie, 161
Single triggers, 54-62; delay-type, 56, 58;
    and double trigger, 55-56; Greener,
    58-59; intermediate pull and, 55; in-

voluntary pull and, 55, 58, **61**; three-pull system and, 56-58, **57**; timing-type mechanism, 56, 58
SKB, 183
Skeet shooting, 8, 33, 39, 158, 197, 198-199, **206,** 207, **211, 212,** 215
Skeuse, Tom, 172
Smallbores, 121-125
Smith, Lyman Cornelius; *see* L. C. Smith
Snap shot, 10
Sodia, Anton, 132
Sodia, Franz; *see* Franz Sodia
Space Gun, 219-220, **220**
Spanish gunmakers, 124-125, 126-130, **127**; AyA, 124-125, **127**, 128, 224; Garbi, 128, 179, 224; Sarasqueta, 128; Union Armera, **127**, 128
Splinter-type fore-end, 16, **23**, 24, **25, 26,** 28-30, **29**
Static action in bolting system, 72-74
Stephen Grant & Joseph Lang Ltd., 116
Stevens, 182
Stocks, finishing of, 96-99
Suhl gunmakers; *see* German gunmakers
Swedish gunmakers, **129**, 130
Swing-past method, 10

T
Target-grade guns, 197-212
Thrust-out technique, 4-11, **5, 6, 7, 8**
Top fastener, 69, 156
Top lever, 66
Tournament guns, 200
Trapshooting, 33, 39, 158, 197, 198-199, **198, 206, 211,** 215, **216**
Trigger switching, 27
Trigger-plate action, 41, 47-50, **48, 49**
Triggers, 51-62; double, *see* Double triggers; single, *see* Single triggers
Trim lines, 98
Trunions, 80
Tula Choke, 206
12/20 concept, 116-120, **117, 118, 119, 120**
Tyrode, Aime Coeur, 147

U
Underbolts, 66-67
Underlever, 66
Union Armera, **127**, 128
U. S. Repeating Arms Company, 166, 224

V
Valmet, 130-132, **131**, 141, 150, 224
Vena Contracta, 117-120
Ventura Imports, 225
Venturi principle, 118

Verrees, Joseph, 138
Vouzelaud, **53**, 124, 141, 144-147, **146,** 196

W
W. & C. Scott, 100, 107-112, **110, 111,** 196, 222
Water table, 64
Watson, 100
Waverly Arms Inc., 225
Wayne, James, 225
Weatherby, Roy, 82, 183-184
Weatherby guns, 76, 183-184, **184**
Webley & Scott, 100, 107, 108-109
Westley Richards, xi-xiii, 41, 62, 66, 70, **71,** 80, 100, 106, 124, **124,** 192, 193, 196, 224
Whatley, Patrick G., 112
Wildflower and Wader set, 104-106, **105**
Wildfowler's Association of Great Britain and Ireland, 104-106
William Powell & Son Ltd., 87, 112, 224
Wills, Jim, 119
Winchester Group of Olin, 165, 184-187
Winchester guns, 48, 50, 103, 124, 184-187, **185, 186, 187,** 212, **212, 216,** 217
Winchester Model 21, 59-62, **59, 91,** 102, 124, 153-167, **153, 160, 161, 162, 164, 165,** 196, 198, 224; action bar of, 156; bending forces and, 156; boxlock, 157; clay-target shooting and, 158; custom-built, 159, 166; development of, 155-158; Grand American, **153, 160, 165,** 166; Pigeon Grade, **28,** 166, **195**; top fastener of, 156; trapshooting and, 158
Wing-gunning; *see* Wingshooting
Wingshooting, xiv, 1-11; aiming, 2-3; gun fit and, 4; hand-to-eye coordination, 1-4, **2, 3,** 9; leading hand grip and, 10; lean and, 6, 8; pointing, 2-3; push-out and, 4; shouldering, 10; snap shot and, 10; sustained lead and, 10; swing-past method and, 10; thrust-out and, 4-11, **5, 6, 7, 8**
Winkler, Benedikt, 132
Winkler, Josef, 132
Wirnhier, Konrad, 205, 206
Wood, Theodore C., 225
Wooden accoutrements, 96-99
Woodward, Thomas, 56, 57
Woodward guns, 56, 58, 79, 128
Woodward-Purdey, 13-14, 24-25, 76, **76,** 80, 81-82

Z
Zoli, 76

Epilogue
The State of the Art

When the artistic and cultural histories of the 18th and 19th centuries are finally written, along with that of the earlier part of the 20th century, they must perforce present massive, respectful chapters covering the handmade firearms of said era. From dueling pistols to game guns, from the first breechloaders to modern over-unders and the finely made Cosmi autoloader, the guns were works of art. Although often having the same profiles, they were works of art, for the hand fitting and extensive engraving and inlays made them one-of-a-kind pieces. Craftsmen stuck with only the most primitive tools, because there were no others. It was an expression of human skills.

I am told that it takes about one thousand hours to build a London "Best" gun today. I don't know what a typical craftsman earns per hour in the English gun industry, but if it takes 30 pounds to keep a man on the job (including overhead, fringes, holidays), one only needs to multiply that figure by a thousand to get an idea what a handmade gun will run these days.

Because it takes more time to cut the receiver of an O/U by hand than it does that of a side-by-side, the cost will be appreciably high. Yet, with a lot of money in the world right now, there is still a business in handmade shotguns. New models have been slow in appearing. However, Holland & Holland has announced a custom-fashioned O/U for sporting clays—the last price I've seen was about twenty-seven thousand dollars.

Ever since the Berlin Wall crumbled, it has become easier to get the legendary Merkel guns, both over-unders and side-by-sides. Wearing some new designations—such as M2000EL and M2001EL for the old M200E and M201E, respectively—the Merkels have been Westernized. The current stateside importer (GSI Inc., P.O. Box 129, Trussville, AL 35173) has prevailed upon Merkel to open the once-narrow bore to U.S. standards.

The Merkel over-unders continue to possess superb pointability, and the sidelock Model 47SL horizontal double pivots nicely from a between-the-hands weight concentration. The guns exude quality and workmanship, but, alas, East German craftsmen now want wages akin to those of the western workers and Merkel prices have risen steadily.

Struggling to keep the Winchester Model 101 concept alive is Connecticut Valley Classics, which has brought out a number of field and clay designs built around the M101 action nucleus.

I do not believe that these H&H over-unders are totally handmade. Some cutting machines are undoubtedly employed. But, what's the difference if the finished gun is superb?

In a surprising development, an enterprising American named Anthony Galazan has backed a new venture in double gun building. Operating under the banner of Connecticut Shotgun Manufacturing (P.O. Box 1692, New Britain, CT 06051), the company began with a Boss-like O/U which has full sidelocks and a trim profile to bring it astride any British or European vertical double in style and handling. Galazan doesn't hesitate to send gns to Italy where the leading names in bulino engraving live. Only the best Turkish Circassian walnut is used blended to the customer's dimensions. At this writing, my information provides a base price of $38,000 without engraving.

Sensing that only a very few sportsmen will spend that much coin of the realm on a shotgun, however superb, Connecticut Shotgun Manufacturing has announced in 1998 a new, more affordable stackbarrel known as the CSM Sporting Series, which is currently made in 12 and 20 gauges. It is also a reasonably low-profiled gun and has a detachable trigger group. This is quite new as we go to press, and I can't add more.

If fans of the Winchester Model 21 have been frustrated lately, they needn't be any longer. The same Connecticut Shotgun Manufacturing Co. discussed above has Winchester tooling and can supply any part(s). In fact, CSM can build a totally new Model 21 if you can afford it. This includes the .410 bore M21.

In a final effort, Galazan has brought back the A.H. Fox doubles, turning out close replicas in several gauges and grades. While machinery is employed at CSM, a large measure of the work is done by hand. Thus, there's a little bit of the old world alove and well in the U.S.

Not all current doubles are pointed toward the highest prices, of course. On the other hand, hunters who want a very good double must realize that it takes more time to produce such a shotgun than it does a field-grade pumpgun; therefore, doubles made with any amount of care and precision will be elevated in price. One such company that provides exceptional value is SKB. In 1998, SKB announced a pair of 12-gauge SxS guns - the Models 385 and 485 - which have excellent handling qualities and are steel shot compatible. The M385 is a box action, while the M425 wears a nicely engraved, but false, sideplate.

Limited numbers of 2-barrel sets in 20/28 are also being assembled by SKB. These can be had with either a pistol or straight grip. Inter-Choke systems are part of the packages. At this writing, all SKB 20/28 sets have 26-inch barrels only.

Miroku of Japan is little known stateside, but it builds a variety of O/Us for the European and U.K. markets plus other nations outside the Western hemisphere. The guns have a winning history in clay shooting, and field grades are quite responsive. The Miroku Mk 38 has met with splendid acceptance. Lamentably, Miroku also makes the Browning Citoris, and its agreement with Browning precludes Miroku sales in the U.S. Sometimes, Miroku O/Us can be had via British Sporting Arms, Ltd., RR #1, Box 140, Millbrook, NY 12545.

The name of Charles Daly has reappeared, a branch of K.B.I., Inc. (P.O. Box 6625, Harrisburg, PA 17112-0625). The new line has both vertical and horizontal doubles, while the SxS group is complete with the grand old Daly names: Empire, Diamond, and Diamond Regent, the latter pair of which are true sidelocks.

In Oregon, a man named Bill Hanus has blended together the features of responsive side-by-sides and called them the "Hanus Birdgun." Currently, these are being built by AyA of Spain. Hanus emphasizes the lesser gauges, beginning with the 16 and working down through the .410. The guns are made with single or double triggers and have the trim British profile and handling qualities (P.O. Box 533, Newport, OR 97365).

Other nations and importers are getting into the act. SIGARMS, Inc., known better as an importer of European pistols, has introduced a pair of Italian-made O/Us that have excellent handling qualities. These are the SA 3 Hunter and SA 5 Upland Hunter. The SA 3 has all-around potential, while the SA 5, available in both 12 and 20 gauge, is a quick-pivoting upland bird gun with European lines. The woodwork is of an advanced grade in the SA 5, which also wears a false sideplate for decor.

Totally new to the American market in the past few seasons are Turkish-made doubles. Unknown to most of the world, Turkey is a tremendous hunting nation second only to the U.S. in number of licensed hunters. A leader in tapping this supply is Tristar Sporting Arms, Ltd. (1814-

SIGARMS Inc. SA 5 SHOTGUN

16 Linn St., P.O. Box 7496, N. Kansas City, MO 64116). There is a full line of O/Us with some affordable side-by-sides. Indeed, the great interest in Turkish guns is that they offer solid quality at moderate to introductory pricing. And much of the work is hand work. For Turkish gunmaking is based on the cottage system wherein the craftsman takes the parts home to fit and finish. And as each man has a specialty, the guns tend to be nicely done.

The Olin[Kodensha plant in Japan, which was built to make Winchester 101s, has been converted into a 3-tiered golf driving range. This same plant made the Parker Reproductions mentioned above, along with the smattering of Classic Doubles. The Classic Doubles never had a chance, but the Parker
Reproductions had some of the best finishes ever in their price range. The interiors didn't reach the same level of workmanship; however, the Repro Parkers have held their prices well as there is a continuing interest and the pieces have superb handling qualities.

Since American mass producers found they couldn't generate a profit from sales of side-by-sides, there have been few entry-level guns at low prices. The exception is the IGA line, which comes from Brazil and is imported by Stoeger Industries (5 Mansard Ct., Wayne, NJ 07470). In recent years, the IGA guns, both SxSs and O/Us, have been given more modern profiles, including straight-gripped English styles. They and the Turkish guns are good starting points for the hunters and shooters who want to spend hundreds of dollars, not thousands.

Despite the virtual collapse of American double-gun making, there is still an active interest in this breed of bird gun. The current world order heads toward a 1-world market, and imports continue; they will undoubtedly remain the staff and stuff of life for doubles fanciers. But if other nations can build them better and attract a market, so be it. America has always dominated the pumpgun field, and craftsmen of the old world invariably seem to have a better touch with gun art than do statesiders.

STOEGER IGA DELUXE UPLANDER SIDE-BY-SIDE

Remington has tried to crack the O/U market with the Peerless, a rather boxy gun with pointing qualities like that of the Model 1100 semiauto. It has not created a substantial market stir, and as this is being written is in redesign.

The state of the art, then, isn't all that bad. Great doubles will be expensive, of course. They always were relative to other things except the great sports cars with equally enormous price tags.

Gradually, however, the intermediate doubles have come closer to the handling qualities of the truly fine game guns. The above-mentioned Hanus Birdgun being a case in pont, along with the SA 5 O/U and obsolete-but-still-quite-available Parker Reproductions. Who knows what can happen when enterprising gunmakers begin to put modern technology to work on lively, well-balanced doubles?